THE
NATIONAL
TRUST

THE FIRST
HUNDRED YEARS

THE
NATIONAL TRUST

The First Hundred Years

MERLIN WATERSON

RESEARCH BY
SAMANTHA WYNDHAM

THE NATIONAL TRUST

The National Trust: The First Hundred Years

First published in 1994 by
BBC Books
and
National Trust (Enterprises) Limited.

Reprinted 1994 and 1995

Revised in 1997 by National Trust (Enterprises) Limited

Text copyright © The National Trust 1994

Designed by Harry Green

A CIP catalogue record for this book is available
from the British Library.

ISBN 0 7078 0233 4 Hardback
ISBN 0 7078 0238 5 Paperback

Typeset by Selwood Systems, Midsomer Norton

Printed and bound in Great Britain by Butler & Tanner Ltd, Frome, Somerset.

Frontispiece

Lindisfarne Castle in Northumberland, a Tudor
blockhouse remodelled in the early twentieth century
by Sir Edwin Lutyens. The castle was given to the
National Trust in 1944 by Sir Edward de Stein
and his sister, Gladys.

Page 6

A drawing by Rex Whistler, commissioned for an early
National Trust publication in 1930.

FOR ALL THOSE WHO HAVE GIVEN
GENEROUSLY TO THE NATIONAL TRUST

'FOR LIFE TO BE LARGE AND FULL, IT MUST CONTAIN THE
CARE OF THE PAST AND OF THE FUTURE IN EVERY
PASSING MOMENT OF THE PRESENT'

JOSEPH CONRAD, *Nostromo*

'THE TRUST IS A NOBLE THING, AND HUMANLY
SPEAKING — IMMORTAL. THERE ARE SOME SILLY
MORTALS CONNECTED WITH IT; BUT THEY WILL PASS'

BEATRIX POTTER

Contents

Her Majesty Queen Elizabeth The Queen Mother at
Polesden Lacey in 1977, receiving a bouquet from
Catherine Blomfield, with Lord Antrim, Chairman of
the Trust from 1965 to 1977.

CLARENCE HOUSE
S.W. 1

I have followed with interest the development of the National Trust since I became President in 1953, the more so because I have known a number of the places now in its care when they were still in private hands, among them Polesden Lacey in Surrey, where The King and I stayed after our Wedding, Fountains Abbey in Yorkshire, and Antony in Cornwall. The tombs of my Bowes ancestors are, indeed, at Gibside in County Durham.

Over the years, I have visited so many of the Trust properties and never cease to be impressed by the way they are cared for and by their diversity. In 1964 I presided at the re-opening of the Stratford upon Avon Canal, in 1990 I went to see the restoration work on Hadrian's Wall, and I have visited innumerable houses which the Trust has saved from almost certain ruin.

In 1970 when I went to Cliveden for the seventy-fifth anniversary celebration the Membership of the Trust stood at 226,000. Now at the approach of its hundredth birthday the number is over two million and I feel sure this trend will continue into the second century.

It is with much pleasure that I commend this history of the National Trust by Mr. Merlin Waterson. It gives a fascinating picture of the way the Trust works to preserve the heritage of the past for the benefit of future generations.

ELIZABETH R
President

1994

PREFACE

FROM THE OUTSET, there has been confusion about when exactly the National Trust was founded. Octavia Hill, who was as closely involved as anyone in its formation, referred in an essay to the founding of the Trust in 1894, the year of its inaugural meeting, extensively reported in *The Times* and other national papers. But in an obituary of the Trust's first Chairman, Sir Robert Hunter, there is an equally clear statement that its foundation was in 1895. It is the date that Hunter, a distinguished solicitor, would probably have regarded as correct, because it was not until 12 January 1895 that the Trust was formally constituted under the Companies Act.

There is another reason for treating 1995 as the Centenary. Understandably, there were no Golden Jubilee celebrations in 1944. But with the coming of peace the following year, the Trust was able to catch the prevailing mood of optimism and a Jubilee appeal was launched which the new Labour government agreed to match pound for pound. In 1995 the Trust will be acknowledging both its foundation and its Jubilee.

To mark the Jubilee, James Lees-Milne edited a collection of essays, *The National Trust: A Record of Fifty Years' Achievement*. This, his published diaries and his recent *People and Places: Country House Donors and the National Trust* (1992) are indispensable to any historian of the Trust. In 1951 Lees-Milne was succeeded as Secretary of the Historic Buildings Committee of the National Trust by Robin Fedden, who also wrote a history of the Trust, *The Continuing Purpose*, published in 1968.

Although only twenty years ago, it is already difficult to understand quite what a hold Fedden had over the Trust while he was Historic Buildings Secretary and Deputy Director-General. Its policies and attitudes were not then enshrined in innumerable management plans and papers for committees. Whenever there was any doubt about how to repair a building, decorate a room or replant a garden, the safest thing was to consult Fedden. Next best was to turn to *The Continuing Purpose*, which is on the table beside me now. The perspective has shifted and the emphasis of this book will be different. But there is not a chance of matching Fedden's characteristic blend of economy and panache.

The other recent history of the Trust, John Gaze's *Figures in a Landscape* (1988), is an invaluable source of information. While Fedden tended to leap from peak to peak, Gaze lingered at every gate and stile with a land agent's eye for detail. He was also infuriatingly modest about his own achievements, although fortunately I have been able to write about these from first-hand experience.

I am extremely grateful to the National Trust's Chairman, Lord Chorley, and to the Director-General, Sir Angus Stirling, for giving me the opportunity to make this contribution to the Trust's Centenary. Lord Chorley's painstaking and detailed comments on my preliminary drafts, drawing on his family's long involvement with the Trust, have been greatly appreciated, and so too has the freedom given me to express my own views, which are not necessarily those of the Council of the Trust. My Regional Chairman, Lord Hemingford, and the Trust's Publisher, Margaret Willes, have both been consistently encouraging.

During the early stages of gathering material it became clear that there were quantities of records and unpublished photographs scattered around sixteen regional offices. The Trust has, quite rightly, always regarded its primary, statutory duty to be the care of property in its ownership, responsibility for which has often been delegated to locally based committees and staff. Only recently has the history of the Trust as an institution received the attention it deserves. One excuse sometimes given to tiresome enquirers by hard-pressed staff was that records had been destroyed during the last war. These gaps could be partially filled by a trawl of the regions, county record offices and the archives of related conservation organisations. During this search it emerged that much of the history of the Trust, including the circumstances which led to its foundation, had been widely misunderstood and misrepresented.

The task of collecting this evidence together has been carried out by Samantha Wyndham. She has also recorded scores of interviews with those associated with the Trust, the transcripts of which will be a valuable addition to a now substantial archive of oral history. While I must accept responsibility for the way this history is written, she has unearthed much of the new material on which it is based and most of the illustrations. The book would never have been finished without her persistence. Nor would it if the Trust's Regional Land Agent in East Anglia, Simon Garnier, had not over several weeks done my job as well as his own, with what appeared disconcerting ease. That burden was shared with other staff at Blickling, particularly my secretary, Frances Martin, who has deciphered my chaotic manuscript.

A word of explanation is needed about my use of Christian names in the text, which may appear inconsistent. There are many examples of different members of the same family being involved in the Trust, beginning with Octavia and Miranda Hill. In such cases I have used Christian names, to avoid confusion.

Many of those who have contributed to this book have done so by a chance remark or a throw-away line in a letter. I hope they will forgive me if I do not mention them all by name. Those who have allowed themselves to be interviewed, have helped with information and hospitality or who have sent written accounts of aspects of the history of the Trust include:

Lord Aberconway, Keith Alexander, Neil Allinson, Richard Ayres, Lord Balniel, Peter Broomhead, Giles and Ginnie Clotworthy, John Coulter, The Earl of Crawford and Balcarres, Nicola Creed, Warren Davis, Susan Denyer, Hugh Dixon, Robin Dower, Patricia Eaton, Edward Fawcett, Stephen Feber, John Garrett, Jessica Gill, St John Gore, Janette Harley, John Harvey, Laurence Harwood, Katherine Hearn, Tiffany Hunt, Gervase Jackson-Stops, Patrick James, Dame Jennifer Jenkins, Claire Jenkins, Mavis Kentish, Sir George and Lady Labouchere, Anthony Lambert, Robert Latham, Colonel and Mrs David Lewis, John Lewis-Crosby, Tony Lord, The Marquess of Lothian, Leslie McCracken, Peter Mansfield, Peter and Fiona Marlow, Gayle Mault, Oliver Maurice, Mr and Mrs Antony Mead, Dick Meyrick, Robin Mills, Colonel Charles Mitchell, Peter Mitchell, Professor Keith Morgan, Sheila Mortimer, Mark Norman, Sara Paston-Williams, Georgina Penfold, Sheila Pettit, Julian Prideaux, Martin Puddle, Commander Conrad Rawnsley, Rosalind Rawnsley, Dick Rogers, Paul M. Rosa, Sir Joshua and Lady Rowley, David Russell, Margaret Sach, Francesca Scoones, David Sekers, Sir John Smith, Michael Taylor, David Thackray, Geoffrey Trevelyan, James Turner, Jean Young, Carew Wallace, Dr S.M. Walters, George Watkins, Sally Woodhead and John Workman.

One or two special debts must be singled out. Sir Jack Boles and Gerard Noel share with Robin Fedden the responsibility for giving me a job with the Trust. They interviewed me in 1970, at 42 Queen Anne's Gate, the ramshackle, elegant, disordered house that then somehow symbolised and served as the Trust's head office; and my gratitude to them continues. Sir John Acland has allowed me to quote from some of his parents' unpublished letters and papers, which cast a new light on the gift of Holnicote and Killerton to the Trust. That he should have given access to these very personal records and should have taken so much trouble to help explain them to me is greatly appreciated. Sukie Hemming commented helpfully on an early draft. Michael Trinick gave two long, recorded interviews, and wrote detailed accounts of several key events. Not for the first time, he has been an invaluable source of guidance and practical help; as has Martin Drury, the National Trust's Historic Buildings Secretary and Deputy Director-General. Lord and Lady Gibson have been similarly generous over many years. Walking with Graham Watson in Upper Wharfedale helped me to understand one of the most remarkable gifts in the history of the Trust. In the summer of 1993 I found myself discussing the origins of the Trust with Ronald Lee Fleming in the unlikely setting of the Baroque riding school at Valtice, in Moravia. He has been assiduous in chasing up documentary evidence for the links between the founders of the Trust and the conservation movement in Massachusetts in the 1890s. The Marquess of Anglesey read my draft in its entirety, corrected several howlers and suggested how to deal with some delicate issues that were troubling me.

My family has seen this book become much more than just a preoccupation. They have had to put up with disappearances that have sometimes been prolonged and often unpredictable, from scribbling on the cliffs above Gunwalloe to days of writing in the Watcher's Hut on Scolt Head. I am grateful for their forebearance. The dedication of the book applies to them, as it does to all my friends in the Trust.

MERLIN WATERSON

CHAPTER ONE

'WORK'

LITTLE WAS LEFT to chance in the arrangements for the gathering on 16 November 1893 at the office of the Commons Preservation Society in Great College Street, Westminster. Those who had promised support represented exactly the right balance of interests from universities, Parliament and the Arts. They ranged from the President of the Royal Academy to the Principal of Owens College, Manchester; from the Duke of Westminster to Professor Huxley, the champion of Charles Darwin. Lord Rosebery, who was to become Prime Minister the following year, had agreed to serve on a provisional council. Artists and architects who had approved the scheme included G.F. Watts, William Holman Hunt and Alfred Waterhouse. *The Times* and the *Daily News* had already been supplied with accounts of what was proposed. A suitable property on the Welsh coast was in prospect and could be alluded to in a tantalising way. Only the best-laid conspiracies have been planned with such meticulous attention to detail.

The printed notice which acted as an invitation to the meeting was headed: 'National Trust for Historic Sites and Natural Scenery'. It proposed the setting up of a body 'to act as a Corporation for the holding of lands of natural beauty and sites and houses of historic interest to be preserved intact for the nation's use and enjoyment.' A reply was requested and the notice was signed: H.D. Rawnsley, Octavia Hill, Robert Hunter. The three founders of the National Trust were by then well used to working in harness.

The momentum of that exploratory meeting was not lost. A list of those to serve on the first Council was drawn up by Robert Hunter. On 16 July 1894, a meeting was held at Grosvenor House to approve the draft constitution. Critics of the Trust, who complain that it has recently become an establishment organisation, too preoccupied with historic buildings, choose to forget that its first

Octavia Hill (1838–1912),
painted by John Singer Sargent in 1898.

Beatrix Potter with her father Rupert Potter and Canon
Hardwicke Rawnsley in the Lake District. The photograph
was taken by Rupert Potter on 11 September 1906.

meetings were held in some of the grandest apartments of the Duke of Westminster's London house in Park Lane. The Memorandum and Articles of Association, again drafted by Hunter, were then forwarded to the Board of Trade. 'The National Trust for Places of Historic Interest or Natural Beauty' was registered under the Companies Act on 12 January 1895.

To celebrate Octavia Hill's sixtieth birthday in 1898, another gathering took place at Grosvenor House, when a group of her admirers presented her with her portrait by John Singer Sargent. It was a tribute which caused her considerable misgivings – presentations and testimonials were, she felt, 'a real oppression and pain to contributors' – and her plain brown dresses offered little scope for Sargent's slick technique. His image is of a benign matron, and she was anything but that. One of her helpers, Janet Upcott, remembers that 'her large brown eyes missed nothing and would flash devastating disapproval'. Her companion, Harriet Yorke, dismissed the portrait: 'Octavia never looked sideways'. At sixty, Octavia Hill's housing schemes, her publications and her work for the poor had given her a reputation which extended from Britain to Germany and the United States.

Hardwicke Rawnsley, Vicar of Crosthwaite in the Lake District and campaigner for any number of good causes, was of striking appearance, as is clear from the large number of photographs of him by his friend, Rupert Potter,

Canon Hardwicke Rawnsley (1851–1920). The photograph,
taken by the Mendoza Galleries, is annotated by Rawnsley:
'Here at the dictate of Mendoza
I sit a most pathetic poser
And dumb from photographic fright
Can neither think a thought or write.'

father of Beatrix. He was an eloquent speaker, a brilliant propagandist and a writer who would pen a sonnet before, during or after any event which seemed to him significant.

There seem to be no painted portraits of Sir Robert Hunter, and few photographs in spite of his distinguished career as Solicitor to the Post Office, for which he was knighted in 1894, and his work for the Commons Preservation Society. His daughter Dorothy recalled his exceptional 'talent for self-efface-

Sir Robert Hunter (1844–1913) in 1907.

ment'. It would never have occurred to him to draw attention to the fact that the idea of the National Trust was his and that he had given it a secure legal framework. As its first Chairman, he was to guide it unerringly through eighteen formative years.

The appearances of a quick and easy birth for the National Trust are deceptive. Years of frustration, personal crises, missed opportunities and struggle lay behind its formation. Its intellectual origins went back further still. To understand why the Trust took the form it did, it is necessary to disentangle the complex web of influences around the three founders. Many of those influences overlap, and there are common themes in the lives of each of them. What gave the Trust its vitality was that their concerns and strengths were complementary. They were also able to compensate for each other's weaknesses.

Octavia Hill's early life was marked by a succession of calamities. She was born on 3 December 1838 in Wisbech in Cambridgeshire, where her father, James Hill, had inherited a thriving corn business, a substantial house and considerable agricultural estates. Within two years of Octavia's birth, her father was declared bankrupt. He had used his inheritance to set up an infant school and an agricultural colony, both modelled on Robert Owen's New Lanark experiments. But his radical, anti-clerical views had outraged most of the influential families in Wisbech, including the Peckovers whose house on the North Brink overlooks Octavia's birthplace and which ironically passed to the National Trust in 1943. James Hill's excursion into radical journalism in the 1840s only compounded the family's financial predicament. His daughters were still struggling to settle his debts twenty years later.

With financial catastrophe came personal tragedy. James Hill suffered a nervous breakdown so serious that to avoid any additional emotional stress his doctors advised that he should be separated from his wife and children. Far too late his wife Caroline acknowledged how misguided this advice had been. The misfortunes she and her daughters experienced taught Octavia Hill that idealism needed to be tempered with realism. It was a lesson which she was to learn all over again from another formative figure in her life, John Ruskin, who, like her father, was to be both an inspiration and a warning. Both relationships were to bring her almost unbearable distress.

By the time Octavia was fourteen, her mother had taken charge of the Ladies' Guild, a co-operative association which gave education and employment to women and children in London and which was supported by a group of prominent Christian Socialists. Octavia supervised some of the children, who were employed making toys and who took home their tiny earnings to help support their families.

The Christian Socialists were to prove another significant influence on Octavia's later work, helping to form her ideas on the most effective forms of charitable work. Her letters show how deeply impressed she was by the preaching of F.D. Maurice, the spiritual leader of the Christian Socialists and one of the most controversial and influential nineteenth-century theologians. Improving the social conditions of the poor was to Maurice as much a Christian duty as saving their souls, and he questioned the teaching of the Established Church on these and other fundamental issues. Not surprisingly, his powerful sermons and his many books and essays met with increasing hostility from large sections of the Church, which tried unsuccessfully to show that he was theologically unsound and a dangerous radical. He was forced to resign his professorship of theology at King's College, London in 1853 and was excluded from some of the Christian Socialists' educational activities which he had helped to initiate.

Undeterred, in 1854 Maurice set up the Working Men's College in Red Lion Square, London, and immediately attracted to it as teachers some of the outstanding intellectuals and artists of the day. Among these was Ford Madox Brown, who painted his masterpiece, *Work*, at the time that he was teaching at the college. On the right-hand side of the picture is a portrait of Maurice talking to Thomas Carlyle, whose writing Brown regarded as 'the cause of well-ordained work in others' and who became one of Octavia's most fervent admirers. The strangest figure in this most didactic of pictures is of 'the ragged wretch who has never been *taught* to *work*'. The artist's explanation of his presence curiously prefigures Octavia Hill's ideas, because the boy has been saved from a life of idleness and crime by 'a love of nature ... and before dawn you may see him miles out in the country, collecting his wild weeds and singular plants to awaken interest, and perhaps find a purchaser in some sprouting botanist.' Like Brown, Octavia Hill regarded work as a moral duty and in later life would frequently refer to her 'housing work' and to 'the National Trust work' in the special sense implied by Maurice and Ford Madox Brown.

Maurice, as much as Ruskin, broadened Octavia Hill's view of social obligations. His belief that spiritual fulfilment was bound up with decent social conditions and with educational opportunities for the poor helped to shape Octavia Hill's life and so ultimately the National Trust. Maurice also wrote powerfully on William Wordsworth and the Lake Poets, and was himself admired by Samuel Taylor Coleridge. Octavia and her sister Miranda saw themselves as Maurice's fellow-workers. Years later, in a letter to Miranda, Octavia referred to Ruskin and Maurice as 'those two men whose presence made London so much of what it is to me'. The bonds with Maurice's family were further strengthened in 1872 when his son Edmund married Octavia's sister Emily.

When Maurice lost his post at King's College because of his unorthodox teaching, this did not discourage Caroline Hill from inviting him to teach her daughter Octavia's toy-makers. Other supporters of the Ladies' Guild objected, but Caroline refused to withdraw the invitation and in 1855 she was dismissed. Two years earlier, John Ruskin had visited the Guild and had met Octavia for the first time. He now offered her employment as a picture copyist.

At the time of their first meeting, Ruskin was already the most influential art critic of his generation. The first volume of *Modern Painters* had appeared in 1843, the second in 1846, both avidly read by Octavia, who knew whole passages off by heart. With the publication of *The Seven Lamps of Architecture* in 1849, followed by the three volumes of *The Stones of Venice* in 1851 and 1853, his reputation had continued to grow. These triumphs had coincided with the failure of his marriage to Effie, who, after they had been on holiday together at Glenfinlas, left Ruskin for John Millais. In 1854, the year that his marriage was annulled, Ruskin had begun teaching at Maurice's recently founded Working Men's College. When she was first employed by Ruskin, Octavia was an impressionable seventeen-year-old and her mentor thirty-six. The warmth of their early relationship and the intimacy of their letters may explain why the rift, when it came, was so traumatic for both of them.

Octavia's copies of pictures by Turner and the Italian Masters struggle to be absolutely faithful to the original, as Ruskin insisted they should. The laboriousness with which she approached her own chosen subjects may explain why she and Ruskin eventually concluded that her energies were better devoted to the social work which had continued to preoccupy her. In 1864 Ruskin put up the money for her to buy three houses in Marylebone, then an area of London of appalling dereliction and deprivation.

The approach that Octavia adopted for the management of Paradise Place, the cruelly ironic name of her houses, could scarcely have been more different from her father's Utopian schemes. Each property was judged on its merits and had to pay its way. Improvements would happen gradually and their effect would be cumulative. It was a scheme which owed its strength to its directness and simplicity. Not only did it work for Paradise Place, but for the increasing number of projects into which Octavia was drawn both in Britain and abroad.

Ruskin's involvement in Octavia's work for the poor reflected the changes in his own perception of the relationship between art and society. 'Beautiful art can only be produced by people who have beautiful things about them', he told an audience in Bradford in 1859. By then he was already working on *Unto This Last*, in which the political, social and economic failings of Victorian Britain were examined with such vigour and passion that after the early chapters had appeared in the *Cornhill Magazine*, publication had to be suspended because of

Work by Ford Madox Brown, painted in 1862–5.
On the far right stands F.D. Maurice, Octavia Hill's mentor,
talking to Thomas Carlyle, her early champion.

furious public objection. Ruskin's critics accused him of being both unbalanced and dangerous; and indeed by the late 1860s Ruskin was convinced that only the wholesale re-ordering of society could rescue it from a state of moral and artistic bankruptcy. While Octavia's work led her to increasingly specific and practical solutions, Ruskin's vision was of a new social order which could only be impeded by tinkering with problems. His diary records on 4 September 1872 a vivid dream of a party at the Working Men's College, where he found himself irritated by the 'vulgar decorations which Miss Hill had got done'. A visit by Octavia the following year to Brantwood, Ruskin's home on Coniston Water in Cumbria, ended in quarrelling. Octavia increasingly disagreed not only about how to tackle social ills, but on how to protect the countryside for the benefit of the urban poor. She must have found Ruskin's growing pessimism debilitating and defeatist.

Some of the countryside most accessible to Octavia's properties in Marylebone and Paddington were the Swiss Cottage Fields, then open and undeveloped as John Constable records in his views from Hampstead. In 1875 Octavia mounted a major campaign to secure them for public enjoyment, recruiting friends to write to *The Times* and relying on the support of professional people 'who will make for once an effort and sacrifice to give £25 or £50 to save a bit of green hilly ground near a city, where fresh winds may blow, and where wild flowers are still found, and where happy people can still walk within reach of their home.' In private she spoke disparagingly of the 'big-moneyed people', including the future President of the National Trust, the Duke of Westminster, who had donated £100. She believed 'more in nobodies than in "somebodies"'. The outcome was a damaging failure, however. Not only did the developers who had bought the Swiss Cottage Fields withdraw their offer to sell, but the money raised had to be returned to subscribers.

She now turned for legal advice to Robert Hunter, since 1868 the honorary Solicitor of the Commons Preservation Society. This link was further strengthened in 1875 when Miranda Hill proposed a 'Society for the Diffusion of Beauty', to be called the Kyrle Society, after John Kyrle, of Ross in Herefordshire, who died in 1724 and who is commemorated in Alexander Pope's *Moral Essays*, for the gift to his home town of parts of the surrounding countryside:

> Who hung with woods yon mountain's sultry brow?
> From the dry rock who bade the water's flow?
> Not to the skies in useless columns toss'd
> Or in proud falls magnificently lost,
> But clear and artless, pouring through the plain
> Health to the sick, and solace to the swain . . .
> The Man of Ross divides the weekly bread:
> He feeds yon almshouse, neat, but void of state.
> Where Age and Want sit smiling at the gate.

The principal activity of the Kyrle Society was to plant trees and flowers in urban areas. There was a decorative branch, energetically supported by the poet and artist William Morris. The Legal Adviser of its Open Spaces sub-committee was Robert Hunter and Octavia Hill was its Treasurer. It was to be a model and a forerunner for the National Trust.

The Commons Preservation Society had been founded by George John Shaw-Lefevre in 1865 to resist the illegal encroachment of common land, so that it could remain available for public enjoyment. From the age of twenty-four, when he became the Society's Solicitor, until his death in 1913, Robert Hunter devoted himself tirelessly to the cause of protecting the countryside. His national reputation was made with the battle to save Epping Forest, once part of the Royal Forest of Essex, from development, which involved the Society in opposing a Government Bill that was supposed to protect public access but in practice confirmed manorial rights of enclosure. Not only was the Bill withdrawn, but a subsequent case heard before the Master of the Rolls, Sir George Jessel, was a personal triumph for Hunter, who assembled over seventy witnesses and so many legal documents that they had to be wheeled into court in a barrow. That judgement was in 1874, the year before Octavia Hill joined the Commons Preservation Society in the aftermath of the Swiss Cottage Fields fiasco and Hunter first became actively involved in the Kyrle Society.

The same year Ruskin encountered a young Oxford graduate, Hardwicke Rawnsley, who wanted to pursue social work. He advised him to meet Octavia Hill, whom he commended as 'the best lady abbess you can find for London work'. Rawnsley had attended the lectures Ruskin had given in Oxford while Slade Professor of Art and subsequently joined one of his more eccentric social experiments, the Hinksey road-menders, who numbered among their recruits the historian Arnold Toynbee and the dramatist Oscar Wilde. Whatever moral and physical benefits Rawnsley derived from his Hinksey experience, they were not enough to prepare him for the rigours of rent-collecting among Octavia's tougher Soho properties and he suffered a nervous breakdown. After a period of recuperation at The Croft on the northern shore of Windermere in the Lake District, he took charge of the Agnes Mission in a particularly poor area of Bristol. Again he found the work too much for him and in 1877, in a state of nervous exhaustion, he returned to the Lake District to become a parish priest of St Margaret's, Wray. That same year Octavia Hill also suffered a nervous breakdown, but for very different reasons.

In 1871 Ruskin had set up the Guild of St George to provide a National Store (words, chosen by him, with a suggestive echo) for the benefit of all. Its three aims were to acquire land to be cultivated or turned into waste or common land as 'may in each case be thought most generally useful'; to provide schools and 'other educational establishments'; and to build museums in which the best works of God and man were to be exhibited. From the start the Guild was hampered by Ruskin's dislike of anything to do with finance and the legal profession – weaknesses which Octavia Hill was rash enough to point out.

Without warning, their disagreements spilled over into print. Ruskin believed and stated publicly that potential benefactors of the Guild 'had been diverted from such intention by hearing doubts expressed by Miss Hill of my ability to conduct any practical enterprise successfully'. In 1877 Ruskin published not only his letters, but also Octavia's replies in *Fors Clavigera: Letters to the Workmen and Labourers of Great Britain*. Within a few months he had launched into a no less destructive dispute with the artist James McNeill Whistler. Unlike Whistler, Octavia was no butterfly, able to respond with amused disdain. She compounded the dissension by telling Ruskin, 'I do think you most incapable of carrying out any great practical scheme. I do not the less think you have influenced, and will influence, action deeply and rightly.'

Octavia had already had one breakdown. This time her collapse was so serious that she suffered from hallucinations, could not sleep and had to abandon all housing work. During the next four years she spent long periods travelling abroad in the company of her friend Harriet Yorke. In her absence a band of carefully chosen and tried helpers continued to run her London properties, allowing her to turn her mind to other things, particularly the preservation of the countryside. As she wrote in 1879 to one of her most trusted friends: 'I hope no one will ever feel wedded to old plans of mine, plans of course – the wisest ones – fit one place and time and not another and one has always to be looking out to see that plans are not blindly adopted, nor unintelligently carried out, else what should have suggested and enlightened becomes a burden and a snare.'

The battles of the 1870s had convinced both Robert Hunter and Octavia Hill of the need for a body to hold open spaces in perpetuity, for public benefit. The preservation societies to which they both belonged were essentially propaganda organisations without the legal status to own property for charitable purposes. The issue was crystallised for them not by threats to a stretch of unspoilt countryside but by the fate of Sayes Court, in Deptford, near Greenwich.

When Octavia Hill and Robert Hunter first encountered Sayes Court, it had a modest, mid-eighteenth-century exterior and a garden of two acres. There was little to suggest that an earlier house on the site had been leased from the diarist, gardener and arboriculturalist John Evelyn by the Russian Tsar, Peter the Great. Since 1723 it had been a workhouse, managed by the churchwardens and overseers of St Nicholas, Deptford. In 1884 the elderly owner, W.J. Evelyn, approached Octavia Hill with the suggestion that the garden should become a public open space and offering a garden building which could be used as a museum.

It would be hard to conceive of a property which encompassed so many of the future purposes of the National Trust. The garden was of exceptional

Sayes Court in Deptford,
painted by Evacustes A. Phipson in 1922.

importance, the historical associations fascinating, and it was a valuable open space in the heart of London Docks. Sayes Court had also been the home of one of the first writers on the effects of pollution. In 1661 John Evelyn presented Charles II with a treatise recommending the planting of trees to 'meliorate the Aer about London' which was contaminating 'buildings, furniture, plate, pictures and hangings; it ruins the gardens, kills the bees, and spoils the taste of fruit'. Evelyn warned that pollution of the air was 'no less fatall than the poysoning of Water'. While he was living at Sayes Court, he chanced upon a young man living in 'a thatched house in a field' near Deptford. He was working on a carving based on Tintoretto's *Crucifixion* in the Scuola San Rocco, in Venice. So impressed was Evelyn that he arranged for the craftsman and his work to be presented to the King. The young man was Grinling Gibbons.

Evelyn's diary entry for 30 January 1698 reports: 'The Czar of Muscovy being come to England, and having a mind to see the building of ships, hir'd my house at Sayes Court, and made it his Court and Palace, new furnished for him by the King.' Although the house was relatively modest, it was next door to the dockyards where Peter the Great could learn how to set about building a

The museum building in the garden
of Sayes Court, *c.*1895.

modern navy for his Russian empire. Warnings of what the Tsar and his entourage
were doing to Sayes Court came to Evelyn from his steward, who reported it
was 'full of people and right nasty'; but it was not until Tsar Peter had left that
the full extent of the damage became known. Evelyn complained so bitterly that
Sir Christopher Wren was commissioned to estimate for repairing the house,
while the King's Gardener, George London, prepared a report on the garden.
Not only the carpets, but the very floors were so stained with ink and grease
that they had to be replaced. The furniture had been used to fuel the stoves; the
pictures for target practice. The garden, with its bowling green and specimen
trees, was wrecked and Evelyn's special pride, the magnificent holly hedge 400
feet long, 9 feet high and 5 feet thick, had been flattened: apparently the Tsar
and his friends had not encountered wheelbarrows before and had devised a
game which involved racing each other through the hedges. It was vandalism on
an Imperial scale. The English Government agreed to compensate Evelyn with
the considerable sum of £350 and ninepence. Twentieth-century vandals were
to treat the surroundings of Sayes Court even more brutally than Tsar Peter.

   The later history of Sayes Court is one of steady decline, with parts of the building being largely demolished and rebuilt, and with little to show that the garden had once been regarded as one of the finest in London. When the lease was renewed in 1820, it was still a workhouse and the churchwardens of St Nicholas were given permission to alter it as they thought necessary. Although what survived in the 1880s was only a sad relic, W.J. Evelyn was in no doubt of its historical importance. Neither were Octavia Hill and Robert Hunter.

Almost immediately it became clear that there were legal difficulties about making a gift of the property, because there was no public body with the necessary statutory powers for preserving it for the uses Evelyn intended. Robert Hunter began one of his exhaustive searches for legal precedents. Writing to Evelyn's agent from the General Post Office on 21 July 1884, he reported:

> I have been again looking as to the various Acts of Parliament proposed to
> facilitate such objects as that which Mr Evelyn has in view: but regret to say
> that none of them seems to me exactly to meet the case. So far as the Recreation
> Ground alone is concerned, use might be made of the Recreation Grounds
> Act 1857 and the land might be validly conveyed to Trustees. But this Act does
> not extend to Buildings or sites of Buildings . . . I suppose an Association for
> the management of land and Museums might be constituted under the Joint
> Stock Companies Act with the license of the Board of Trade . . . On the whole
> I think the best course will be for Miss Hill and Mr Evelyn to determine what
> form they would like the proposed dedication to the public to take . . .

Hunter also wrote to Octavia Hill about these discouraging findings, saying that 'I have taken some little trouble to look into the various Acts of Parliament and I have been unable to find that any means exist of making this building over to any Metropolitan Local Authority.'

On 8 August Octavia thanked Hunter for his summary of the legal position and reported that Evelyn seemed to have decided 'to transfer the land and buildings to trustees, with power to hand over to a public body afterwards'. Hunter was now convinced that the most appropriate public body for preserving Sayes Court would be a specially created corporate company under the Joint Stock Companies Act. 'I think such a company as you suggest would be valuable and that Sayes Court might well be handed over to it', Octavia wrote on 22 August, adding: 'at any moment some other important scheme may present itself and our body ought to be ready.' She continued:

> I think you see it is most important to get this land given by Mr Evelyn. He is
> an old man, and I shld. think an eccentric man; once given to good trustees
> we shld. have time to decide how to transfer or cooperate best. It is exactly a

> place fit for the sort of body you name as there will be a good deal of expense
> wh. might be easily recouped, it will be a question who will incur the risk . . .
> I am very low in spirits seeing so much work I ought to do and having nothing
> like time to deal with it. It will be a great comfort to think this scheme of the
> Company is progressing.

During the ten years that it took to bring that body into existence, the chance to save Sayes Court was lost. By the end of the Second World War the house and the garden building had been razed.

That September, 1884, Hunter was due to deliver a speech to the congress of the National Association for the Promotion of Social Science in Birmingham. He used it to explain the proposal that he and Octavia had been forming for a new body, capable of acquiring land and buildings for public benefit, developing this theme with the clarity and conviction which characterised everything he wrote. 'The central idea', he explained, 'is that of a Land Company, formed, not for the promotion of thrift or the spread of political principles, and not primarily for profit, but with a view to the protection of the public interests in the open spaces of the country.' In what was to prove to be in effect a draft of the first National Trust Act, of 1907, he outlined the functions of the proposed company, clause by clause, including: 'the acquisition and holding of properties to which common rights are attached; the acquisition of manors . . .; and the maintenance and management of gardens in towns as such, and the maintenance and man-agement of any buildings connected with them as places of resort for recreation and instruction.' This last clause was prompted by the situation Hunter had encountered at Sayes Court, which, although not referred to by name, must be the property he had in mind when he mentioned 'a gentleman in the neigh-bourhood of London' who had 'offered to dedicate to the public a couple of acres of open land with a building capable of being used as a Museum or Lecture Hall'.

There were other prophetic passages in the speech. The reference to using properties as 'places for instruction' implied an obligation to educate visitors, as well as providing for their enjoyment. Hunter envisaged income being raised from farms; and where 'there was any building to keep up, some small charge for admission might be imposed'. His plan was 'capable of being adopted locally as well as generally' and he foresaw a regional organisation dealing with cities like Birmingham and its surrounding neighbourhood, with counties, and with districts like the Potteries.

Encouraged by the enthusiastic reception of his speech and offers of financial

(*Above*) John Ruskin (1819–1900) in his study at Brantwood on Coniston Water.
Cumberland, painted by his secretary, W.G. Collingwood,
a supporter of the Trust's work in the Lake District,
including the acquisition of Great Gable in 1924.

(*Left*) The Hinksey road-menders, Ruskin's
experiment in honest labour for
Oxford undergraduates, including
Hardwicke Rawnsley.

support, Hunter agreed to have the address printed by the Commons Preservation Society under the title 'A Suggestion for the Better Preservation of Open Spaces'. A supplement on 'Illustrations of the workings of the proposed Society', giving examples of what could have been saved and of needless litigation, was presented to the Commons Preservation Society on 4 February 1885 and was then circulated, with the pamphlet, to the Kyrle Society and the Metropolitan Public Gardens Association. On 10 February Octavia pointed out that 'a short expressive name is difficult to find for the new company'. Her letter continued:

> What do you think of 'THE COMMONS AND GARDENS TRUST for accepting, holding and purchasing open spaces for the people in town and country'? I do not know that I am right in thinking that it would be called a Trust. But if it would, I think it might be better than 'Company' – you will do better, I believe, to bring forward its benevolent than its commercial character. People don't like unsuccessful business, but do like charity where a little money goes a long way because of good commercial management. You are certainly right in thinking that many would work for us who would not join the other Society. We want some good practical men of business added to our committee.
>
> I think we might be right too in getting on with the plans for Sayes Court. Nothing would help us more than good practical work put well before the public.

The mention of the 'other Society' presumably refers to the Commons Preservation Society. Her use of the word 'Trust' may have prompted Hunter to pencil at the top of the letter: '? National Trust. RH'.

At this point the idea ran into further difficulties. Shaw-Lefevre, the Vice-President of the Commons Preservation Society, had misgivings that a new body might weaken the standing of the parent organisation he had founded. He was a powerful opponent, who in his early twenties had photographed the siege of Sebastopol during the Crimean War and ridden on horseback from Vienna to Constantinople. It was Shaw-Lefevre who had been responsible for Hunter's appointment in 1868 to the post of honorary Solicitor to the Society. To compound the problem, Shaw-Lefevre had just suffered the most bitter disappointment of his political career, losing in the general election of 1885 the Reading seat which he had held since 1863, and with it the prospect of ministerial office. Hunter and Octavia Hill had the greatest respect for Shaw-Lefevre and were not prepared to press ahead if it meant antagonising him. Any disloyalty to such a close colleague would have been totally alien to Hunter's character.

To try to break the deadlock a meeting was called on 16 February at the house of James Bryce, MP, a botanist, mountaineer and champion of university education for women, who was to serve on the Trust's first Council. With Bryce's encouragement, Hunter and Octavia Hill agreed to adopt an alternative approach, proposing an 'Open Spaces Preservation and Land Development Society'. The proposition was reported on favourably in the Commons Preservation Society report for 1884–5, and a subscription list was opened, but again this failed to find favour with Shaw-Lefevre.

In October 1889 Octavia Hill wrote disconsolately to Hunter: 'Mr Shaw Lefevre does not rise to the idea of the new Society.' A catalyst was needed, preferably from far afield, and it came from Hardwicke Rawnsley. In 1883 he had moved from his living at Wray to Crosthwaite, to a post which his bishop reckoned 'as near heaven as anything in this world can be'. Rawnsley had accepted the living in preference to others because he had become immersed in the life of the Lake District, valued his friendship with Ruskin who lived nearby at Brantwood and whose wood-carving classes he attended, and because he had already set out on his crusade to protect the countryside around Keswick.

News that a syndicate of quarry owners was planning a railway into the heart of Borrowdale leaked out shortly before Rawnsley moved to Crosthwaite. Initially he looked to Ruskin for support, only to receive on 3 February the most discouraging reply: 'You may always put my name – without asking leave – to any petition against any railway anywhere – But it's all of no use. You will soon have a Cook's tourist railway up Scawfell – and another up Helvellyn – and another up Skiddaw. And then a connecting line, all round.'

Like Octavia Hill before him, Rawnsley consulted Hunter and the Commons Preservation Society, at that time fiercely resisting the incursion of railways across the remaining commons around London. The Society agreed to support a 'Borrowdale and Derwentwater Defence Fund' and soon *The Times*, the *Spectator* and *Punch* had taken up the cause. So successful was the campaign that not only was the Borrowdale railway defeated, but so too were proposals to extend railways to Ennerdale and Ullswater.

The next campaign to concern Rawnsley was the resistance to the closure of long-established rights of way on Latrigg Fell, at the foot of Skiddaw. His position was a delicate one, because the owners of the estate were his parishioners; but so too were the children who at Easter 'used always to go with their parents to the top of Latrigg . . . to "trundle the eggs"'. Rawnsley wrote eloquently on the rights of local people, but did not join the mass trespass which in 1887 finally ensured that Latrigg's footpaths remained open.

Benny Horne, Sir Robert Hunter, his daughter Winnie Hunter
and Canon Hardwicke Rawnsley in the Lake District, *c.*1900.
Benny Horne was a close friend of the Hunter family and worked
as solicitor to the National Trust until 1942.

Rawnsley had come to realise that rather than fight each threat as it arose, more consistent protection was required. In 1883 he had formed the Lake District Defence Society, which he intended should be a propaganda and campaigning body, to 'work in co-operation with the Commons Preservation Society and the Kyrle Society'. He did not envisage it having powers to own land, nor did he predict the opposition of local people, many with vested interests. At just the time that Hunter and Octavia Hill were encountering obstacles to furthering their plans for a national trust, Rawnsley was experiencing similar frustrations with his Lake District Defence Society. What finally brought their ideas together was a renewed threat to Derwentwater.

In 1893 came the announcement that some of the most beautiful and historic parts of the shores of Derwentwater, including the Falls of Lodore, were to be

Lodore Falls on the shores
of Derwentwater, Cumberland,
painted by Francis Towne in 1786.

sold. Coleridge had described the Lodore Falls as 'beyond all rivalry the first and best thing in the whole Lake Country' and they had been painted by Francis Towne, Turner and many other artists. Even if they could be protected in the short term, Rawnsley soon realised there was no statutory body capable of preserving them in perpetuity. He needed the help of Hunter and Octavia Hill. In turning to them both he provided exactly the emotive issue needed to resolve the impasse with Shaw Lefevre. Further encouragement came from Massachusetts, where their ideas had helped with the formation of the Trustees of Public Reservations.

There is an intriguing circle of events which links the conservation movement in Massachusetts with the National Trust. In 1886 a young landscape architect, Charles Eliot, visited Europe to build on the education he had received at Harvard, where his father, Charles W. Eliot, was President and where he was taught by Ruskin's close friend and future literary executor Professor Charles Eliot Norton. In London he met James Bryce who was at the time actively supporting the efforts of Octavia Hill and Robert Hunter to form the organisation that was to become the Trust. Bryce was a frequent visitor to the United States who had first stayed at the President's House at Harvard in 1870 and who was later to be a much respected ambassador at Washington. Charles Eliot's diary notes that while in London he visited the offices of the Commons Preservation Society and was given a set of its reports. He then travelled to Cumberland, specifically to learn about Rawnsley's Lake District Defence Society. By a stroke of good fortune he found Rawnsley at home and they talked in the Vicarage garden about Bryce's 'Scottish Mountains' bill, about the damage to natural scenery caused by railways and about conservation issues in both the United States and the Lake District.

On his return to America, Charles Eliot pursued the idea of forming a body with the object of taking into ownership land to be held for preservation. In 1890 he put his proposal to the President of the Appalachian Mountain Club, George C. Mann, who supported a resolution to invite societies and individuals to meet to consider a plan for preserving natural scenery. The scheme drafted by Eliot was approved and on 2 April the Appalachian Mountain Club resolved to call a meeting 'of persons interested in the preservation of natural scenery and historical sites in Massachusetts'. By July there was a formal proposal for the establishment of the Trustees of Public Reservations, Massachusetts and on 21 May 1891 the necessary legislation was passed. Eliot was made Secretary of the new corporation. The speed with which Eliot achieved his objectives and the long struggle to form the National Trust make a telling contrast.

Eager to exploit the opportunity presented by the threat to the Falls of Lodore, Octavia Hill deployed the contacts and influence accumulated during thirty years of work for the poor and underprivileged. 'If Sir Robert Hunter will help us, and the Duke of Westminster will allow us to meet at Grosvenor House, the scheme will go forward', she told Rawnsley. She had learnt that whatever her earlier misgivings about the 'big-moneyed people' might be, they could be useful. The Duke of Westminster, a noted philanthropist and long-standing supporter, agreed to become President of the proposed trust. At the inaugural meeting, held at Grosvenor House on 16 July 1894, the Duke was in no doubt of the significance of what lay ahead: 'Mark my words, Miss Hill, this is going to be a very big thing.'

Rawnsley opened the meeting by explaining the objects of the proposed trust and by referring to the way in which *The Times*, *Daily News* and *Spectator* had reported the exploratory gathering the previous autumn in the office of the Commons Preservation Society. He mentioned the success of the Trustees of Public Reservations, Massachusetts, and their constitution of 1891 which had been carefully studied and which provided a useful guide. When he said they were really establishing 'a great National Gallery of natural pictures' and 'but for such action ... many a lovely bit of English landscape would be irretrievably ruined', there were cheers.

The initial resolution was moved by Octavia Hill: 'That it is desirable to provide means by which landowners and others may be enabled to dedicate to the nation places of historic interest or natural beauty, and that for this purpose it is expedient to form a corporate body, capable of holding land, and representative of national institutions and interests.' She went on to explain that 'the trust, like St Francis of old, would be strong in its poverty, and, like him, would appeal for gifts' and it would 'save many a lovely view or old ruin or manor house from destruction and for the everlasting delight of thousands of the people of these islands.' Her brother-in-law Edmund Maurice, whose father had been such an inspiration to her, seconded the resolution. Walter Crane pledged the support of the Society for the Protection of Ancient Buildings. The Earl of Carlisle, a trustee of the National Gallery, hoped that 'the Society might also act as an educator'.

The first meeting of the Executive Committee of the Trust was held in February 1895 in 1 Great College Street, with Sir Robert Hunter in the chair and with Rawnsley as Secretary. There was the offer of a property, Dinas Oleu on the Merioneth coast of Wales, to consider. Its donor, Mrs Fanny Talbot, had been a generous supporter of Ruskin but had lost confidence in the Guild of St

A regatta at Barmouth on the Merioneth coast of Wales in 1909.
Dinas Oleu, $4\frac{1}{2}$ acres of cliffland above Barmouth
(immediately left of the house near the top of the cliff),
was the Trust's first property, given by Mrs Fanny Talbot in 1895.

George, whose financial affairs lurched from crisis to crisis after the resignation of the two original Trustees, William Cowper-Temple and Sir Thomas Acland. She now looked to Ruskin's one-time protégé. Rawnsley had visited the gorse-covered cliff of Dinas Oleu above Barmouth, and his imagination had been stirred when he was told that its name meant 'Fortress of Light'. A group of children had captivated him when they danced and 'doffed their ragged petticoats'.

Mrs Talbot explained her intentions: 'I am so grateful for this chance, for I perceive your National Trust will be of the greatest use to me. I have long wanted to secure for the public for ever the enjoyment of Dinas Oleu, but I wish it to be put into the custody of some society that will never vulgarise it, or prevent wild Nature from having its own way ... I wish to avoid the abomination of asphalt paths and the cast iron seats of serpent design'. Her wishes and Rawnsley's report satisfied the Executive Committee. 'We have got our first piece of property', noted Octavia Hill. 'I wonder if it will be the last.'

CHAPTER TWO

FROM FEN
TO FELL

Dinas Oleu was not the only property in prospect before the National Trust was fully on its feet. The first Council (see p. 280) included a member nominated by the Entomological Society, Herbert Goss, and at the meeting on 26 April 1895 he reported on the possibility of acquiring the only substantial area of East Anglian fenland still undrained. Wicken Fen, some

Sedge-cutting in Wicken Fen, Cambridgeshire: Early Morning
by Robert Walker MacBeth, 1878.

seventeen miles north west of Cambridge, had been the haunt of moth and butterfly collectors since the 1850s. So popular was it that in 1879 there were complaints that the number of lamps in use on the Fen at night gave the appearance of street lights. Wicken is an early example of a fragile property already threatened with over-use in the nineteenth century; of enthusiasts destroying the thing they have come to admire. Goss reported to the Council that 'Wicken Fen was the haunt of much wild life and of the rare swallow-tailed butterfly and

Alfriston Clergy House in Sussex, the National Trust's
first historic building, undergoing repairs in 1896.

urged the desirability of acquiring some portion of it.' Since 1890 there had
been persistent rumours that the Sedge Fen at Wicken was to be drained,
encouraging the naturalists working there to find a way of securing its long-
term protection.

The first plot of two acres of Wicken Fen was bought from an entomologist, J.C. Moberly, in 1899. The Trust had acquired its first nature reserve. Even more significant, it had secured the support of some of those who were to be pioneers of nature conservation in this country. One of the contributors to the costs of early acquisitions at Wicken was Charles Rothschild, a leading entomologist, the founder in 1904 of the Society for the Promotion of Nature Reserves and a benefactor who in 1912 made possible the purchase of Blakeney Point, in

Norfolk. The Council of the Trust were in no doubt of the importance of Wicken Fen, as 'the first instance in which a property has been acquired partly on the grounds of its scientific interest' and they drew attention to 'the value of the work of the National Trust to all lovers of natural science'.

If Wicken Fen provided a model for how the Trust might approach nature conservation, the purchase and repair of Alfriston Clergy House, in Sussex, set a standard for the care of historic buildings. Again, negotiations began early. On 26 July 1894 the vicar of Alfriston, the Rev. F. W. Beynon wrote in desperation to Canon Rawnsley. The fourteenth-century timber-framed Clergy House had been abandoned by the vicar in the early nineteenth century, divided into cottages and by 1879 was in such decay that the bishop had authorised its demolition. A local appeal for its repair had failed and the building was only reprieved thanks to the efforts of the Sussex Archaeological Society. On 16 April 1896 the house was sold to the Trust by the Ecclesiastical Commissioners for the nominal sum of £10. At that point the headaches began.

Octavia Hill greatly admired the house, which she described as 'tiny but beautiful, with orchard and a sweep of lowland river behind it', and she involved herself in both the fundraising for repairs and the way they were to be carried out. Money came in painfully slowly, but she would not countenance the thought of failure, insisting that to allow the Clergy House to deteriorate further would be 'a sort of breach of trust ... because it is ours now, given in the expectation we could preserve it. Besides, all this hope is a great factor in inspiring people to work and gift, and if our National Trust failed in these small schemes in this the opening of its work, it would throw back the future work.'

Another moving spirit behind the repair was Sir Robert Witt, later to be Alfriston's first tenant and the first honorary Secretary to the National Art-Collections Fund. The Society for the Protection of Ancient Buildings (SPAB), founded in 1877 by William Morris, also guided the work, agreeing with Octavia Hill that they should 'restore it, in so far as that odious word means preservation from decay'. Remarkably, those responsible recognised that although modest in size, Alfriston was an example of a medieval hall-house – the open hall stretches the whole height of the house, as was common in much grander buildings – and its original structure was scrupulously respected.

New uses for historic houses presented problems from the start. In 1900 the Trust purchased Long Crendon Courthouse, in Buckinghamshire, a fourteenth-century half-timbered building probably used as a wool store originally. The intention was that part should serve 'as a holiday home for London boys' to attend art classes organised by C.R. Ashbee, architect, craftsman and town-planner who was a SPAB committee member and also on the Council of the Trust. At a late stage Octavia Hill intervened, so infuriating Ashbee that in 1901 he resigned from the Council. He wrote deploring the decision that the 'beautiful Court House is for the present at least to remain a mere dead lumber house with no humanity in it but just to be looked at by Tourists.'

Octavia Hill continued to exert a powerful hold on the Trust, partly from the force of her personality and partly because of her own generosity. She and Miranda Hill began assembling countryside properties in Kent at Ide Hill and Mariner's Hill, nearby, in 1899. The principle of building up estates in small pieces, like jigsaw puzzles, was established.

One of the events which had brought Octavia quiet pleasure was the healing of the rift with Ruskin. Three years before his death Ruskin had responded to the 'demands and entreaties' of a mutual friend, Sydney Cockerell, for a reconciliation with Octavia. Ruskin's letter about their quarrel was magnanimous, heaping all the blame on himself and asking her forgiveness not just 'for error merely but for total wrongness in all one's thought – in all one's anger – in all one's pride'. Octavia for her part told Cockerell that in spite of the rift, 'All that Mr Ruskin is and has always been of good and great is quite independent of such things'.

A less complimentary description of Ruskin in old age was noted by a young woman who kept a secret journal, written in her own code, describing her father's political and artistic friends. At one moment earnest, at the next disrespectful and very funny, the journal is a record of exceptional talent and intelligence. Its author, Beatrix Potter, was, much later, to use that talent to transform the Trust's work in the Lake District. Writing on 22 November 1883 when she was seventeen, Beatrix noted: 'soon after we came back to town Papa bought a curious book at the second-hand booksellers. Ruskin's *Modern Painters*. It had Mr Ruskin's autograph on the title page, stating that he gave the book to D.G. Rossetti. Interesting copy, not that I think much of either chappy.' She encountered Ruskin in person in March the following year at the Royal Academy:

Mr Ruskin was one of the most ridiculous figures I have seen. A very old hat, much necktie and aged coat buttoned up on his neck. Lumpbacked, not particularly clean looking. He had on high boots, and one of his trousers was tucked up on the top of one. He became aware of this half way round the room, and stood on one leg to put it right, but in so doing hitched up the other trouser worse than the first one had been. He was making remarks on the pictures which were listened to with great attention by his party . . .

Although they were reconciled, Octavia found Ruskin a pathetic relic as he drifted into insanity. When he died at Brantwood on 20 January 1900, Rawnsley proposed a memorial to him on Friar's Crag, overlooking Derwentwater. It was to be a monolith of Borrowdale slate. Below a portrait of Ruskin in bronze relief were his own words: 'The first thing which I remember as an event in life was being taken by my nurse to the brow of Friar's Crag on Derwentwater.'

Rawnsley's compulsion to erect memorials, which was almost as obsessive as his sonnet writing, originated in his visit to Egypt in 1890 when convalescing from a heart attack. He was deeply moved by the sight of the pyramids, but seems to have concluded that other forms of memorial would be more appropriate in the Lake District. In 1891 he commemorated two Lonsdale shepherds in a simple runic cross inscribed 'Noted breeders of prize Herdwick sheep'. The same year a stone slab, with Wordsworth's poem 'Fidelity' on it, was dragged up Helvellyn on a sledge and erected above Striding Edge, as a tribute to a dog which stayed by its dead master's side for three months.

Another memorial, and one which was to set a precedent for the Trust, was the acquisition by public subscription of Dove Cottage at Grasmere, where William Wordsworth lived with his sister Dorothy and where he wrote much of his finest poetry. Although the National Trust has never owned or been directly involved with Dove Cottage, and its trustees have always been independent, Rawnsley was in 1890 made their first Chairman. Wordsworth's response to natural scenery, his respect for ordinary country people and insistence on the freedom to roam the hills which is implicit in *The Prelude*, all helped to shape the Trust's philosophy. Wordsworth's 'Goody Blake and Harry Gill' must be among the most sustained diatribes against a callous landowner and farmer ever written, with all the more impact for coming from the pen of a land agent's son. In *A Guide to the Lakes* of 1810, Wordsworth identified 'persons of taste throughout the whole island who . . . testify that they deem the district a sort of national property in which every man has a right and interest, who has an eye to perceive and a heart to enjoy.'

Samuel Taylor Coleridge was another powerful influence on the Trust. While they were both working on the poems which were to appear in *Lyrical Ballads*, Wordsworth stayed with Coleridge at his cottage at Nether Stowey in Somerset. It was where *The Ancient Mariner* was written and where 'a person from Porlock' interrupted his composition of *Kubla Khan*. To Octavia Hill the purchase of the cottage by public subscription in 1909 was significant because of Coleridge's association with F.D. Maurice. When Wordsworth's birthplace in Cockermouth in Cumberland was acquired in 1938 to save it from being demolished to make way for a bus station, one of the subscribers was the Canon's second wife, Eleanor Rawnsley.

On the opposite side of Derwentwater from Friar's Crag there is an area of wooded park with Catbells as a backdrop. This is the Brandelhow Park estate of over 100 acres, which was offered to the Trust in 1902, provided the purchase price of £6,500 could be raised within six months. The negotiations were so fraught that at one stage Rawnsley wrote testily to the Trust's Solicitor:

> I should very much wish you should call the attention of the lawyers of the Brandelhow Estate to the fact that owing to their not having made any progress my long journey and all it cost of time was taken absolutely in vain ... If they do not wish or intend to sell us Brandelhow lock and stock as was originally intended why not say so. This beating about bushes and keeping a very simple matter hanging in the wind is very annoying.

It was the Trust's first major appeal in the Lake District, and thanks to the efforts of Octavia Hill and Rawnsley, it achieved far more than the sum needed. Queen Victoria's daughter Princess Louise played her part. The appeal leaflet went to all 'lovers of Ruskin'. It was also sent by the fundraising committees organised by Rawnsley to factory workers in Manchester, Liverpool, Leeds, Birmingham and Keswick. One contributor, referring to himself as 'a working man', apologised for being able to send only two shillings: 'I once saw Derwent Water and can never forget it. I will do what I can to get my mates to help.' Octavia Hill recalled a contribution of 2s 6d from a factory worker in Sheffield who said that 'All my life I have longed to see the Lakes' and then added, 'I shall never see them now, but I should like to help keep them for others.'

No acquisition by the Trust explains so clearly the social and moral objectives that motivated the founders. Describing Brandelhow to an audience in Oxford, Octavia Hill wished they could all see its beauties for themselves: 'It commands views of Skiddaw in one direction and Borrowdale in the other, from its slope you can see the whole space of the lake set with its islands, it has crag and meadow and wood, on it the sun shines, over it the wind blows, it will be preserved in its present loveliness and it belongs to you all and to every landless man, woman and child in England.'

During the months that Octavia was working so hard to raise money for

Hill Top, Beatrix Potter's farmhouse
in Sawrey, and her illustration of it in
The Tale of Jemima Puddleduck.

Brandelhow, one of the Trust's first life members, Rupert Potter, was staying at the neighbouring estate, Lingholm. He rented in successive years Fawe Park on Derwentwater, Ees Wyke near Esthwaite and Wray Castle on Lake Windermere for family holidays, introducing his daughter Beatrix to the Lake District. Rupert Potter's photographs show how often Canon Rawnsley called to see them. It was in September 1901 that Beatrix Potter began work on *Squirrel Nutkin*, which was published by Frederick Warne in 1903. Her preliminary sketches of Derwent Bay were painted in the summer of 1901, and the illustration of the squirrels preparing to sail over to Owl Island in the following months. At the time Canon Rawnsley was struggling with the purchase of the Brandelhow estate, Beatrix Potter was preparing drawings of that same part of Derwentwater for use as illustrations.

Without Rawnsley's encouragement Beatrix Potter might never have

St Herbert's Island, Derwentwater, and 'Owl Island' from *The Tale of Squirrel Nutkin*, both drawn by Beatrix Potter at the time of the acquistion of Brandelhow, Derwentwater.

published her children's stories. He encouraged her to draw up a list of six publishers, all of whom turned down *The Tale of Peter Rabbit*. Hoping that it would have the same success as his recent *Moral Rhymes for the Young*, Rawnsley then rewrote *Peter Rabbit* for her in verse:

> . . . Grim Mr McGregor
>   a garden sieve brought
> Ha! Ha! Mr Rabbit
>   I've got you! he thought
> 'Don't count all your chickens
>   before they are hatched'
> The young sparrow cried out –
>   'Little rabbit aint catched!'
> And just as he spoke
>   Peter made up his mind
>   Slipped his arm from his jacket
> and left it behind . . .

Exactly how Beatrix explained to the Canon that she wanted to retain her own crisp prose is not recorded. She decided that she would meet the costs of publication herself, issuing the first of her stories in December 1901, selling some at 1/2d each and giving others to friends.

A necessary preliminary to the opening of Brandelhow by Princess Louise was the penning of Rawnsley's sonnet, 'Opening of Brandelhow':

> And here may mortals, weary of the strife:
> Of inconsiderate cities hope to come:
> And learn the fair tranquillities of Earth.

The day of the opening, 16 October 1902, was anything but tranquil, as Octavia Hill reported to her sister Miranda:

> The scene was really most beautiful, and very funnily primitive. The great tent was blown to atoms when it was being erected, and the little red dais was out under the free sky with the great lake and splendid mountains, and golden bracken slopes around us, and the nice North country people quite near, and so happy and orderly. The Princess was most kind and really deeply and intelligently interested in the National Trust work, said she would like to do more, told me of beautiful old houses, will be our President. My heart is very full of the thought of all who helped to get this land.

The photographs taken at the time show dignitaries gathered anxiously round the dais, clearly apprehensive about the weather.

The opening ceremony at Brandelhow
on Derwentwater, Cumberland, 16 October 1902.

Wicken Fen and Alfriston Clergy House set important precedents. Rawnsley now applied his energies to the protection of archaeological sites. An attempt in 1898 to acquire the remains of the Roman fort at Borrans Field in Westmorland had fallen through, but Rawnsley was not to be deterred. The purchase was finally completed in 1913 and the same year Rawnsley, as joint donor, steered the Stone Circle at Castlerigg, in Cumberland, into Trust ownership. This free-standing circle of prehistoric megaliths is of exceptional importance to archaeologists, but its appeal also lies in its dramatic situation on a ridge which looks across to one of the most majestic mountains in the Lake District, Blencathra.

The Trust began to acquire more modest structures. The close links with the SPAB ensured that, from the start, advice was readily to hand. The repair in 1904 of the Old Post Office at Tintagel in Cornwall, a fourteenth-century stone house, was supervised by the architect Detmar Blow, and although

The Old Post Office
at Tintagel in Cornwall,
bought by the
National Trust in 1903.

contemporary photographs show that he was prepared to make changes to some of the windows and to the chimneys, he was both restrained and respectful in what he did. Rawnsley worked particularly hard to save the ancient bridge spanning the Derwent River at Portinscale in Cumberland, although it was to be only a reprieve. Winster Market House in Derbyshire, dating from the late seventeenth century, was bought in 1906, the Priest's House at Muchelney in Somerset in 1911, and Chantry Chapel, Buckingham in 1912.

From the outset there were disagreements about the relative importance to the Trust of buildings as opposed to countryside. 'All my friends seem keener about beautiful open space ... We don't seem to reach the antiquaries and artists', Octavia Hill confessed. But the delight which both she and Rawnsley took in historic buildings ensured that responsibilities for both were honoured. This conflict, however, caused one of the few serious rifts with Harriet Yorke,

Barrington Court in Somerset, *c.*1890.
Two of the ground-floor windows were removed and replaced
with bricks by the farm tenant, who used parts of
the Elizabethan house as a cider store.

always known by friends in the Trust as The Keeper, while Octavia Hill was called The Lion. The acquisition of Barrington Court in Somerset confirmed Harriet Yorke's worst fears that maintaining historic buildings could have dire financial consequences. This substantial mid-sixteenth-century country house was particularly admired by Rawnsley, who wrote about its condition when it was being used as a cider store by the farm tenant:

> A good insight into Elizabethan ways was gained by our visit to the huge open garrets, with little recesses for cubicles to accommodate the servants, which ran from end to end of the house. We were not astonished to hear that at one time five hundred Parliamentary soldiers were accommodated in this attic. The only creatures accommodated there now are the owls, and though the windows have been built up to prevent their easy entrance, they still find their way thither, and as our hostess told us, make a noise at night as if people were shuffling about and dragging weights over the rough boarding.

The considerable sum for purchase and initial repairs amounting to £11,500 was raised relatively quickly and Barrington was transferred to the Trust in 1907. Then the real financial problems began. Thirty years later any suggestion that the Trust might take on another major country house would provoke the former Secretary of the Trust, Nigel Bond, to counter: 'Remember Barrington!' It is still a drain on the Trust's funds.

Hunter continued to supervise the legal work involved in these purchases and Octavia Hill assisted with the fundraising. When one of the founders wrote to another, the letter was often annotated and then passed on to the third. Until his death in 1899, the Duke of Westminster continued to receive copies of much of this correspondence. One of the most useful things he did for the Trust was to help dissuade Rawnsley from accepting the Bishopric of Madagascar, offered in 1898 by the Archbishop of Canterbury.

Only too aware of the threats caused by its proximity to London, Hunter was also at work on the beginnings of a major area of protection around Hindhead, close to his Surrey home. To the east of the village lies the Devil's Punch Bowl and Gibbet Hill, with Inval and Weydown Commons to the south east. The greater part of this area, some 750 acres in all, was given in 1906 by the Hindhead Preservation Committee, which Hunter had nurtured.

Although his letters show that Hunter took the keenest interest in the details of every transfer, ensuring that enthusiasm was tempered with realism and that all the necessary legal safeguards were there, he was at the same time refining the first of the National Trust Acts, which became law in 1907. Acquisitions such as Wicken Fen had already given the Trust experience of the complexities of managing sites important for their natural history, and this may be reflected in the tortuous wording of the Act: 'The National Trust shall be established for the purposes of promoting the permanent preservation for the benefit of the nation of lands and tenements (including buildings) of beauty or historic interest and as regards lands for the preservation (so far as practicable) of their natural aspect features and animal and plant life.'

Parts of the Act were taken straight from the Articles of Association of 1894, which Hunter had also drafted. The social objectives which lay behind the formation of the Trust were succinctly covered by the words 'for the benefit of the nation'. The succeeding clause gave the necessary powers to pursue that public benefit in the widest possible way. The Trust was to maintain and manage its land: '. . . as open spaces or places of public resort and buildings for purposes of public recreation resort or instruction . . . and make all such provisions as may be beneficial for the property or desirable for the comfort or convenience of persons resorting to or using such property.'

Responsibility for the policies and ultimate control of the National Trust lay with the Council, composed of fifty members, twenty-five elected and twenty-five nominated by distinguished bodies such as SPAB, the British Museum, the National Gallery, the Commons Preservation Society (subsequently renamed the Open Spaces Society) and the Royal Academy. This division of the Council into elected and nominated members may have been suggested to the founders by those they consulted in the United States. The Appalachian Mountain Club – founded in 1876 and the parent organisation of the Trustees of Public Reservations, Massachusetts – has a constitution which stipulates that there should be on its governing body five councillors 'chosen to represent the departments of Natural History, Topography, Art, Exploration and Improvements'. By requiring nominations from respected institutions, the constitution of the National Trust ensured that its Council was equipped to deal with its wide-ranging obligations.

The Act of 1907 provided the National Trust with such a secure statutory base that no further legislation was needed for thirty years. The National Trust Acts that followed built on Hunter's framework but did not supersede it. His achievement is all the more remarkable, because the Act was drafted without the aid of counsel. Instead Hunter could draw on his experience of having drafted over forty successful Bills as Solicitor to the Post Office and having prepared Lord Balcarres's Ancient Monuments Protection Bill in 1900. Of all the powers conferred on the Trust by the Act of 1907 the most important was the right to hold land inalienably. This means that Trust property, once it has been declared inalienable, cannot be sold or mortgaged, nor can it be developed or acquired by any other body, except with the express consent of Parliament. It is doubtful whether Parliament, when the Act became law, appreciated the full significance of these powers of inalienability. Sir Robert Hunter may well have done.

As the Trust's first Chairman, Hunter also established a clear, efficient way of considering potential acquisitions and making decisions about the care of properties. The Council met only annually and was not involved in the day-to-day running of the Trust, which was in the hands of the Secretary, initially Lawrence Chubb, succeeded in 1896 by A.M. Poynter, by Hugh Blakiston in 1899, by Nigel Bond in 1901 and by Samuel Hamer in 1911. All matters of major importance were referred to the Executive Committee, which has continued to exercise this role throughout the history of the Trust. The need for effective regional representation was recognised from the very earliest years. At the

Executive Committee meeting on 19 January 1897, when Sir Robert Hunter was in the chair and the two other founders were present, there was sympathetic discussion of a proposal to divide the country up into districts under the supervision of local secretaries. The first task to be undertaken by these secretaries would be the compiling of regional surveys, dealing with buildings, archaeology and natural history. (For the National Trust's committee structure, see table on p. 280.)

A very precise and carefully annotated amateur watercolour records a meeting of the Trust's Executive Committee on 15 April 1912 at 25 Victoria Street in London. It shows Professor Frank Oliver standing to speak 'on the charm of Blakeney Point', the Norfolk coastal property that was to be bought by the Trust that year, thanks to the generosity of Charles Rothschild and the Fishmongers' Company. On the opposite side of the table is the distinguished literary critic, scholar and future Chairman of the Trust John Bailey. As a Norfolk man himself, Bailey could be relied on to support Oliver's recommendation. The Treasurer, Harriet Yorke, sits next to Oliver and is holding her head in her hands, as treasurers are required to do when acquisitions are in prospect. Rawnsley is to the right of the Chairman, Sir Robert Hunter, and is poised to intervene. Hunter himself is following Oliver intently. On the wall above him hangs a portrait of Shaw-Lefevre, founder of the Commons Preservation Society. Octavia Hill was not in fact present, because by this time she was seriously ill with lung cancer, but she is shown in her usual chair. By one of those curious coincidences of history, on the day that this meeting took place, disaster struck the *Titanic* in mid-Atlantic.

The following summer, on 13 August 1912, Octavia Hill died. She had been greatly saddened by the death of her sister Miranda in May 1910 but had continued to work assiduously for the Trust. Janet Upcott recalled how Octavia would 'sweep into the office every morning – a small, stocky figure laden with account books – and work with a diligence expected of everyone.' Those who came below her expectations or who disagreed with her often got short shrift. C.R. Ashbee once referred to her as 'that most lovable of great little women, Octavia Hill', but he was not uncritical of her: 'She was of the women whose function in life it is to manage – keep you in order – see that you work on set lines, and with a hard stern power of regulating her own life she expected other folk to do likewise ... she was just a moral force that could take curious and tremendous forms.' He then compared 'the dear old Lady's way of ordering things' to those of 'a seaside lodging-house landlady'.

National Trust Executive Committee Meeting on
15 April 1912, painted by 'TMR' in 1924.

She did not invariably win over those who thought to give property to the Trust. When she and two colleagues visited Worth Forest in Sussex, tentatively offered to the Trust by the explorer, poet, politician and ceaseless philanderer Wilfrid Scawen Blunt, he was unattracted by the 'three old women like the witches in Macbeth'. Blunt resolved there and then on a different future for his patrimony: 'If such are to be its guardians, it would be a desecration.'

Octavia Hill's qualities would scarcely have appealed to Blunt. Those who worked most closely with her recognised that such strength of purpose inevitably meant that she was not always an easy companion. She recognised this herself and acknowledged to helpers her 'faculty of always saying the wrong thing'. That she was prepared to pursue what she believed in passionately, even if it sometimes meant offending sensibilities, was ultimately a strength, as Robert Hunter recognised. In his appreciation of her he recalled 'her power of brushing aside all subsidiary details and piercing to the heart of any question, her careful choice of methods and her scrupulous regard for the rights and wishes of those who supplied her with funds, and her courage and boldness in carrying through any enterprise of which she approved.' He rightly recognised that it was her 'moral and intellectual stimulus' which was her most lasting contribution to the Trust.

Hunter's own health was failing, but he was determined to see the purchase of Box Hill, in Surrey, concluded if at all possible. The day following the news of Sir Robert Hunter's death, on 6 November 1913, at Haslemere, came the announcement that the acquisition of Box Hill had been successfully completed.

The most telling tribute to Hunter came from Henry Fawcett, the Postmaster General who had appointed him Solicitor to the Post Office. Fawcett commented that 'he had never known a professional man who had done so much professional work for nothing'. Sadly, the obituary by Canon Rawnsley which appeared in *Cornhill Magazine* in February 1914 included one highly misleading section which was to cause Hunter's family considerable distress. Having praised his work for the Commons Preservation Society, Rawnsley turned to Hunter's part in founding the Trust:

> In 1895 more work came to him to do that perhaps was nearer his heart than any he had yet undertaken for the public benefit. Circumstances had made the writer feel that it was imperative that some association should be formed for the securing and the permanent holding of places of historic interest and natural beauty. The first person consulted was Robert Hunter. He threw himself into the scheme at once, but begged that Miss Octavia Hill might be consulted.

If Octavia had been alive, Rawnsley might have been reminded that Hunter had first proposed such a body at a public meeting in 1884; and the very name 'National Trust' was his suggestion. 'The Troubadour of the College', as Rawnsley had been known at Balliol, sometimes hit the wrong note. As his widow Eleanor wrote, 'Hardwicke's nature had more than its full share of the universal need for sympathy'. Although incensed, Hunter's daughter Dorothy left her own hand-written memoir to put the record straight, but published nothing. That is exactly how Hunter would have wished it to be.

Hunter would have been the first to acknowledge that the idea of a National Trust could never have been brought to reality without the imagination, energy and influence of the other two founders. The passion which underlies the work of Octavia Hill and Rawnsley carried with it a deep emotional involvement that left them at times overwrought. Hunter's rock-like integrity, his exceptional administrative ability and the modesty and warmth of his generous personality complemented their qualities ideally. In the vast number of letters which passed amongst the three founders there are frequent expressions of dissatisfaction with the inadequacies of governments and even an occasional hint of impatience with the first President of the National Trust. There seems never to have been a disagreement with each other or the slightest hint that they were not completely united in a common purpose.

The part Rawnsley played during the remaining seven years of his life were indispensable to the success of the Trust. His place in its history was already secure and needed no exaggeration. Just as Octavia's single-mindedness was an essential part of her and the Trust's make-up, so Rawnsley's egotism continued to fire both his own and other people's enthusiasm. Between them the founders not only assembled an extraordinary number and variety of properties, but by example they also helped to define what the Trust's ideals and objectives should be. It is worth examining these in detail, because at later stages in its history some of these aims have been questioned. Whenever it has deviated from its original purposes, either by going beyond them or by taking too constricting a view, the National Trust has tended to compromise itself.

The Trust's first duty, so clearly set out in the Act of 1907, was to hold places of historic interest and natural beauty for permanent preservation. That the Trust should not attempt to separate its responsibilities or put its properties into neat compartments was of fundamental importance to Octavia Hill and Rawnsley, who were fully aware of the infinitely complex relationship between landscape and man's use of the land, between natural history and human endeavour. They had been taught by Ruskin to see how botany, geology and architecture were interrelated; that art was the most developed response of the human spirit to natural beauty. 'How all things bind and blend themselves together,' Ruskin wrote at the end of *Praeterita* and so expressed not just the essence of his beliefs, but also what the Trust should aspire to.

Hunter was careful not to restrict the definition of 'public benefit' in the Act by being too specific about exactly what was meant. His life's work, as well as that of Octavia Hill and Rawnsley, are a clear guide to what was intended. The right of access, where it could be legally established and would not cause damage, had occupied Hunter all his professional life. It was what Rawnsley had fought for at Latrigg. Octavia Hill's aim was to protect places of beauty for their own sake, but also to provide 'open air sitting rooms for the poor'. As the Act put it rather more drily, the Trust's properties were to be maintained as 'open spaces or places of public resort'. The possibility of conflict over public access was recognised from the outset. Miranda and Octavia Hill delighted in the pleasure that the Kyrle Society's excursions into the countryside brought to their tenants from London's East End. But Octavia also observed that 'picnic parties carry London noise and vulgarity out into woods and fields, giving no sense of hush or rest'. Respect and appreciation of the countryside were to be achieved through education, or 'instruction' as the Act termed it.

Octavia Hill would surely have been puzzled by the hostility which the word élitism arouses today. The aims of first the Kyrle Society and then the Trust were to make what was beautiful and enriching available to everyone. Octavia was clear about the distinction between élitism and exclusiveness. She identified 'the desire to keep up an appearance' as accursed and wrote that 'exclusiveness . . . is eating out the heart of English life'. The Trust should never confuse élitism with the canker of exclusiveness.

Both Rawnsley and Octavia Hill devoted much of their lives to educational work. Music, literature and the art of decoration were among the activities of the Kyrle Society. Similarly Rawnsley would take the children from Crosthwaite School to visit Keswick Museum and the countryside around Derwentwater. The beehives in the school garden and the barometer to be used by children were gifts from him. When Grange Fell in Borrowdale came on the market in 1910, Rawnsley moved quickly to secure a five-year option to buy, helped raise the full sum by appeal, and then retained one farm to endow a scholarship for Keswick School, which he had helped to found. The role of the Trust as an educator, which the Earl of Carlisle had spoken about at its inaugural meeting, strengthened the case for the acquisition of properties such as Wicken Fen and Blakeney Point. Both were to be open air laboratories, one for the use of Cambridge students, the other for University College, London, where Oliver was Professor of Botany. Oliver had started to bring his honours students to Blakeney Point in 1910 to use the field laboratory there and to assist with his study of the physiography of shingle beaches and salt-marsh. In one of her letters Octavia Hill warned against regarding 'the education of childhood as if childhood were the time of education, when, after all, it is manhood when the noble kind is possible'.

More difficult to pin down is exactly where Octavia Hill and the other founders stood politically. As with Rawnsley and Hunter, Octavia's family background and early life inclined her towards radicalism. However, the Christian Socialism which F.D. Maurice espoused has little in common with twentieth-century socialism, and was specifically denounced by Marx as 'holy water'. Maurice was opposed to trade unions and against electoral reform (as Octavia was against women's suffrage). To Maurice socialism was the opposite of unbridled individualism and materialism. This was not just a theological or political position to adopt: as unashamed romantics, the founders of the Trust loathed materialism and preferred heroic values to the pursuit of self-interest. Certainly any state-imposed socialism would have been anathema to Octavia who was consistently hostile to local authorities. Nor did she believe that better housing conditions would be achieved by government-imposed solutions. 'Almost all public bodies do things expensively; neither do they seem fitted to supply the various wants of numbers of people in a perceptive and economical way,' she said publicly.

What is certain is that the Trust's founders were driven by a sense of moral commitment: a social purpose lies at the root of every clause of the National Trust Act of 1907. They mixed zest with zeal, and they were extraordinarily energetic. Most important of all, they were able to pass their ideals on to others.

CHAPTER THREE

'MUST ENGLAND'S BEAUTY PERISH?'

MEMBERS RECEIVING THE Annual Report for 1918 may have wondered whether the National Trust could survive. It had lost Sir Robert Hunter and Octavia Hill just before the war. Canon Rawnsley was still active, and its second Chairman, the Earl of Plymouth, brought useful contacts with the Tate Gallery – he was Chairman of the Trustees – and with the National Gallery. In 1895, when the Trust was founded, there were 110 members, paying an annual subscription of 10s; life membership cost £20, and honorary membership was given to those who donated £100 or more. Membership in the first years grew steadily; 260 in 1900, 450 in 1905, 630 in 1910, and 670 at the outbreak of the First World War. But nevertheless, the war saw membership decline and the pace of acquisition slacken. The Trust's report must have made melancholy reading. Fortunately there was more going on than the Secretary, Samuel Hamer, realised.

Hamer was one of those who migrated to the Trust from the Kyrle Society. As a young man he had been chief promoter of the theatricals which Miranda Hill organised for the tenants of her sister's East End properties. These took place in St Christopher's Hall, Marylebone, which had been built by Harriet Yorke, who also met all expenses. Hamer recalled many years later that Octavia joined in the opening game of 'curtsying', and that on one occasion a member of the cast insisted on reciting the stage directions with the lines of his part. At weekends Hamer would sometimes stay at Crockham Hill with Octavia Hill, who would send him out to walk footpaths which in some way or other were obstructed. 'What if the path goes by the landowner's front windows?' Hamer once asked, only to be told: 'You must say you have a *right* to be there and you *mean* to go on.' He was by nature conscientious but irresolute.

Hamer was Secretary of the Trust from 1911 to 1933. Professor Chorley, a Council member during the 1920s, described Hamer as 'a pleasant little man capable of turning over wheels which were already moving, but certainly not endowed with drive enough to make them revolve faster', while James Lees-

Milne remembers 'a shy lethargic individual' who sat at meetings 'with his eyes shut, blandly sucking at an old pipe and emitting little smoke'. Those at the Trust's London office, by then 7 Buckingham Palace Gardens, seem to have been only vaguely aware that plans were afoot for the Trust's responsibilities to be greatly enlarged in Derbyshire, in Norfolk and in the Lake District. In these and other areas the idea of what the Trust might be capable of had taken hold.

The inspiration for the Trust's work in Derbyshire derives from a day in 1916 when F.A. Holmes, a Buxton businessman with a deep love of the Peak District, was walking in Dovedale. The sound of axes and the felling of great trees echoed around Hurt's Wood. Those trees had been painted by countless topographical artists during two centuries, and would have been seen by Elizabeth Bennet on her visit to Dovedale described in *Pride and Prejudice*. They were being felled on the pretext that the timber was needed for the war. Holmes found an ally in a future benefactor of the Trust, Sir Geoffrey Mander, MP for Wolverhampton. Questions were asked in the House and the felling stopped. There then began a long and frustrating correspondence with Hamer about how Dovedale might be brought under permanent Trust protection. Holmes was to persist and, thanks to the generosity of a Manchester businessman, Sir Robert McDougall, most of Dovedale was to pass into Trust ownership in the 1930s.

Similar frustration began to be felt by the Trust's supporters in Norfolk. In 1922 Professor Oliver organised the purchase of the Lifeboat House on Blakeney Point to provide a base for Bob Pinchen, the Watcher. The following year Scolt Head Island was acquired through the joint efforts of Oliver and Dr Sydney Long. As honorary Secretary of the Norfolk and Norwich Naturalists' Society, Long was responsible for fundraising, and on 11 June 1923 the island was handed over to the National Trust 'so that it may be preserved for ever as a nature reserve'.

Work was soon put in hand to build a Watcher's Hut, so that the terneries could be constantly protected from egg thieves, predation and disturbance. The Norwich architect Stuart Boardman came up with a design using a flint chimney, timber clapboard and oak shingles, and before the end of the year the building was ready. The December meeting of the Norfolk and Norwich Naturalists' Society was attended by Emma Turner, a distinguished ornithologist in her late

(*Overleaf*) Wolfscote Dale in the Peak District, Derbyshire.
The dale, given to the National Trust in 1948,
is close to the connecting valley of Dovedale,
much of which was acquired in the 1930s.

Russell Colman, President of the Norfolk and Norwich Naturalists' Society,
handing over the deeds of Scolt Head to Viscount Ullswater,
Vice-President of the National Trust, 11 June 1923.

fifties, who had spent parts of the previous twenty summers living on an island
in Hickling Broad, taking the photographs which were used in her *Stray Leaves
from Nature's Notebook*, published in 1929 by Country Life. When at the end of
the meeting Long confessed, 'I cannot find a watcher for Scolt Head', Miss
Turner volunteered, 'Why not me?' During the ensuing months 'England's
loneliest woman', as *The Times* had dubbed her, was relentlessly pursued by the
national press.

For two summers Miss Turner led a strenuous existence on Scolt, protecting
the terns nesting on the sand and shingle ridges and keeping scientific records.
One of her visitors was the young Alfred Steers, the future Professor of Geography
at Cambridge, whose studies of Scolt were to span 65 years and who was to
serve on the Trust's Properties Committee. Steers once found Miss Turner in
the sand dunes, engaged in pistol practice.

When the opportunity arose in 1925 to acquire Cley Marshes, Dr Long
again looked to the Trust. It is an area of exceptional importance for breeding
birds, including bitterns, but money was a problem and his patience wore thin.
Long's solution was to form the Norfolk Naturalists' Trust in 1926, the first
of the county naturalists' trusts. Although Oliver and Long may have felt

disappointment at the time that such a step was necessary, the development of county trusts with such strong local support has been for the good, and many work closely with the National Trust.

John Bailey, who had become Chairman in 1923, also found Hamer at times reluctant to pursue the Trust's interests with sufficient vigour. Commenting on correspondence with a prospective donor, Bailey had to tell Hamer to make clear that 'we decline to be treated as children'. If the Trust was to grow, stimulus would have to come from outside. Fortunately it had begun to interest those who would give its work new impetus, regardless of the supine Secretary at 7 Buckingham Palace Gardens.

Awareness of the appalling carnage of the Great War had gradually shaken even Hardwicke Rawnsley's optimism. In 1917 he bought part of High Rigg Fields overlooking Derwentwater, presenting to the Trust a knoll which he had prematurely named Peace How. One of Rawnsley's last but most inspired contributions to the Trust was to propose that the dead should be commemorated in gifts of land. Accordingly in 1920, the year that Rawnsley died, the summit of Scafell Pike was given by the 3rd Lord Leconfield (the future donor of

(*Overleaf*) The Sandham Memorial Chapel, Hampshire,
with wall paintings by Stanley Spencer, based on his
experiences during the First World War, while serving
in Salonika.

Petworth House in Sussex), as a memorial to the men of the Lake District who had fallen in the Great War.

The suggestion that the Fell & Rock Climbing Club should make their own gift to the Trust in memory of their colleagues was first aired by H.P. Cain at a meeting of the club in February 1919. Various suggestions had been put forward but it was Cain who interjected: 'Let's buy a fell'. At the annual general meeting Cain proposed that the club should enter into negotiations 'with a view to

Herbert Porritt Cain, a member of the Fell & Rock
Climbing Club in the Lake District from 1908
until his death in 1927. He also served on the
Council of the National Trust from 1923 to 1926.

purchasing Pillar Rock or part of Great Gable', to be handed over to the National Trust. An approach was made to the owner of Pillar Rock, Lord Lonsdale, but he rejected the suggestion. That might have been the end of the matter.

By all accounts Cain was a dynamic, attractive person and he was to have a lasting impact on the Trust. Not in fact a great climber, he had walked every fell over 2,500 feet in the Lake District. His personal qualities and his humour ultimately ensured his election to the presidency of the Fell & Rock Club and to an invitation to serve on the Trust's Council, which he did from 1923 to

1926. One of his friends wrote of him that 'having become convinced that a thing was good, he would pursue it with passion, overcome the difficulties in the path with cheerful determination, and, when the end was achieved, look back as if the whole affair had been child's play.' In this spirit he now pursued the idea that Great Gable should be bought for the Trust.

The lengthy negotiations began with efforts to purchase Row Head Farm at Wasdale, but the offer to sell was later withdrawn. Cain and other officials of the club then tried another tack, and proposed to the owner, H. W. Walker of Seascale, that the club should buy all of the Great Gable fells over 1,500 feet. His response was now generous and a huge acreage was bought for £400. At the annual dinner of the club, in October 1923, the deeds of the land were handed over to the Trust's representative, Sir Francis Acland, MP. The 1,184 acres comprised two groups to the north and south of Styhead Pass, including the summits of Kirk Fell, Great Gable, Green Gable, Brandreth, Grey Knotts, Base Brown, Lingmell, Broad Crag, Great End, Seathwaite Fell, Allen Crags and Glaramara.

The unveiling of a bronze plaque just below the summit of Great Gable on 8 June 1924, and the press reports which followed, helped to bring the Trust back into national prominence. Hamer had sent his apologies, saying he had been advised 'that I should not undertake the expedition'. The principal speaker was Geoffrey Winthrop Young, the avatar of all climbers and the leading mountaineer of his generation, later President of the Alpine Club, initiator of the British Mountaineering Council and of the Outward Bound Movement, and author of one of the great classics of mountain literature, *On High Hills*. Young had served with the first British Red Cross ambulance unit in Italy, alongside G. M. Trevelyan, a lifelong friend who was to play an important part in revitalising the Trust. Seriously injured during the war, Young had had his left leg amputated. He resumed his climbing career, using a slender steel leg with a specially adapted gripping plate at the end.

The day of the dedication was wet and windswept, and Young had to be helped up Great Gable by Hilda Gnosspelius, the sister of one of those to be commemorated, H. L. Slingsby. There were about five hundred people present to hear the President speak slowly and with emotion of the 'great mountain park which lay in mist and silence below and around, and which for memory, had been presented to the nation, a possession for ever'. Then Young paid his tribute in 'a trumpet voice' so that 'climbers who had only reached the top of Green Gable, across Windy Gap, said afterwards they had heard every word':

Upon this mountain summit we are met today to dedicate this space of hills to freedom. Upon this rock are set the names of men – our brothers, and our comrades upon these cliffs – who held, with us, that there is no freedom of the soil where the spirit of man is in bondage; and who surrendered their part in the fellowship of hill and wind, and sunshine, that the freedom of this land, the freedom of our spirit, should endure.

A relief map of Great Gable fells had been made by W.G. Collingwood, a painter and antiquary, formerly secretary to Ruskin at Brantwood, friend of Rawnsley and an indefatigable walker of the fells. Cain now read from the inscription below the relief: 'in glorious and happy memory of those whose names are inscribed below, members of this club, who died for their country in the European War, 1914–18, these fells were acquired by their fellow-members and by them invested in the National Trust for the use and enjoyment of the people of our land for all time.'

There were long reports in *The Times* and most other papers from the *Aberdeen Press* and the *Yorkshire Herald* to the *Manchester Guardian*. 'The World's Greatest War Memorial' was how the *Graphic* described it, beneath a full page picture of Wastwater, seen from Great Gable. To those who criticised all this publicity as unseemly, Cain's answer was simply 'a secret virtue is often more intolerable than a public vice'.

When Cain took his place on the Trust's Council he had the opportunity to see at first hand how the Trust's London office operated. Hamer, somewhat disarmingly, described a typical day's work: he would arrive between 11 and 11.30am, read his mail, dictate a few letters to his secretary, Miss Spencer-Wilkinson, then walk across Green Park for lunch and to read the papers, returning to the office at about 3pm to sign letters before departing at about 3.30pm. It was, Cain reported to his friend Professor Chorley, what was known in the war as 'a cushy job'. Clearly Hamer was not the person to take the Trust forward on his own initiative. That was to come from those whom Bailey now began to draw into the Trust.

The most important of these was G.M. Trevelyan, the friend of Geoffrey Young. They had known each other long before serving together at Piave, on the Italian front. Trevelyan's *Garibaldi and the Thousand*, published in 1909, is dedicated to Geoffrey and Hilton Young, who accompanied him on his walks across Italy and Sicily, and who took many of the photographs used for illustrations. There are connections between Trevelyan's admiration for Garibaldi and his later commitment to the Trust. As Trevelyan's biographer, David

Great Gable from Scafell,
painted by Delmar Banner in 1945.

Cannadine, has written, Garibaldi 'loved nature and he loved liberty: the two
things about which Trevelyan himself cared most'. There is no better way of
understanding how he saw the relationship between landscape and history, and
why he was attracted to the Trust, than by tramping, with Trevelyan's book in
one's rucksack, in the footsteps of Garibaldi and The Thousand on the long
march from Marsala to Palermo. Trevelyan and the Youngs stopped at every
wellhead, trod every path on that route, and when they wanted to describe the
mountains around Monreale, it was comparisons with the Lake District which
came to mind. At the time that the Youngs and Trevelyan first became involved
with the Trust, it was supported by fewer than a thousand members and it too
had embarked on a quixotic and improbable adventure.

As well as writing the books that made him the most widely read historian
of his generation, Trevelyan was to work strenuously for the Trust, using his
increasing influence and prestige for its benefit. Before the First World War, he

had lectured alongside John Bailey at the Working Men's College, and the two men had developed a lasting friendship, Trevelyan dedicating *English Songs of Italian Freedom* to Bailey, because of their shared 'attitude to literature and life'. It was their 'love of poetry in particular, not as unrelated to ethics, to history, to public affairs ... that binds you and me together', Trevelyan wrote.

Chorley was another lecturer at the Working Men's College, brought into active involvement with the Trust by Cain's unexpected death. Few of those

John Bailey, Chairman of the
National Trust from 1923 to 1931.

who walked and climbed with Cain knew that he had a weak heart. The Fell & Rock meet in March 1927 was in Langdale and while returning from a walk up Rossett Ghyll, Cain collapsed and died. He had spoken frequently òf the importance of the Trust to Chorley, who being London-based was the obvious person to succeed him on the Council. For over forty years Chorley played a central role in the affairs of the Trust and his son was to become Chairman in 1991.

All these cross-currents and friendships were important, because they brought together those who were to extend the National Trust's philosophy and define its ideals in ways which equipped it to deal with the challenges of the middle years of the century. It was Bailey, for instance, who summed up the Trust's responsibilities towards preservation on the one hand and access on the other: 'Preservation may always permit of access, while without preservation access becomes for ever impossible.' The Trust's objectives were set out with renewed vigour in G.M. Trevelyan's *Must England's Beauty Perish?*, a passionate and eloquent plea published in 1929.

Bailey also enlisted the help of those with administrative skills and experience on to the Executive and the Finance and General Purposes committees. R.C. Norman, a future Chairman of London County Council and of the BBC, and brother of the Governor of the Bank of England, began to shape the Finance Committee into an effective body. A Publicity Committee, on which Chorley served, was set up in 1928, and membership began to increase. In 1920 there were 713 members, by 1925 this had increased to 973 and by 1930 membership stood at 1,959.

The timidity with which the Trust's committees regarded historic buildings after the Barrington Court fiasco was gradually overcome, thanks to the generosity of a man whose wealth and influence reassured the doubters. The Marquess Curzon of Kedleston, former Viceroy of India, had a passionate regard for what he described as 'beautiful and ancient buildings, which recall the life and customs of the past, and are not only an historical document of supreme value, but are a part of the spiritual and aesthetic heritage of the nation, imbuing it with reverence and educating its taste.' Curzon had bought the fifteenth-century Tattershall Castle in Lincolnshire in 1911, after its fireplaces had been looted by a firm of antique dealers for export to America. The medieval fireplaces were brought back in triumph and the keep repaired with scrupulous care by William Weir, an architect in whom the Trust and the SPAB had complete confidence. Weir was employed again for the repair of Bodiam Castle, the late fourteenth-century castle in Sussex that Curzon had purchased in 1917. Both Tattershall and Bodiam came to the Trust on Lord Curzon's death in 1925. Lord Esher's tribute is revealing of both men: 'His heart was sound enough, but his temper was hasty. What of that? A minor fault.'

The effectiveness of this new leadership for a new era was quickly demonstrated by a succession of major acquisitions. In 1924 Viscount Grey of Falloden, the former Foreign Secretary and a native of Northumberland, wrote to *The Times* strongly supporting the efforts of the county Natural History Society to buy the Farne Islands and present them to the Trust. Grey explained

Bodiam Castle in Sussex, bought by Lord Curzon in 1917 and repaired by William Weir.

the quite exceptional ornithological importance of the Farnes, describing how they were then the northernmost breeding place of the Sandwich tern. Almost certainly it was his close friend, future biographer and fellow Northumbrian, Trevelyan, who had enlisted his support. What *The Times* readers would not have known was that behind the distinguished political career was personal tragedy: the death of his wife, the burning of his home and the loss of his eyesight through overwork, so that, as Trevelyan explained, 'the bounty of nature's loveliness was spread before him, invisible'. Grey had been virtually blind for eight years when he wrote his appeal for the Farnes: £2,200 was successfully raised and the islands became Trust property in 1925.

Two years later Lord Grey opened the newly acquired nature reserve at

Hawksmoor, near Cheadle. In 1926 a local ornithologist, J.R.B. Masefield, a cousin of the Poet Laureate, secured an option to buy 208 acres of Staffordshire woodland, in which were nesting hobby, bittern, dipper and water-rail. This gave the opportunity for the Trust to launch an appeal strongly supported by the Chairman of the County Council and the Lord Lieutenant. Lord Grey's speech at the opening ensured reports in both the local and national press. The involvement of leading figures in the county meant that the approach to fundraising was simple and remarkably effective, encouraging involvement at a local level and contributing to the Trust's steadily growing reputation nationally.

The purchase of woodland near Berkhamsted in Hertfordshire followed this pattern, but in a more dramatic and highly publicised way. In 1925 the Trustees of Lord Brownlow's Ashridge estate had announced that an area of several thousand acres around Aldbury and Ivinghoe Beacon were to be put on the market to pay death duties. Initially the reaction of the office at Buckingham Palace Gardens was that there was insufficient time to acquire them for the Trust, but Trevelyan, who then lived at Berkhamsted, soon brought his influence to bear. He addressed public meetings and persuaded a local resident, Mrs Renée Courtauld, to donate £20,000 to the appeal, which she did anonymously. As often happens with the Trust's boldest efforts at acquisition, the momentum was now irresistible. On 20 October 1925 there was a letter in *The Times* appealing for £80,000 to secure 1,600 acres. It was signed by Stanley Baldwin – on whose recommendation Trevelyan had been appointed Regius Professor of History at Cambridge – Ramsay MacDonald, and the Earl of Oxford and Asquith: a tally of three Prime Ministers. The final stages of negotiations were not straightforward but Bailey and Trevelyan handled them with skill. 'We were near shipwrecked' wrote Trevelyan afterwards, reckoning that it was John Bailey who ensured that, over Ashridge, the Trust was 'saved by . . . skilful steering'. The Trust was back on the national stage.

Bailey and Trevelyan were not only decisive leaders; they also clarified the Trust's objectives in the minds of its committees, members and the general public. Trevelyan's 'Plea on behalf of the National Trust' of 1929 restated many of the principles set out in its Act of Parliament. He chose as his title, *Must England's Beauty Perish?*, to show that this was not to be a dry or academic treatise, but a passionate appeal for help to protect places which could continue to enrich the nation's life.

Experience and dread necessity have compelled those who care for the preservation of natural beauty to regard the National Trust as their best friend.

Every month those who scent the danger in the wind threatening some loved place come to us bearing precious gifts which we are to preserve, not indeed locked away, but as the public heritage ... But every increase in the number and area of our properties means increase in our financial liabilities. *We have no central endowment. We have at present less than a thousand annual subscribers. We must get rid of both these handicaps if we are to win the race that lies before us.*

Trevelyan was himself one of the Trust's greatest benefactors. His drive and generosity helped to secure the Longshaw estate in Derbyshire, the Newtimber estate on the South Downs, land around Housesteads Fort on Hadrian's Wall in Northumberland and great stretches of the Lake District. He used his friendship with Stanley Baldwin and the author John Buchan to encourage major donations from the Pilgrim Trust, a charity set up in 1930 by the American railroad tycoon Edward Harkness, to provide grants for educational, cultural and social causes: Baldwin was Chairman and Buchan one of the trustees. Ties of similar importance were made with the Youth Hostels Association. Its members may not have realised that their President's walking companions had to plead with Trevelyan to limit their excursions to a gentle twenty-five miles a day; or that as a young man he regularly led the field in the Man Hunt, in which Geoffrey Young, the future Chancellor of the Exchequer Hugh Dalton and others chased each other over the Lake District fells for three days. Recent descriptions of him as a humourless old man asleep in Trust committee meetings have left a very partial and misleading picture of G.M. Trevelyan.

'The importance of the Trust is a measure of the constant diminution of all that is lovely and solitary in Britain,' Trevelyan wrote. He first mentioned a major Trust initiative to save the coast in a letter to Hamer, of December 1930. The scheme he put forward was for the Trust to carry out a survey of stretches of unspoilt coastline which might, with the help of the Pilgrim Trust, be acquired before they came on the open market. The Secretary of the Pilgrim Trust, Tom Jones — 'a patriotic Welshman' — had particularly in mind the Pembrokeshire coast, which Trevelyan had personally visited earlier in the year, reporting back that 'the idea of *saving the coastline* in various regions, including Pembroke, might perhaps appeal specially to the chiefs of the PT and of the NT.' Trevelyan went on:

It would require preliminary investigation, not of course carried out in the name of the Pilgrim Trust and perhaps not even in that of the National Trust. Some moderate sum would have to be devoted to this investigation. Our present idea is that many headlands, and cliffs and lowlands of the sea coast could be secured in districts not yet touched by development . . . all parts of the coastline are particularly liable to ultimate injury by development, and are yet particularly loved by the holiday maker – and the nature lover in whose interest it is urgently desirable that they should be preserved in their natural beauty.

Here was the germ of an idea for a national campaign to protect the coastline. The level of support that Trevelyan had hoped for from the Pilgrim Trust did

C. P. Trevelyan (later Sir Charles and donor of
Wallington in Northumberland) and G. M. Trevelyan
walking on the Devon coast, c.1906.

not materialise and it was to be over thirty years before Enterprise Neptune brought Trevelyan's scheme to reality. It was to be the most effective campaign in the history of the Trust, and its greatest achievement.

Must England's Beauty Perish? has a revealing section on 'nature and history', which gets to the heart of why Trevelyan believed the role of the Trust to be so important. He noted an increasing enthusiasm for ancient monuments and 'a growing tenderness for old houses'. 'Visits to historic scenes and buildings have become one of the most inspiring methods of modern education', he wrote, preparing the ground for Lord Lothian's initiative a decade later. He also reaffirmed the belief of the Trust's founders in the intimate relationship between buildings and landscape:

> In this way men and women brought up amid the rawest modern surroundings of city sights and sounds, obtain, as an invaluable corrective to their mental and imaginative outlook, an affectionate sympathy with the very different lives of their ancestors. And this effect is most powerfully produced when the building of 'historic interest' stands in its setting of 'natural beauty' as Bodiam Castle amid its meadows and trees.

Most deeply felt of all was Trevelyan's plea for support for the Trust on the grounds of what he called 'spiritual values': 'The happiness and the soul's health of the whole people are at stake. The preservation of natural beauty as an element in our nation's life is a cause that deeply concerns people of every sort who are working to maintain any ideal standards and any healthy life ... without vision the people perish, and without natural beauty the English people will perish in the spiritual sense.'

CHAPTER FOUR

SUCCESSION AND INTERVENTION

A COMPLEX PATTERN of relationships linked scientists working on Blakeney Point with those carrying out research at Wicken Fen. Their findings were to have far-reaching consequences for the National Trust. Among the pupils that Professor Oliver took to his field laboratory at Blakeney was Arthur Tansley, in due course to be a pioneer plant ecologist and the first Chairman of the Nature Conservancy. As with several other leading figures in the development of nature conservation in this country, Tansley did much of his work on National Trust properties, served on its committees and contributed to some of its most forward-looking publications.

In the early 1920s Tansley was teaching in the University Botany School at Cambridge. He already had a national reputation: in 1913 he had been made first President of the British Ecological Society and in 1917 editor of the *Journal*

Professor Frank Oliver with students
at Blakeney Point, Norfolk.

of Ecology, a post he held for twenty-one years. An enthusiastic supporter of the Cambridge Botany School Ecology Club, he organised in 1921 a bicycle excursion to the nature reserve at Wicken Fen. One of those in the party was Harry Godwin. Tansley's interest in plant ecology had been nurtured by Oliver; now Tansley was to launch Godwin on a lifetime's study of succession in semi-natural vegetation. This was of more than just academic significance. It was to lead to a far clearer understanding of the processes taking place on nature reserves, and consequently to an awareness of new obligations facing the Trust.

What Godwin observed at Wicken was that, left to themselves, plants of the open fen would progressively give way to woodland species, particularly if falling water levels caused the peat to dry out. Drainage of the farmland around Wicken meant that this was a constant problem, unless a high water table was artificially maintained by pumping into a long-established network of ditches. Changes were accelerated when plants colonised the edges of dykes or open water. Although such processes had been observed by others, Godwin recorded them through scientific monitoring of small plots which were regularly resurveyed. Godwin published a lifetime's work at Wicken in 1978, in his *Fenland: its Ancient Past and Uncertain Future*. Similar systematic analysis was applied by Godwin to the study of plant communities in the Norfolk Broads.

Godwin also studied the effects of the harvesting of sedge, which had been practised by the villagers of Wicken for centuries. Plant succession was, he found, diversified by such traditional activities, with different species responding in different ways to cutting. A fuller understanding of these processes was dependent on more scientific evidence of the history of plant communities. Godwin needed to go back far beyond the recent history recorded in his trial plots, and with Tansley's encouragement, he turned to the study of pollen analysis, which was just beginning to be developed in Sweden and north-west Germany. He also enlisted the help of historians, geologists and archaeologists to help him piece together a chronology for the different deposits in the Fens. At a meeting of the Royal Society in 1935 Godwin described how, by analysing the tree pollen preserved for centuries in successive layers of Fenland peat, it had been possible to trace changes in different tree species over long periods. This in turn could lead to a greater understanding of the composition and structure of other, related vegetation in wooded areas.

These findings transformed the study of ecology. They were also to have a lasting impact on the way nature reserves were managed. No longer was it enough to assume that the Trust or other conservation organisations had done

Bi-plane at Blakeney Point, crashed during the vegetation survey
on 25 July 1922. The pilot appears in a subsequent photograph,
apparently unharmed apart from a bandaged head.

their job once sites of nature conservation importance had been taken into
ownership. Without an understanding of previous patterns of land use, such as
grazing or coppicing, nature reserves would develop in ways which might be
detrimental to their plant communities and their whole ecosystem.

As the wider implications of Godwin's discoveries came to be understood,
so the word 'conservation' was increasingly used to describe the active management of nature reserves and the enhancement of their wildlife populations.
At the same time what had previously been described as 'preservation' now
acquired pejorative overtones, implying a negative, even negligent attitude. In
practice the distinction was often meaningless and at times showed the worst
sort of academic detachment from the realities of conservation. Often protection
from development or commercial exploitation is the first step in conserving and
managing a site in a responsible way.

In 1947 Tansley became the Trust's honorary Adviser on Ecology. The
following year a leaflet, 'Notes for the Guidance of Local Committees who
are responsible for the Management of Properties of Nature Conservation
Importance' was issued – anonymously – to which both Tansley and Sir Edward

Salisbury, the honorary Adviser on Botany and Zoology, seem to have contributed. The Trust could no longer plead ignorance of the importance, for instance, of sheep grazing to Box Hill or of coppicing at Selsdon Wood, and its committees tried to act accordingly. At some properties shortage of money, manpower and machinery meant that the Trust failed to conserve valuable plant communities; problems which were greatly exacerbated by the Second World War. Lack of resources did the damage as often as ignorance. But the Trust had been taught by Tansley, Godwin and others that protection, preservation and conservation were interrelated responsibilities. That in turn pointed to more knowledgeable and ultimately more professional ways of looking after countryside properties.

Some of these tensions found expression in the Annual Report for the Trust's Jubilee year in 1945, and it is tempting to see the hand of Tansley in the section dealing with nature reserves:

> Nature's tempo brings changes too slow to be easily seen. At Wicken Fen the group of scientists and others who form the Trust's Local Committee have long worked on the intricate problems of maintaining, in spite of nature's tendency to change, static conditions on a property rich in natural history interest dependent on those static conditions. On stretches of downland, on heather-clad moors or in Sussex copses different conditions have been studied, and now the lessons learned at Wicken and elsewhere can show how better to preserve over a long term not only natural history interest but wild beauty for the enjoyment of the public. In this field the Trust has already acquired a unique experience and is still experimenting.

The Trust's practice at Wicken had not always measured up to this ideal, because the local committee was chronically short of funds. By the 1920s Wicken Fen was already heavily in debt to the Trust's pitifully small General Fund and required a subsidy of over £500 a year to maintain even a semblance of effective management. Regrettably, Sir Edward Salisbury later resisted efforts to have the 'Notes' revised, so laying the Trust open to the criticism that its nature conservation practices were outdated.

The enlisting of authorities such as Tansley on to the Trust's committees suggests a growing awareness of the need for better informed management. There were other changes. At the age of eighty-one Harriet Yorke relinquished

The Naturalists painted by Leslie Watson on an East Anglian heath
in the summer of 1949. A. G. Tansley (second from the left) became
the National Trust's honorary Adviser on Ecology in 1947.

the post of honorary Treasurer but continued to serve on the Council and Executive Committee until her death in 1930. The few remaining links with the founders were being severed. In 1931 the Chairman, John Bailey, died. Ronald Norman was felt by many to be the ideal choice to succeed: he had joined the Executive Committee in 1918, was an outstanding Deputy Chairman of the Trust and could be relied on to act wisely and decisively. Just occasionally he was impulsive, but spontaneity can be an asset on committees. He was elegant, had effortless charm and a modesty which meant that he was liked – adored almost – by the staff. To Hamer's secretary, Miss Spencer-Wilkinson, he was 'that beautiful man'. James Lees-Milne regards this as an understatement and prefers to describe him as simply 'the most charming and most handsome man who has ever existed'. Lord Reith, not noted for generous praise, was enormously impressed by his skill as a chairman, his intellectual capacity and his fastidious taste, confirming that Norman was 'kind in the highest degree'. Reith also referred to his 'essential modesty' and it was partly this, and partly the fact that he was not himself a great landowner in touch with potential donors of estates, that persuaded Norman to decline the chairmanship. He agreed instead to help Trevelyan to find someone suitable.

First choice was H.A.L. Fisher, the distinguished historian. When he too declined, Norman approached the Marquess of Zetland. As Curzon's secretary and then biographer, Zetland was familiar with the Trust's work. He accepted the offer and immediately put his great experience of government at the service of the Trust. Even in 1935 when he was made Secretary of State for India, he continued to take the closest interest in the Trust's affairs, summoning the Secretary round to the India Office to run through Executive Committee agendas and ensuring that he was fully briefed on potentially controversial issues. This punctiliousness extended to his dress, which was slightly dandified and made him look as if he was wearing a corset. He was rather pompous and to some of those who worked with him often seemed unimaginative; but he had an incisive intellect which he applied tirelessly to the good of the Trust and was able to bring a committee to a decision without bullying. Zetland continued to serve as Chairman until 1945.

There could scarcely be a more bizarre alliance than that between Lord Zetland and Ferguson's Gang. This notorious group of zealots was drawn to the Trust by what might be called the Octopus connection. When in 1913 Lord Curzon spoke at the opening of Colley Hill in Surrey, he referred to London as 'a great octopus stretching out its tentacles in order to lay hold of the rich

William Brigg and his twin brother John handing over
the deeds of East Riddlesden Hall in Yorkshire to the
Marquess of Zetland on 31 May 1934. Zetland was
Chairman of the National Trust from 1931 to 1945.

pastures and leafy lanes of the countryside'. The metaphor gave Clough Williams-
Ellis the title of his *England and the Octopus*, an eloquent, powerful and irreverent
plea for the protection of the countryside; and it was the publication of this book
in 1928 which led a group of sympathisers to pledge themselves to 'destroy and
frustrate the Octopus'. At moments of greatest need, when the future of a
potential acquisition was hanging in the balance for want of a few hundred
pounds, masked members of the gang would burst into the Trust's offices and
deposit bundles of notes and coins in front of an incredulous Lord Zetland or a
bemused Samuel Hamer.

The true names of the gang have never been revealed, but the original
members and inner circle were known as Ferguson, Sister Agatha, Kate O'Brien,
the Nark, Bill Stickers, the Bloody Bishop and Red Biddy. Another member of
the gang, Black Maria, could be relied on to produce large sums of money at
need with no questions asked. Their achievements were as improbable as their
names: the preservation, restoration and endowment of Shalford Mill, an

eighteenth-century watermill near Guildford; the rescue of the Old Town Hall at Newtown on the Isle of Wight; and the acquisition of Mayon Cliff in Cornwall, which they celebrated in song:

> Up on the cliffs by Mayon Castle,
> What 'as you seen to make a fuss?
> Up on the cliffs by Mayon Castle
> There I seen the Octopus!
>
> What was the Octopus a-doing?
> East of the Longships as you go?
> E'd some bricks and a load o' concrete
> For to start on a bungalow . . .
>
> Save me barrow, me old ring barrow,
> Take it safe to the National Trust
> Save me castle, me old cliff castle,
> Save us all from the Octopus!

Perhaps most valuable of all, their exploits were followed avidly by the national press. 'Masked lady weighed down with silver' ran the headline in *The Times* of 1 February 1933. The article reported that the National Trust had secured an endowment for Shalford Mill, in strange circumstances:

> On January 13, when the day about Victoria was slipping into an unpleasant evening, cold and wet, a taxicab stopped outside 7 Buckingham Palace Gardens. A lady, heavily masked, got out and announced herself to the commissionaire as 'Red Biddy' of 'Ferguson's Gang'. She was bent with the weight of a heavy bag and desired to see the Secretary, with whom, without lifting her mask, she deposited £100 in silver . . . she left, as she had come, recognised by no-one.

In November *The Times* revealed that 'The Smasher' had left a further £200 and he too had gone unrecognised. Not all their gifts were in cash. At Christmas one year the Secretary received a small bottle of ruby-coloured liquid labelled 'Sloe Gin of Ferguson's Gang, gathered, matured and bottled by Black Maria and Bill Stickers'. Nor was their acquisitiveness solely for the benefit of the Trust.

The interior of Shalford Mill in Surrey.
The eighteenth-century watermill – headquarters
of the anonymous members of Ferguson's Gang –
was given to the Trust in 1932.

The Old Town Hall at Newtown, Isle of Wight, photographed by
a member of Ferguson's Gang in 1933, prior to restoration.

After the dinner on 28 February 1935, to celebrate the Trust's fortieth anniversary, a member of the Gang was found to have pinched the Dorchester's entire supply of toothpicks. Occasional back-sliding happens among even the most beneficent *banditti*. The Trust, if not the Dorchester, was fully compensated for any embarrassment by Ferguson's visit to Broadcasting House that same year. In his talk, the masked leader of the Gang gave away nothing but his sex; and the Trust received £900 and 600 new members.

Hamer retired as Secretary in 1933, although he remained on the Publicity Committee, an acknowledgement of over twenty years at the centre of the Trust's affairs. His successor was Donald MacLeod Matheson, who seems to have puzzled and intrigued even those who worked closest with him.

There was no doubt about Matheson's intellect, which made him a match even for the Trevelyans when they taxed their visitors with quizzes after dinner at their family home of Wallington in Northumberland. His dedication to his work meant that he would often stay in the office until midnight, catching up with correspondence and correcting minutes. Concerns about his health had encouraged him to leave his job of Assistant Secretary to the Gas, Light & Coke

Company and accept a much lower salary from the Trust. He was not the last person to imagine that working for the Trust would be a gentle, as well as civilised occupation. During his period as Secretary the Trust began to adopt a more professional approach to public relations, turning to good advantage contacts with the BBC where his sister, Hilda Matheson, was Director of Talks. To the friendly, informal office at Buckingham Palace Gardens Matheson brought efficiency, dedication and a sensitivity to the feelings of others that Zetland sometimes lacked. On occasion he would disconcert the owners of country houses by arriving on a motorcycle, which at night he rode without a headlamp but with a torch in his mouth.

In the 1930s the Trust advanced on a broad front. Tansley and Godwin were helping to develop the management skills needed to look after its nature reserves and woodland. It was beginning to appreciate that public support would depend on modern methods of communication, including broadcasting. In 1936 the first Regional Committee was set up in Northern Ireland and proved extremely effective. Its first property, Killynether House and its surrounding woodlands in County Down, was acquired the following year and thanks to the generosity of the Pilgrim Trust and help from the Youth Hostels Association of Northern Ireland, White Park Bay in County Antrim was purchased in 1938. The tragic break-up of country houses and their estates was a problem which was addressed in 1934, at the Trust's Annual General Meeting.

In *Must England's Beauty Perish?* Trevelyan noted that 'of all the *lands* in our possession far the greater part is uncultivated ground . . . of no agricultural value'. In the 1930s that also was changing. The Trust had to learn how to look after great agricultural estates. Almost by accident it was taught how to do so by a woman at least as remarkable as Octavia Hill. Both were artists. Beatrix Potter brought delight to countless children through her books. Beatrix Heelis, as she became on her marriage to William Heelis, brought vision, determination and extraordinary generosity to her work for the Trust. Just as she understood exactly how to thrill children by scaring them, so she knew when to terrorise the Trust, for its own good.

At an early age Beatrix Potter learnt what it was to be undervalued and patronised. A stubborn streak which she inherited from both her mother and

(*Overleaf*) White Park Bay in County Antrim, Northern Ireland, was bought in 1938 with the help of the Youth Hostels Association of Northern Ireland and the Pilgrim Trust.

father meant that she was hurt but undeterred by discouragement. Repressive and stuffy her parents may have been, but they numbered among their friends outstanding artists and writers. The radical politician John Bright was a frequent visitor to their London house and so too was John Millais. Beatrix was particularly fond of William Gaskell, husband of the novelist and a Unitarian minister immersed in social work. When news of his death came in 1884 she recorded in her journal that: 'If ever any one led a blameless peaceful life, it was he .... There has always been a deep child-like affection between him and me.' Although she was later dismissive of the Unitarians, her essential goodness and uncomplicated beliefs never deserted her: in her Will she stipulated that her bible was to remain on the washstand beside her bed at Hill Top, her farm between Esthwaite Water and Windermere.

The friendship with Hardwicke Rawnsley was of lasting importance to her. As the royalties from her books increased, she used them to purchase property in the Lake District, first in 1905 to buy Hill Top, and then to acquire the other estates that she ultimately passed over to the National Trust. By the time she married William Heelis in 1913, her writing of children's books was nearly over and she was committed to being a Lake District farmer and the wife of a country solicitor.

The way her life appeared to change course has prompted speculation about the influence William Heelis had on her creative writing and illustrating. Beatrix Potter's interest in the protection of the natural beauty of the Lake District is apparent from her very earliest visits there. The mutual respect with which she and the local farming community regarded each other was increasingly important to her, as was her very happy marriage. Her own simple explanation for why she largely abandoned her literary work is enough. She subjected her eyesight to hours of strain while working on her exquisite studies of fungi and on the minute detail and delicate touches of colour in her illustrations. She began to realise, as have other illustrators such as Edward Lear and Charles Tunnicliffe, that to continue to work to the scale necessary for her books would mean feebler drawings and rapidly deteriorating sight. As she told her publisher in 1921, 'I am utterly tired of doing them and my eyes are wearing out.' Again, when she was working on *The Fairy Caravan* in 1929 she acknowledged, 'My eyes have lost the faculty for seeing clean colours.' Instead she directed her powers of creativity into work for the National Trust.

Troutbeck Park Farm lies at the head of the Troutbeck Valley, with nearly 2,000 acres of sheep grazing running up towards the Kirkstone Pass. In 1923 it came on the market and immediately attracted the interest of developers keen to build houses in the valley bottom. With the proceeds from her books Beatrix Potter purchased the farm and then asked the Trust whether, on certain strict conditions, it would accept it on her death. She told Hamer that she intended it should be kept together as an entity, 'that a good intelligent solvent tenant is preferable to a rack rent' and that the traditional farmhouse furniture should be retained. 'Lakes housewives are accustomed to the care of old oak furniture', she wrote, and added notes on precisely how the farm should be stocked with pure Herdwick sheep, the sturdy Lake District breed so well suited to grazing the fells.

In 1927 she used her illustrations to support the Trust even more directly. Fifty drawings were sent to one of her American admirers, Bertha Mahony of the Boston Bookshop for Boys and Girls, 'to save a strip of foreshore woodland and meadow, near Windermere Ferry'. Her 'friends in Boston' contributed £104 and Cockshott Point was secured. They were told that 'it will be thrown open to the public next summer – to the great pleasure of strangers from the Lancashire mill towns who like to picnic beside the lake'.

Two years later she became not just a benefactor of the Trust, but also its farm manager. In October 1929 the Monk Coniston estate of 4,000 acres near Coniston Water came on the market, and 1,500 acres including Monk Coniston Hall were immediately purchased. This left seven farms, the famous beauty spot of Tarn Hows, cottages and open fell. She proposed to Hamer that she should buy this remaining 2,500 acres, selling on part to the Trust when the necessary money had been raised, and retaining the remainder which she would farm herself and leave to the Trust on her death. She congratulated the Chairman, John Bailey, on his 'dignified appeal' in *The Times* and added: 'Those of us who have felt the spirit of the fells reckon little of passing praise; but I do value the esteem of others who have understanding. It seems that we have done a big thing; without premeditation; suddenly; inevitably – what else could one do? It will be a happy consummation if the Trust is able to turn this quixotic venture into a splendid reality.'

The Trust's suggestion that she should assume responsibility for running the whole estate she welcomed with amused approval: '. . . and I have a personal gratification – they have asked me to manage it for a time, 'til it is in better order; . . . interesting work at other people's expense!' Just how much she had to teach the Trust is evident in her letters about repairs to Yew Tree Farm, Coniston: 'The mason Cookson and his labourers have been most conscientious in their work doing it old fashioned style . . . I can only say if I have spent too much I am totally unrepentant. I consider Yew Tree as a typical north-country farmhouse, very well worth preserving. Besides, you cannot let a farm without a habitable house.'

Beatrix Potter took immense trouble over the preservation of features which were part of the history of her buildings. She was no less concerned to ensure that her tenants could earn a reasonable livelihood. To help the tenant of Yew Tree Farm she provided some of her own furniture for the parlour where his wife was to serve teas to visitors. The relationship between commerce and conservation was to her straightforward. If income could be provided to further the aims of the Trust, without compromising its objectives, there was no need for qualms. Her books paid for most of her acquisitions. Farmers' teas would help pay the rent. She consoled herself with a misquotation from the Scriptures: 'Blessed are they that expect very little for they shall *not* be disappointed.'

The relationship with the Trust was not always to be so cosy as it was over the purchase of the Monk Coniston estate. Major H.M. Heyder, the Trust's honorary Forestry Adviser, simply could not understand her insistence on tree felling 'in her own way, on picturesque lines'. He confessed that 'I have always thought it somewhat odd that a lady, who has a perfectly competent husband, should insist on managing every detail of farms and woodland problems herself'. Beatrix Potter had encountered similar prejudices when as a young girl she had submitted an impeccably researched and illustrated paper 'On the Germination of the Spores of Agaricineae' to a meeting at Kew, which she was not allowed to deliver in person and which was read for her by the Assistant Director, George Massee. 'I opine that he has passed several stages of development into a fungus himself', she had noted in her private journal. Over thirty years later she was not inclined to keep such feelings to herself.

In 1931 she bought Thwaite Farm, Coniston. The Trust was told the farm would be transferred straight away provided the gift remained anonymous. When her name appeared in the next Annual Report, she wrote: 'I'm very much annoyed about it . . . You had better tell Prof Trevelyan what he has done. Willie and I made up our minds to give a good deal more if my mother had died last time when she was so ill. *Now I won't.* It must take its chance.'

If Beatrix Potter had a low opinion of academics, it was nothing compared with her views on the inadequacies of land agents. Whomever the Trust appointed to be its first full-time agent in the Lake District was bound not to come up to expectations. The choice of Bruce Logan Thompson was in fact an

The kitchen at Townend, a seventeenth-century Lake District
farmhouse in Troutbeck village. Townend was owned by the Browne
family for 300 years and acquired by the Trust in 1947.

inspired one. He had qualified for the Bar, but had then worked at Buckingham
Palace Gardens as the Trust's Assistant Secretary. He clearly found some of the
committee work uncongenial and is remembered for one heroic interjection
when he felt the Trust's ideals were being compromised: 'Gentlemen, I do beg
of you that you have some regard to zeal for the Cause!' In 1930 Thompson had
published a book about the Trust's Lake District properties, which he knew
well, as his home was in Westmorland. When in 1932 he was offered the chance
to become the Trust's Northern Area Representative, he leapt at it.

Bruce Thompson established a reputation for fairness and integrity. After thirty years of work in the Lake District it was said of him that 'not a farmer, not a shepherd did not know and love him'. Beatrix Potter was the exception. She clearly took pleasure in having her own preconceptions confirmed, writing to tell the Trust's Secretary that Thompson 'seems to have no understanding about anything; and he is not learning either'. It had always been her belief that '*an absentee landlord with a typical Land Agent*, I think that is the system that has made what socialism exists in the countryside . . . The typical agent has the faults of the idle rich, with bumptiousness added.' One of the reasons why she advised the Trust against taking on as tenants 'semi-genteel outsiders' was that 'their morals are sometimes bad; or they are people who run [up] debts to tradesmen'. Lake District farmers – honest but untidy – were preferable.

Whatever anguish he may have felt over his conflicting loyalties, Matheson had to reply tactfully to each fusillade from Beatrix Potter. 'A man cannot help having been born dull', she wrote on one occasion: 'Thompson is supercilious as well. He destroyed the finest group of oaks on Thwaite, dealing with a man he had been warned against . . . He seems to have no sense at all. And not capable of learning. Indeed, excusably; because it is impossible to inculcate a pictorial sense of trees arranged in landscape, when imagination is a blank.'

Her final verdict on Thompson was also her verdict on the organisation which she supported with such insight and generosity: 'The Trust is a noble thing, and humanly speaking – immortal. There are some silly mortals connected with it; but they will pass.'

Beatrix Potter died on 22 December 1943. Her property went to Willie for his lifetime, and on his death in 1945, all her cottages, farmhouses, and 4,000 acres of land passed to the National Trust. She left instructions that the rooms and furnishings at Hill Top 'may be kept in their present condition', that her farms should be let at moderate rents and that the landlord's flocks of sheep on the fell farms should continue to be of the pure Herdwick breed.

CHAPTER FIVE

ENGAGING
AESTHETES

T HERE ARE MOMENTS in the history of the National Trust when
the mood changes. It is as though one symphonic movement has come to an
end, and another begins, in a different key and with new thematic material. The
musical analogy is worth pursuing because it is revealing of other things. Miranda
and Octavia Hill loved putting on amateur productions of comic opera for their
East End children. Singing was to Octavia 'a complete way of pouring out all
which is too strong, too deep and sad and joyous to be kept to oneself', and she
had a beautiful contralto voice. Their friend Arthur Rackham was often roped
in to paint the sets. In the 1920s, the scene changes. What the generation of
Bailey and Trevelyan longed to hear was the sound of the Northumbrian pipes
on a windswept hilltop. Then the reedy strains of that particular rural idyll began
to seem rather monotonous. An increasingly influential figure in the Trust's
affairs as Chairman of the Country Houses Committee was the witty and urbane
Oliver Brett, later 3rd Viscount Esher, who had little use for the stout walking
boots worn by those he called 'mangle-wurzels'. It was time for another change
of scenery and the Trust would look to the likes of Rex Whistler and John Piper
for designs.

The changes that transformed the Trust in the mid-1930s cannot be attributed
to a new chairman or secretary, nor were they the result of conscious decisions
made by any committee. It was more a matter of the Trust reflecting and
responding to what was going on around it. Without this shift in attitude, the
Trust would never have found itself so deeply involved in the fate of country
houses.

The story of the Country Houses Scheme has often been told. Its inspiration,
Lord Lothian, makes an impassioned plea in 1934 that the Trust should rescue
country houses and their owners in distress. A young champion, James Lees-
Milne, steps forward. He declares that his passions are not 'for flesh and blood'
but for 'bricks and mortar'. Filled with missionary zeal he rides out, either on a
bicycle or in the Trust's ancient and unreliable car, on his quest to palace after

palace. Thanks to his tact and youthful enthusiasm many of the finest of these houses now belong to the Trust. All this is true; but there is more to the story than that.

As has been shown, the Trust's commitment to the preservation of historic houses goes right back to the founders. Partly because of Ruskin's influence,

James Lees-Milne, Secretary of the
Country Houses Committee from 1936 to 1951,
painted by Derek Hill in 1951.

their efforts were directed to what were loosely thought of as medieval buildings, although this did not preclude an interest in Tudor houses such as Barrington Court. Manor houses particularly interested Robert Hunter, because he not only appreciated their historic value, but saw that manorial rights over large areas of common land would be secured at the same time. The Trust was consequently very much in tune with what the architectural historian John Cornforth has called 'the cult of the castle and the manor house', which took hold in the 1930s. Among the buildings restored with care at that time and which influenced taste considerably were Ightham Mote and Sissinghurst Castle in Kent, Ockwells in Berkshire, and Westwood Manor in Wiltshire. In due course the Trust was to own or hold covenants over all these houses.

During the 1920s the Trust began to show more confidence in its ability to look after its buildings, some relatively modest, others involving a major commitment. In 1925 it accepted the Chadwich Manor estate on the south-west edge of Birmingham as a gift from Edward and George Cadbury, members of a family who were to be outstanding benefactors of the Trust. As well as a late seventeenth-century house, now leased, the gift included over 400 acres of agricultural estate. As Bailey wrote to *The Times*, 'Access will be given where possible up to the hills. But the farms will remain farms and will not become parks or playgrounds.' It was an important precedent. A succession of smaller houses of great historical importance followed. The gift in 1928 of Stoneacre in Kent gave the Trust responsibility for a fine medieval yeoman's house, with great hall and crown-post roof. In 1938 the architect Sir Herbert Baker gave Owletts in Kent, a Caroline house which had been in his family since 1794.

Paycocke's, a sixteenth-century merchant's house at Coggeshall in Essex, caught the eye of the young Edward Noel-Buxton, MP when he was travelling between Westminster and his north Norfolk constituency. He acquired it in 1904 to ensure its preservation and because it provided a convenient place for him to stay *en route* for London. Between times it could be used by friends such as Gustav Holst, who would enjoy its small garden and fine carved and panelled rooms. Lord Noel-Buxton's involvement with the Trust is a bridge back to the ideals of its founders and forward to those responsible for the Country Houses Scheme. As a young man Noel-Buxton involved himself in the Christian Social Union and in efforts to improve living conditions around Spitalfields in east London. In Parliament he was a supporter of Lloyd George's social legislation and was in contact with the Prime Minister's Private Secretary, Philip Kerr, later Lord Lothian. In 1919 he joined the Labour Party and in 1924 became Minister of Agriculture. The gift of Paycocke's to the Trust in 1924 reflects the increasing interest in early Tudor houses at that time and helps to explain the social and political ideas which influenced such donors. Lord Noel-Buxton's reasons for making the gift are partly explained in an essay he called 'Giving Without Tears' which appeared in 1940 in the *Contemporary Review*. In it he argued strongly for charitable giving as a way of avoiding tax. Noel-Buxton also noted prophetically – both for his family and the Trust – that 'children may bitterly resent the alienation of part of what they regard as their patrimony'.

The case for tax concessions to the owners of historic buildings was first put to the Chancellor of the Exchequer by the Trust in 1923. The approach was discreet and it fell on deaf ears: public opinion had yet to be mobilised. Discretion

"This is my last warning, Charles. If you do not mend your ways I shall leave the estate to you instead of to the National Trust"

H. F. Hoar "PUNCH" Jan. 22. 1947.

and understatement were not the hallmarks of Clough Williams-Ellis, who devoted a devastatingly witty and outspoken chapter of *England and the Octopus* to 'The Great House: its conservation and conversion'. In 1928 this can scarcely have pleased all his readers:

> One hears and one reads a good deal of sentimental gush about the heart-break of old-established landowners forced to sell their ancestral acres through the hardness of the times. Not infrequently, however, they are in low water through their own folly or mismanagement, or they have expensive tastes incompatible with the low returns from landowning. Briefly, though they may be attached to their inheritance, there are other things they care for more... The most genealogically and antiquarian minded of us would scarcely quarrel even with a fifteenth earl for selling his historic seat rather than stint the education of his offspring. The cynical indifference, however, with which too many vendors seem to regard the ultimate fate of what they sell, cannot but make one a little

suspicious of their auction-room anguish. They take no effective steps to prevent the instant desecration of their ancestral groves and meadows by mean buildings, the ruthless destruction of all the amenity that generations have created and guarded, or even of the mansion house itself. Having themselves cleared out, they just let the whole place and its neighbourhood go hang.

Clough Williams-Ellis then made a cogent case for a more responsible approach to taxation, arguing that substantial remissions from rates and tax should carry very definite obligations as well as privileges. He proposed that the editor of *Country Life* should be asked to draft a list of those houses which 'really deserve protection as national monuments and as characteristic and precious parts of England'. There would be no difficulty in establishing criteria for preservation:

> ... it is unthinkable that the great houses of England should be allowed to perish away – the really great houses, that is – those that are great in their architecture, their associations and the beauty of their settings, and not merely great in size. Size, indeed, has nothing to do with their claim to be preserved: it is quality, not bulk, that has survival value, as the unintelligent brontosaurus found to its cost.

England and the Octopus mixed indignation with a gadfly's contempt for the attitudes which allowed so much destruction of what Clough Williams-Ellis valued. At the time this was not a fashionable stance, and he and a few others were lonely voices in a wilderness of philistinism. Why it proved so difficult to change attitudes was that his opponents were not philistines out of ignorance, but by education and choice. They had been taught in the great public schools that team spirit and athleticism were the proper training for life; that the reading of novels was suspect and a love of poetry or music worse. Interest in the visual arts was at best soft, but it might also have sinister implications.

In his autobiography, *Another Self*, James Lees-Milne describes how his father, a fine gardener and a skilful carpenter, loathed decoration of the Georgian period: 'Any furniture of an age later than oak was utterly taboo with him.' George Lees-Milne so despised intellectuals that any poetry books found after the school holidays would be thrown into the stoke-hole furnace. As his son recalled, art was anathema:

> His deadliest, most offensive adjective was 'artistic'. It denoted decadence, disloyalty to the Crown, and unnatural vice. To be called artistic by him with a biting sneer used to make me shake like an aspen leaf. I really believe he would have expected any man but his son, thus described, to challenge him to a duel for the rankest insult.

Over half a century later all this seems very strange. A sign that attitudes towards the arts were changing is evident in the growing interest in Georgian art and architecture, which Robert Byron, Lord Derwent, Christopher Hussey and Professor A.E. Richardson were nurturing. Byron and Derwent were among those who formed the Georgian Group in 1937. For Lees-Milne (another founder member) his moment of decision was when he witnessed as a guest the deliberate mutilation of statues in the grounds of Rousham Park in Oxfordshire. The incident, he wrote, 'brought home to me how passionately I cared for architecture and the continuity of history, of which it was the mouthpiece'. It was to be a revelation of immense personal significance for Lees-Milne and consequently for the Trust as well:

> Those Rococo rooms at Rousham, with their delicate furniture, and portraits of bewigged, beribboned ancestors, were living, palpable children to me. They and the man-fashioned landscape outside were the England that mattered. I suddenly saw them as infinitely fragile and precious. They meant to me then, and have meant ever since, far more than human lives. They represent the things of the spirit.

The language is remarkably similar to that used by Trevelyan to describe his feelings for the landscapes of Northumberland and the Lake District. Lees-Milne brought a commitment no less passionate and no less eloquently expressed to the preservation of the country house.

At the National Trust's annual dinner in 1933, the Director of the Courtauld Institute, Professor W.G. Constable, spoke about the urgent need to protect the growing number of country houses at risk. His points about preferential rating and taxation were echoes of what Clough Williams-Ellis had proposed. The issue became more urgent the following year, when Sir Charles Trevelyan sounded out the Trust on the transfer of his seventeenth-century house, Wallington, and its 13,000 acre estate. In the circumstances his brother, G.M. Trevelyan, could not take on the role of public advocate. With the agreement of Lord Zetland, Matheson approached a man who had the ear of the government and whose own home, Blickling Hall in Norfolk, had already suffered as a result of death duties.

Lord Lothian took an ironic view of the succession duty of around £300,000 that had forced him in 1932 to sell some of the most valuable books from Blickling's library. Between 1916 and 1921 he had been private secretary to Lloyd George when Prime Minister and so had been involved in the drafting of much of his fiscal policy. On succeeding in 1930 to the title of Marquess of

Lothian, and with it four important historic houses, he found himself replying to Lloyd George's letter of congratulation:

> Largely as a result of your all too admirable work a well diluted peerage is now possessed of almost no power, and I discover that I shall have to pay to our exhausted Exchequer almost 40% of the capital value of a mainly agricultural estate. In my capacity as an ordinary citizen I think highly of these arrangements but as an inheritor of a title and estates thereto they will prove somewhat embarrassing.

To avoid further depredations he gave Newbattle Abbey to the universities of Scotland to be used as an adult education college. At the time this was a new role for a country house and one which Lothian worked hard to make a success. Ferniehirst, a border fortress, was let for a modest rent to the Scottish Youth Hostels Association. Blickling was to be a weekend retreat and a place where he and his political friends could discuss the deteriorating international situation. When staying at Blickling, Lothian chose for himself the more austere rooms on the north side of the house. He encouraged his guests to shoot and enjoy his cellar, but as a Christian Scientist he participated in neither himself. Like Matheson, whose sister Hilda was a friend, Lothian frequently travelled by motorcycle. For the coronation of George VI at Westminster Abbey in 1937 he turned up in an Austin 7.

His own experience of succession duty had in 1930 prompted Lothian to write a long letter to *The Times*, urging that income from the taxation of land should be reinvested by the government in agriculture. A lively correspondence followed. He also challenged the Chancellor of the Exchequer, Sir John Simon, on the way agricultural land was valued for probate. In these disputes he was often arguing with colleagues and friends. Some, including Stanley Baldwin, had borrowed Blickling for weeks at a time. Lothian had the right contacts with the government to give the Trust's negotiations renewed impetus and he was the ideal choice of speaker at the Trust's Annual General Meeting on 19 July 1934. He spoke eloquently but few could have predicted just how far-reaching the consequences would be:

> The National Trust has already done a remarkable work in securing in perpetuity for the nation many places of historic interest or natural beauty, and in awakening opinion to the importance of preserving these from destruction, defilement or abuse. I am going to ask you to-day, however, whether it is not possible for the National Trust to extend its protecting arm, in a more definite and considered manner than it has hitherto done, over another part of our national treasure

now threatened with partial destruction – the historic dwelling houses of our country.

I venture to think that the country houses of Britain, with their gardens, their parks, their pictures, their furniture and their peculiar architectural charm, represent a treasure of quiet beauty which is not only specially characteristic but quite unrivalled in any other land. In Europe there are many magnificent castles and imposing palaces. But nowhere I think are there so many or such beautiful country manor houses and gardens, and nowhere, I think, have such houses played so profound a part in moulding the national character and life. Yet most of these are now under sentence of death, and the axe which is destroying them is taxation, and especially that form of taxation known as death duties.

He reminded his audience that the current rate of estate duty stood at 50%. Even Mr Lloyd George's famous budget was relatively moderate. It has been the war and the post-war depression which have raised the rates so devastatingly high. The really high rates have only been in operation for about 15 years. Nor has the full impact of the present system yet been felt. Heirs sell their securities or their books or their valuables before they break up their estates. But once sold these assets cannot be used a second time. Moreover, in the old days these houses were largely maintained by the yield of the agricultural property which surrounded them. But as every landowner knows, since the opening up of agricultural export from the New World, and the growth of direct taxation, the net yield of agricultural property has been immensely reduced. ... This speech is not intended to be an attack on death duties or surtax. ... There is, indeed, much to be said for them as an instrument of social justice, though far more careful study should be made of their practical effect. But let no one mistake that they spell the end of the old rural order.

The first step Lothian proposed was for the National Trust to agree a list of houses of 'real historic interest and artistic merit'. A draft had already been prepared by *Country Life* identifying 60 large and 600 smaller dwelling houses that qualified: 'it is surely not an unmanageable proposition to set to work to preserve them'. He then suggested that these should be exempt from death duties 'provided the house, gardens and historic contents are preserved as a whole and provision made for access by the public from time to time. Death duties should only be levied if the organism, so to speak, is broken up.' The cost to the Treasury would be small in relation to the public benefit: 'Such action is a natural part of that new order of planned private enterprise which is increasingly coming to replace both the unrestricted individualism of the early capitalistic era and the universal socialisation of early Socialist thinkers.'

The particular role he envisaged for the National Trust was to take on the responsibilities of the private owner, when the alternative was the sale of a house and the disposal of its contents, saving not just the building but perpetuating its vitality. 'Why should not the National Trust equip itself to hold properties

Philip Kerr, 11th Marquess of Lothian (1882–1940),
from a drawing by A. de B. Footner.

bequeathed or given to it?' he asked. 'What matters is that these houses, except perhaps the most monumental, should be lived in by people who care for them and also are prepared to make them not merely private homes, but places of hospitality and converse, for those engaged in politics, in literature and the arts, or in some aspect of local or international life.' His ideal was for these houses to continue to be 'living centres of beauty and hospitality and discussion in the form appropriate to our more democratic and far more mobile age. There should be enough land or endowment to cover the cost of maintaining the structure and this endowment should be exempt from taxation.' It was this proposal which was novel and it would, Lothian knew, require new legislation. He concluded

(*Overleaf*) Blickling Hall in Norfolk. The house and its
surrounding estate of 4,768 acres were acquired in 1940,
under the will of the 11th Marquess of Lothian.

by asking for sympathetic consideration of these steps 'which might be taken to preserve for posterity in living form a national treasure of beauty and inspiration which is quite unique in the modern world'.

Lothian followed up his speech with a long and detailed letter to Matheson. He predicted the Trust would need to set up its own professionally competent department of estate management to meet these new responsibilities. If the scheme was successful, then he predicted in time 'a very considerable amount of property will come into its hands'.

At first Lothian and Zetland had in mind a 'Country Houses Association' in which both the Trust and private owners would act together to secure fiscal concessions. A great deal of time and effort went into trying to prepare a co-ordinated approach to the government, with the Trust acting as honest broker. Zetland personally drafted proposals for a joint management committee that would act as 'the organic link between the Association and the National Trust'. To try to learn from practice abroad, the founder president of La Demeure Historique, the Duc de Noailles, was invited to London to address a reception called by the Trust in the rooms of the Royal Geographical Society. But the French model, which involved very modest financial help for private owners, did not find favour with government ministers. Not surprisingly, many country house owners were lukewarm about a partnership with the Trust and uncertain about how it would work in practice. The Trust had therefore to decide whether to press ahead with a much less ambitious scheme or risk further protracted and possibly fruitless negotiation. Zetland's response was decisive: 'the only effective way of preserving the country houses permanently will be getting them transferred to the National Trust'.

With hindsight it is easy to suggest that an opportunity was missed. It might have been possible to persuade the government to make major tax concessions to a body rather similar to the Historic Houses Association that was set up after the war. The Trust could have continued to act as some sort of negotiator between private owners and the government. It certainly made well-intentioned and strenuous efforts to do so, but time was running out. War looked inevitable. There was a solution within the Trust's grasp that would save some great houses at least and the government was willing to act. Zetland and Lothian were politicians and they opted for pragmatism. They could not risk letting the opportunity slip.

A Country Houses Committee was set up in March 1936 and James Lees-Milne appointed its first secretary. The following year the legislation which

Lothian had advocated – enabling the Trust to acquire and hold land or investments to act as endowments for great houses – became law in the National Trust
Act of 1937. What was new in the Act was the provision for donors to provide
endowments in these forms in the knowledge that once the gift to the Trust was
completed, no further tax would be payable.

One of the principles that Octavia Hill had instilled in the Trust was that
each property should be self-supporting, either through occupation by a tenant
with responsibility for all maintenance, or through rental income to meet all
future expenses. In the Trust's early years, assessments of whether properties
were adequately funded were based more on optimism than careful calculation.
Those responsible for the Country Houses Scheme knew that the acquisition of
great estates would occur only if the provision of endowments brought tax
advantages to the donor, in that a capital sum for upkeep would go much further
in the hands of the Trust than if continually eroded by taxation. It was also
increasingly important that the basis of the future funding for each property was
carefully scrutinised by the Finance Committee, which had to be satisfied that
the endowment, whether in land, capital or shares, would be sufficient to meet
future costs.

The Act also extended the purposes of the Trust to include 'the preservation
of furniture and pictures and chattels of every description having national or
historic or artistic interest'; and it provided for 'the access to and enjoyment of
such buildings places and chattels by the public'. Lothian was now able to ensure
that on his death Blickling would pass to the Trust; but as a very fit man in his
fifties there was no reason to suppose that this would take place for many years.

Almost immediately the Trust's new statutory powers made possible a gift
which appeared then and since to be highly improbable. Sir Geoffrey Mander
offered the Trust Wightwick Manor, a house less than fifty years old. The
architect, Edward Ould, was responsible for many of the buildings of Port
Sunlight, Lord Leverhulme's model suburb on the opposite side of the Mersey
from Liverpool. Port Sunlight would have met many of Octavia Hill's criteria
for improved working-class housing, but it was difficult to make a case for
Wightwick Manor being of outstanding historic interest. The house was mock
half-timbered Tudor, on the outskirts of Wolverhampton, with a small but
interesting garden designed by Alfred Parsons. There had to be special pleading.
Sir Geoffrey Mander was an energetic supporter of the Trust in the House of
Commons, particularly over unsympathetic planting by the Forestry Commission
in the Lake District. He was prepared to offer a substantial endowment in the

form of shares in the family's paint and varnish manufacturing business. Sir Geoffrey was also a friend of Sir Charles Trevelyan. Like Wallington, Wightwick is a house with Pre-Raphaelite associations: there are well-preserved Morris wallpapers, de Morgan tiles and Kempe glass. The Director of the Victoria and Albert Museum, Clifford Smith, confirmed that it would in time be regarded as decoration of considerable historical importance. Sir Geoffrey and his second wife were already adding Pre-Raphaelite furniture and pictures to the collection. Lady Mander was young, a brilliant literary historian, waspish, witty and very pretty. The Trust was persuaded.

Armed with the small booklet setting out the intentions of the Country Houses Scheme, Lees-Milne now embarked on the visits he describes so vividly in his diaries. He listened attentively to Lord Berwick's accounts of ghosts at

Attingham Park. He heard Sir Henry and Lady Hoare of Stourhead dispute whether it was during the First World War or in Paris during the Commune that they had been forced to eat rats. At Wallington he had to endure the Trevelyans' quizzes. At Lacock Abbey he coped with Miss Talbot's dances – *thés dansants* or were they tarantelle? – in the swirling smoke from a green yule log. Despairing Lady Newton of Lyme Park would describe the taxation policies of

(*Left*) The Great Parlour at Wightwick Manor in the
West Midlands, the first house to come to the Trust under the
Country Houses Scheme. (*Above*) Sir Geoffrey Mander with his
second wife, the writer Rosalie Glynn Grylls and their
children John and Anthea, in the Library at Wightwick Manor.

successive governments as though she was Marie Antoinette in the tumbril. He even survived visits to West Wycombe, that 'den of ancient vice' as Esher called it, where the Hell Fire Club had met in the eighteenth century. For some, his restraint and discretion reassured. The Hoares probably associated him with their only son and heir who had been killed during the First World War. Others found that his love of architecture and old houses meant that he could share their affection for their family home without embarrassment. Thanks to Lees-Milne and to Esher, the scheme and the way it was implemented proved a triumph.

Even after 1938, when Lord Lothian had accepted the offer to become British Ambassador in Washington, he continued to correspond with Matheson about the Country Houses Scheme. During 1939 and 1940 Lothian subjected himself to a punishing regime of lecturing across America, with the object of turning public opinion in favour of joining the struggle against Hitler. He was responsible for conducting the Destroyers for Bases negotiations that marked a key stage in the delicate process of bringing America into the War. At great personal risk to his own position, he met in Washington Adam von Trott, who was to be executed by the Nazis for his part in the plot against Hitler of July 1943. Lothian was in constant touch during these months with both Roosevelt and Churchill, who found him a 'deeply-stirred man'. On a brief return visit to Blickling, in October 1940, he was undismayed that the house was occupied by the RAF and arranged that more comfortable furniture should be made available. He returned to Washington in November to work on a major speech to be delivered in Baltimore on 11 December, but the papers that reported it across America also carried news of his death from uraemic poisoning, hastened by over-work. Drafting a letter to Roosevelt, Churchill referred to Lothian as 'one of our greatest Ambassadors to the United States', but then changed this to 'our greatest Ambassador to the United States'. Initially sceptical of his abilities, Churchill had come to regard Lothian as 'a man of the very highest character and of far-ranging intellectual scope. All his life his mind played about broad issues of human progress.'

Lothian's legacy was a gift on a huge scale. Blickling is an architectural masterpiece, but it is more than that: it is a building that exemplifies the poetry of architecture, from the first glimpse of towers and gables framed by clipped, undulating yews, to the last fleeting reflection in its crescent lake. Its plasterwork, tapestries and books are all superb. The estate includes over a hundred houses and cottages and 4,700 acres of wooded Norfolk countryside. If the Trust proved to be capable of looking after Blickling, it could be the worthy guardian of any other country house.

As Lothian had foreseen, the Trust would need to develop new skills to care for such places. It would also need to show imagination in how they were used. In his speech to the Trust in 1934 Lothian had warned that country houses should not become 'melancholy museums' but should continue to nurture creativity, 'setting a standard of beauty, in garden and furniture and decoration by which later generations can mould their own practice even though they have come to live under more collective conditions'. His own use of Blickling had demonstrated what he had in mind. The inaugural concert in 1937 of the Norfolk Rural Music School had been held in the Long Gallery, at which Ralph Vaughan Williams had given an address. Lothian had welcomed the staging of a pageant in 1938 to raise funds for the repair of the parish church of neighbouring Aylsham, when the house had been floodlit. In a Codicil to his Will which he personally drafted he specified that it should be 'a place from which public or intellectual or artistic activities go forth and in which persons or conferences of persons interested in such things are entertained'. There was never a conflict in Lothian's mind between this continuing vitality in the life of a country house, and its value as a place for spiritual refreshment. In 1934 he had referred to the country house as 'a treasure of quiet beauty'. He himself would slip away to the Secret Garden when he was in need of tranquillity during his brief visits to Blickling in 1939 and 1940. He wanted to extend that opportunity to a wider public.

If there is a central theme to Lord Lothian's life it is his commitment to resisting social and cultural exclusiveness. As he wrote in 1927, he did not want to see modern civilisation turned back, but wished instead to 'purify and ennoble it by saving people from making prosperity an end in itself, and by putting back into it the quiet and peace-giving love of spiritual things which is the true end of civilized life'. By guiding the National Trust into new areas of conservation and through the gift of Blickling he gave tangible expression to that ideal. Writing of Lord Lothian in 1940, Lord Esher acknowledged that 'it was really entirely due to his inspiration that the Country Houses Scheme of the Trust was initiated'. Within a few months of the bequest of Blickling, Sir Charles Trevelyan gave his Wallington estate to the Trust. These gifts were an affirmation that generosity and creativity were not to be extinguished by the war which was tearing Europe apart.

The Country Houses Committee, under the chairmanship of Lord Esher, could now get into its stride. As the decisions it was making were so momentous, its authority and influence increased proportionally. Its style was very different from the Estates Committee, still chaired by G.M. Trevelyan. Lord Esher was a source of infinite delight for those not on the receiving end of his sometimes wounding humour. He could be devastatingly rude. On a visit to a house not

(*Overleaf*) The North Gallery at Petworth House,
West Sussex, acquired in 1947.

owned by the Trust he asked, 'who is that very ugly woman in the picture over the mantelpiece?' and received the reply from his host, 'My wife'. Some staff adored him, others were nervous and apprehensive. The secret was either to make him laugh, or to let him get his own way. With Lees-Milne as its Secretary, the Country Houses Committee was in the ascendant.

Lord Esher's position was made even more powerful when in 1945 the 28th Earl of Crawford succeeded Zetland as Chairman of the National Trust. During the middle years of this century Lord Crawford occupied an unrivalled position in the artistic life of the nation. As a scholar of paintings and of literature he shared the enthusiasm of those on the Country Houses Committee, although he also loved the countryside and natural beauty. The fact that his home was in Scotland meant that much of the day-to-day direction of the Trust's activities was left to Esher.

Another change which tipped the balance still further in this direction was the resignation of Matheson in 1945. The previous year he had been given six months' leave of absence because of illness, and both Esher and Lees-Milne advised against his return. Two brief interludes ensued during which first a civil servant, George Mallaby, breezed in and out of the post of Secretary, followed by a retired Admiral, Oliver Bevir. Lees-Milne and Esher dismissed Bevir as 'a nice Philistine' and Robin Fedden labelled him 'King Low Brow'. When Bevir resigned in 1949, Jack Rathbone was appointed on Esher's recommendation and continued as Secretary for nearly twenty years. The battle against the Philistines had been decisively won.

The powerful position which the Country Houses Committee had so quickly established made possible the Trust's startling successes during and immediately after the War. The pace of acquisition reflects both the energy with which Lees-Milne trekked around the country, often in difficult conditions, and the extent to which a tiny administrative staff – first at Buckingham Palace Gardens, then migrating to the Pavilions at Runnymede and on to West Wycombe Park – could improvise solutions to every problem. During the war years Packwood House, Dinton Park and Hyde's House, West Wycombe Park, Lindisfarne Castle, Lacock Abbey, Speke Hall, Gunby Hall and Hatchlands all came as gifts to the Trust. Lyme Park, Cotehele, Attingham Park and Petworth followed in 1947; Ham House in 1948; and Osterley Park and Horton Court in 1949. This was only possible because of the close and creative partnership between Esher and Lees-Milne.

Inevitably there were drawbacks. Some of the houses came with great estates

Miss Matilda Talbot handing over the deeds of Lacock Abbey in Wiltshire
to Oliver Brett, 3rd Viscount Esher, Chairman of the Country Houses
Committee, in 1944. To the right of Lord Esher sit Hubert Smith, the Trust's
Chief Agent, and Eardley Knollys, Representative for the South West.

which, as Lothian had foreseen, needed professional management. The land
agents recruited for the task sometimes felt they were excluded from the charmed
circle which seemed to be running the Trust. They did not enjoy being the butt
of Esher's jokes or being called 'mangle-wurzels'. Nor did they all approve of
the way that the Trust's benefactors were deliberately diminished if political
views differed, as they did with G.M. Trevelyan, whose false teeth were another
source of merriment. Such things are not forgotten.

A restricted view was sometimes taken of the purposes of the Trust. In
Another Self Lees-Milne mentions his tendency to agoraphobia. He has also made
no secret of the fact that his loyalties were first to the houses, then to the families
that had created them and only then to the National Trust: 'I love the Trust, in

so far as one can love an instrument.' The statutory duty which the Trust had to preserve country houses 'for the benefit of the nation' was interpreted in a narrow way. This was certainly not what Lord Lothian had intended.

Blickling came through the war relatively unscathed. Parts of the park had been ploughed up in the 'dig for victory' campaign, a substantial area of Great Wood had been felled and wartime buildings were scattered around the house like confetti. All this could be put right, but finding a use for the house was more of a problem, as neither Lord Lothian's successor in title, nor the sons of his great friends Lord and Lady Astor, wished to take up the invitation to live at Blickling. At this point the Trust was approached by Somerset de Chair, a Norfolk MP, who explained that he was a great friend of the late Lord Lothian and was prepared to lease the whole of Blickling. To the dismay of Lord Lothian's sisters, the Trust agreed. When de Chair formed an attachment with the daughter of the manager of a local cinema and left Blickling, his wife Thelma stayed on, marrying another MP, Sir Jocelyn Lucas. The Trust felt it was fortunate to have found a tenant willing to take some of the responsibilities of Blickling off its hands, but for the moment at least Lord Lothian's wishes had been overlooked.

During the twenty-five years that Lord Esher was Chairman of the Country Houses Committee, from 1936 to 1961, its achievements were prodigious. But there was a price. His consummate skill as a chairman and public speaker, his single-mindedness and his intellect were vital to the success of the Country Houses Scheme. But his influence was divisive. Part of the reason for his sometimes dismissive behaviour was perhaps that his father misjudged his abilities and refused to allow him to go to university. This may have explained his dislike of academics and his habit of invariably addressing G.M. Trevelyan, Professor of Modern History at Cambridge, Master of Trinity College and a member of the Order of Merit, as 'Mr Trevelyan'. Esher was never wholly at ease with those like Chorley and Trevelyan who were outside his circle. He found them stuffy, and they thought him frivolous, which was in fact mistaken: on the really important issues he was usually extremely wise, with a strong liberal conviction that made him dislike Tories and socialists about equally. His teasing of Trust staff was merciless but even-handed: while Lees-Milne relished jokes at his expense, the Solicitor and some of the Agents did not. Totally unambitious himself, Esher found ambition in others ridiculous and funny.

The passion that Esher and Lees-Milne felt for country houses meant that they were unashamed zealots, prepared when necessary to provoke what they perceived as the powerful and well-established figures on the Estates Committee.

West Wycombe Park in Buckinghamshire. The house was
given to the Trust in 1943 by Sir John Dashwood.

Esher was also conscious of the extent to which Lord Crawford left so much of
the running of the Trust to him, remarking to a member of staff, 'Don't you
think it ridiculous that the Chairman of the National Trust should live in
Scotland and come down to England once a month for a week of meetings?'

There were seeds of future discord.

CHAPTER SIX

DONORS AND
DYNASTIES

O N THE MANTELPIECE in the dining-room of Shaw's Corner at
Ayot St Lawrence in Hertfordshire, the unlovely Victorian villa bought by
George Bernard Shaw in 1906, stand photographs of Lenin, Stalin and the early
Bolshevik Dzerzhinsky. Shaw merrily described himself as a Bolshevik and was
equally enthusiastic about democratic socialism and communism. His writings
on the Soviet Union were given some credibility by a two-hour interview with
Stalin during a visit to Russia in 1931. Also present were Nancy Astor and Lord
Lothian. 'When are you going to stop shooting people?' Lady Astor asked the
smiling and apparently benign Stalin. The only comment the press could extract
from Shaw after the meeting was that 'Stalin has splendid black moustaches'. All
three in that strangely assorted deputation ensured that their houses – Blickling,
Cliveden and Shaw's Corner – passed to the Trust.

Shaw was not alone in his infatuation with communism. When in March
1937 Sir Charles Trevelyan spoke on the wireless of his intentions to give the
Wallington estate to the National Trust, he preached a sermon on socialism: 'To
me, it is natural and reasonable that a place such as this should come into public
ownership, so that the right to use and enjoy it may be for ever secured to the
community. As a Socialist, I am not hampered by any sentiment of ownership. I
am prompted to act as I am doing by satisfaction at knowing that the place I love
will be held in perpetuity for the people of my country.'

Sir Charles had initially sounded out the Trust about the transfer of Wallington in 1934, a month before Lord Lothian's speech at the annual meeting.
His plans for Wallington clearly acted as a spur to the Country Houses Scheme.
Subsequent negotiations with Sir Charles were punctuated with such mis-
understanding and back-pedalling that his brother, Professor G.M. Trevelyan,
had to be enlisted as arbitrator. What was finally agreed was a Deed of Settlement,
signed by Sir Charles in September 1941. This did not immediately transfer
ownership but was an irrevocable commitment that on Sir Charles's death
Wallington would pass to the National Trust. Victorian novelists made frequent

George Bernard Shaw in the Drawing Room at Shaw's Corner in Hertfordshire.
Shaw gave the house to the National Trust in 1944 and the contents,
acquired under his will in 1950, remain largely as in his lifetime.

use of such arrangements, known legally as an 'entailment', and in both fiction and real life there was rich potential for resentment and strained relationships.

As with so many subsequent gifts, a Memorandum of Wishes proved a useful device for securing family interests of importance to Sir Charles. These could not become legal rights without compromising the donor's tax position, the Trust's charitable status, or both. Subsequently the Trust has treated these Memoranda as morally but not legally binding – a solution of benefit to all but the legal profession. In the case of Wallington, Sir Charles used the Memorandum of Wishes to reserve numerous interests to himself, such as exercising the right to fell softwoods on the estate. This caused the Trust misgivings, but as the reservation was for Sir Charles's lifetime only, a long-term view could be taken.

The motives for Sir Charles's gift were mixed. To the public at large he wanted it to be seen as the expression of his socialist beliefs. Sir Charles was convinced that the landed aristocracy would either be swept away or would dwindle and die. He was able to reassure his family that 'the old place has a future if there is a future for anything', and at the same time retain most of the pleasures of living at Wallington. What incensed other country house owners, and did little to help the Trust, was his assertion that the only way to preserve great estates was to give them away.

To ensure that there could be no doubt about his allegiances, the hammer and sickle was painted on one of the Wallington gate-piers. His son George was effectively disinherited. It is a measure of just how complex attitudes and loyalties were within the Trevelyan family that, far from distancing himself from the Trust, Sir George Trevelyan was to make his own quixotic contribution to its work, through the Attingham Adult Education College, of which he was the first Warden. Established by Shropshire County Council in 1947, this was the National Trust's first, and for many years, only experiment in turning over most of a country house to an educational use. An offshoot of lasting influence was the Attingham Summer School, which Sir George Trevelyan and Helen Lowenthal, then in charge of education at the Victoria and Albert Museum, launched in response to a suggestion from an American, Mrs Roberts Wood Bliss. Another supporter was Lydia Bond Powell, keeper of the American Wing at the Metropolitan Museum, New York, who convinced the Trust's Deputy Secretary, Joshua Rowley, that the Trust was dragging its feet both in the conservation of the contents of its country houses and by not taking advantage of the opportunities they afforded for teaching about the decorative arts.

Grave doubts were expressed by the Trust's Solicitor about the propriety of using Trust funds for any purpose not spelt out in its Acts of Parliament, but he was reassured by Rowley's discreet diplomacy. The first 'National Trust Summer School on Great Houses', as the brochure described it, took place in July 1953, with 22 Americans and 8 British scholars being conducted on a grand tour of country houses, some belonging to the Trust, many in private ownership. Forty years on, the Attingham Summer School continues, benefiting both Americans and, increasingly, students from central Europe.

During and immediately after the Second World War the Trust received property on a vast scale. The families of some of those benefactors – the Aclands of Killerton in Devon, the Trevelyans of Wallington, the Dashwoods of West Wycombe Park, the Fairfax-Lucys of Charlecote in Warwickshire and the Hoares of Stourhead – may have questioned the decision to relieve them of responsibility for the care of their ancestral homes. To some it may seem inadequate consolation that they still have, and some exercise, the right to live on their former estates. What is easily forgotten is that at the time there was a widespread conviction that the war would mean the end of one social order and the beginning of another.

The belief that there could be no going back was articulated most forcefully by Sir Richard Acland, the donor of that great tract of Exmoor that came with the Holnicote and Killerton estates. He had entered Parliament in 1935 as a Liberal, but was converted to socialism the following year on reading Maynard Keynes's *General Theory*. It was not until the outbreak of war that his talents as a

Sir Richard and Lady Acland celebrating victory
in the General Election of 1935, in which he
became Liberal MP for Barnstaple in north Devon.

polemicist brought him a national following. In 1940 he published *Unser Kampf*, sub-titled *OUR Struggle*, an answer to Hitler's *Mein Kampf*, which sold a staggering 132,000 copies at 9d each. Its success gave him the satisfaction of a place in the Nazi Black Book, which listed those to be imprisoned or executed following a German invasion. Central to Sir Richard's message was the belief that 'only under common ownership can we abolish class distinction, unemployment, inequality and strife.' 'Will you agree with us', he wrote in *The Manifesto of the Ordinary Man*, 'that there is no hope until the world is based on the common decency, generosity, and humanity of ordinary people?' Two years later, with the author J.B. Priestley and a Marxist veteran of the Spanish Civil War, Tom Wintringham, he launched the Common Wealth Party, which enjoyed spectacular success in by-elections but which did not survive the Labour landslide in 1945. Much of Sir Richard's later life was taken up with teaching and campaigning against nuclear weapons, at one stage bringing him into open conflict with the Trust.

The name of Common Wealth, devised by J.B. Priestley, summed up their shared aspirations. It stood for 'the common ownership of all land and of all the great resources of our country, and this not for the sake of making anybody materially richer but as the inescapable foundation for a more morally based way of public life.' These aims remained the cornerstone of Sir Richard's beliefs, but they sat uneasily with his family inheritance. His initial idea was to dispose of Holnicote and Killerton on the open market, even though there could scarcely have been a worse moment for a hasty sale. His wife Anne had managed the estates single-handed during the early years of the war. The task would have been a daunting one for anyone in her early twenties, but for Anne Acland there were physical obstacles to contend with: the ravages of polio had affected her spine, lungs and legs, a splint encasing her from hips to armpits. To carry out what she saw as her and Richard's responsibilities, she had learnt to ride a bicycle to take her round the farms, enduring frequent falls and injuries. Nothing had prepared her for the moment when, at a point of crisis in the Common Wealth Party, Richard revealed his intentions. She later recorded how, in mid-October 1942, he 'sprung the idea on me that the estates are sold and money given to C.W.' Anne's reaction was to resist strongly. 'The estates are important not only as property; they are communities of people', she noted, implying how her sense of social obligation differed from her husband's. Richard could not really share her feelings, confessing to her that he was 'better at making intelligent conversation to a pine tree than to a farm tenant'. As a compromise they agreed that part of the estates should be sold to the National Trust and the remainder transferred as a gift. However, the terms of the transaction meant that the political stakes were high: without careful handling, its disposal could have compromised Richard, while its acquisition might well have spelt disaster for the Trust.

A highly unusual arrangement for the protection of part of the Holnicote estate had been made a quarter of a century earlier. In 1917 Sir Richard's great uncle, Sir Thomas Acland, leased his 8,200 acres of moorland around Dunkery Hill, Winsford Hill and the wild Horner Woods to the Trust for 500 years, on the understanding that his successors would continue to receive all rental income. Under the agreement the family was not permitted to profit from any building development on the estate. As the then Chairman of the Trust, Lord Plymouth, explained in a letter in *The Times*, the Trust had obtained such control 'as may be necessary to preserve the property, so far as possible, in its present beauty and natural condition'. When Holnicote passed to Sir Richard in 1927, his hands were already tied by the 500 year lease of these moorland areas, although he owned most of the farmland. To complicate matters still further, in October 1943 Sir Richard was faced with death duties, legacy duty and estate duty on parts of his estates; 546 acres of Holnicote and 730 acres of Killerton were bound by a Marriage Settlement given to Sir Richard; and he had already committed £11,000 to help launch Common Wealth. All these legal and financial commitments had to be reconciled. He was also in a hurry: any transfer to the Trust had to be concluded by Christmas.

At other moments in the Trust's history he might well have been told that he was asking for the impossible. Goodwill alone would not have been enough. Then, fortuitously, the Trust received in 1943 a munificent legacy from Mrs Ronald Greville, as well as her Polesden Lacey estate, near Dorking in Surrey. The financial obstacles to the acquisition of Holnicote and Killerton could be overcome, provided the Trust contrived to find a route through a legal and political minefield. Other events coincided in a useful way. In 1943 Anthony Martineau joined the staff as Assistant Secretary and the following year was appointed Solicitor to the Trust, a title subsequently changed to Legal Adviser. Martineau saw the potential pitfalls of the arrangements proposed by Sir Richard and immediately became involved in both the exact terms of the transfer and in the way it was explained publicly. Then and since, his interventions were regarded as tiresome and pedantic, particularly by those anxious to conclude negotiations speedily; but without such a strict legal conscience the Trust might well have put at risk its charitable status by appearing to use its funds for political purposes.

Those risks were very real in the case of Holnicote and Killerton. The Greville Fund was used to meet an assortment of financial liabilities that Sir Richard had either committed himself to, or inherited. He had to find the purchase price of a house for himself and his wife, provide for the education of their children and his own living expenses, and secure £11,000 to clear up what he called his 'Common Wealth tangle'. Sir Richard satisfied himself that what he was doing was transferring property of a value which greatly exceeded these liabilities, so that the Trust's payment of £120,000 could not be directly attributable to any specific financial obligation. Nevertheless, there was an element of special pleading when Sir Richard acknowledged that 'from a money point of view the whole thing is as broad as it is long'. What matters now is that

a sale of Sir Richard's estates on the open market was averted and instead there was to be protection in perpetuity of 10,000 acres of Exmoor and 6,300 acres of the Killerton estate, with its house, garden, the village of Broadclyst and the hamlet of Budlake. At the end of January 1944, the tenants of both estates witnessed the formal handing over of the title deeds to the Chairman of the Estates Committee, Professor Trevelyan. That this was achieved says much for the resourcefulness of the Trust at that time. Matheson was spurred on by his admiration for Sir Richard and the sympathy he felt for his political views. When handing over the deeds, Sir Richard referred to Trevelyan's 'long and close connection with my family on both sides.'

At such a grim stage of the war, when the Trust was struggling with what many must have felt were irrelevancies, Acland's gift brought a renewed sense of purpose. The fact that some landowners fulminated in *The Times* against Acland for betraying his class meant that the significance of what he had done could not be overlooked; nor could the sheer extent of the property involved, at that time the largest acreage ever transferred to the Trust.

Over the next forty years Sir Richard was at intervals to feature prominently in the Trust's affairs. Although he did not hunt himself, he took a public stand on the issue of deer hunting, which he urged should continue on the Holnicote

Dawn near Luccombe on the Holnicote estate in Somerset,
which was transferred to the Trust, together with the
Killerton estate in Devon, by Sir Richard Acland in 1944.

estate. As the dispute about blood sports became steadily more contentious, he argued all the more forcefully that the banning of hunting would damage rather than encourage responsible management of deer on Exmoor. On this issue he supported the Council of the Trust. But when in 1979 the Trust negotiated with the Ministry of Defence over the building of an underground military headquarters on inalienable land at Bradenham in Buckinghamshire, the same energy and oratory that Sir Richard brought to all his activities were poured into ferocious denunciation of the Trust (see p. 215). Until his death in 1990 he was among the Trust's most generous benefactors, most ardent supporters and sternest critics.

The same passionate commitment was brought by Sir Richard's younger brother, Cuthbert – Cubby as he was invariably known – to his work for the Trust in the Lake District. Cubby Acland joined the staff of the Trust in 1946, initially in the south east; then seizing the opportunity to move to the Lakes, where he was made Area Agent in 1949, he worked there until his retirement in

1973. Never overtly political like his brother, he shared the same conviction that the countryside should be available for ordinary people to enjoy. When Cubby appointed Neil Allinson to be the first warden in the Lake District, he was given specific responsibility for improving public access. Camp sites were to be provided and caravans allowed, but with the utmost care taken over their siting and screening. One of the very first National Trust shops was set up in Bridge House, over Stock Ghyll in Ambleside, Cumbria. Modest information rooms – referred to by the staff as 'Cubby holes' – appeared in towns and villages so that visitors might learn about the Trust. Old barns were adapted for use by young volunteers keen to work for the Trust in the Lake District. These provisions were intended to benefit not only the Trust but the local communities and tenant farmers who needed to supplement their incomes.

In all this Cubby Acland was paternalistic and at times fiercely autocratic. He persuaded manufacturers of tents to include in their leaflets a note saying which colours were approved by the National Trust (or rather, by Acland). He brushed aside objections that subfusc tents made the job of the mountain rescue teams more difficult. Local Authority officers who presumed to disagree with him were told that eventually they would come to realise just how wrong they had been, and would be grateful that he had persisted.

The energy with which Cubby furthered the work of the Trust, the pace of acquisition in the Lake District and the widespread appreciation of what he achieved there meant that criticism of his style of management was rarely directed at him personally. Resentment at what was in some quarters felt to be Trust arrogance was, however, stored up for his successors. He deserves to be judged not just by the record of protection in the Lakes during those years. Cubby Acland helped to extend the Trust's understanding of what was meant by enjoyment of the countryside. In this way he came closer to the spirit of the Trust's founders than some other staff who were his contemporaries.

Like the Aclands, the McLaren family is rooted in radical politics. Henry McLaren served as Parliamentary Private Secretary to Lloyd George, preceding Philip Kerr in that post. His father, the 1st Lord Aberconway, was given the names Charles Benjamin Bright, after his uncle John Bright. His mother Laura was an ardent supporter of women's suffrage; and her father, Henry Davis Pochin, was a radical MP, as well as an outstandingly successful industrial chemist. The loss of his seat in Parliament in 1922 allowed Henry McLaren to devote more time to horticulture. It was due to his powers of persuasion and his ability as an organiser that a rather reluctant Trust was persuaded to become a protector of great gardens. Among the finest of these is Bodnant, in north Wales, which he gave to the National Trust in 1949 to set both a standard and a precedent.

Concern about the gardens of its historic houses had already led the Trust to enlist outside help. When Montacute in Somerset was acquired in 1931, through the SPAB, the care of the formal garden posed as many problems as the empty house. A small group of advisers was recruited, among them the architectural editor of *Country Life*, Christopher Hussey, and Henry McLaren, who became President of the Royal Horticultural Society in 1931 and who succeeded his father as 2nd Lord Aberconway in 1934. They made an effective committee, agreeing among other things to sack the local gardening firm and persuading the Trust to employ its own gardeners. Lord Aberconway also involved the RHS's advisory staff.

The proposal that the Trust and the RHS should jointly set up a Gardens Committee to administer and raise funds for the maintenance of a few of the best gardens of England was first aired at a meeting in November 1947, convened at the Trust's offices by Lord Aberconway. Lees-Milne supported the idea, noting that 'there are thousands of English people who love gardens even more than buildings, and would willingly subscribe to such a fund'. Hubert Smith, Chief Agent since 1941 and a knowledgeable gardener, was also enthusiastic.

The Secretary, Admiral Bevir, was sceptical, however. He was worried about the financial implications of the scheme, and feared that the Trust might be drawn into arrangements which departed from the established practice of insisting on capital endowments. There were also doubts about whether the Trust's statutory obligations to preserve places of historic interest or natural beauty could be extended to the protection of gardens created in the recent past. But Aberconway was adept at setting objectives that neatly complied with the Trust's aims and indeed went beyond them. He told the Annual General Meeting of the RHS in March 1948 that 'only gardens of great beauty, gardens of outstanding design or historic interest would be considered', adding the carefully chosen words, 'and those having collections of plants or trees of value to the nation either botanically, horticulturally or scientifically'. Although the scheme gave the Trust the confidence to acquire many great gardens – negotiations for the

(*Overleaf*) The east court pavilion and
herbaceous border in the garden at Montacute House
in Somerset, acquired by the Trust in 1931.

gift of Nymans in Sussex began in 1948, and for Mount Stewart in Co. Down, Northern Ireland the following year – joint fundraising proved only a partial success. Vita Sackville-West, who with her husband Sir Harold Nicolson had created the garden at Sissinghurst Castle in Kent, made a radio broadcast appeal in 1948. She also supported an approach to the Queen's Institute for District Nurses which, before the days of the National Health Service, had raised funds by special openings of private gardens. With many of their medical objectives taken under the wing of government, it was suggested that some of the money from these openings might be devoted to preservation of gardens by the Trust. After initial hesitation the Institute agreed, and what has become the National Gardens Scheme was launched. These contributions, channelled into the Trust's Gardens Fund, still generously assist some of the finest gardens in its care; but any hope that it might provide the equivalent of endowments has long been abandoned.

Just as Blickling set the seal on the Country Houses Scheme, so the gift of Bodnant gave credibility to the Trust's role as gardener. It is rare that a garden enriched by several generations of plantsmen should also be a masterpiece of formal design. The terraces at Bodnant are just that, with the mountains of Snowdonia as a backdrop. The conception was Henry Aberconway's, as was the addition of the Pin Mill, a previously derelict building of about 1730, brought from Gloucestershire in 1938 and re-erected at the southern end of the canal on the lowest terrace.

There are two dynasties of distinguished gardeners at Bodnant. Like his father, who died in 1953, Charles, 3rd Lord Aberconway, was President of the Royal Horticultural Society, serving from 1961 to 1984. Frederick Puddle was Head Gardener from 1920 until his retirement in 1947, when he was succeeded by his son Charles. Martin Puddle, Charles's son, has been Head Gardener since 1982. The relationship between the two families, both committed to preserving and enhancing the beauty of Bodnant and each dependent on the other for achieving that aim, has been subtle and effective.

The first garden to be acquired through the scheme was not Bodnant but Hidcote in Gloucestershire, given by Major Lawrence Johnston in 1948. Since 1907 he had developed a garden of infinite variety and richness out of 280 acres of farmland in the heart of the Cotswolds. As so often, it was a complex web of influences that drew Johnston to the Trust. One of his closest female friends was Norah Lindsay, whose work for Lord Lothian had so enormously enhanced the garden at Blickling. A neighbour was George Lees-Milne, the owner of a fine garden at Wickhamford Manor, whose son, James, was in no doubt of the exceptional merits of Hidcote. Johnston's original intention was to leave the garden to Norah Lindsay, but when she predeceased him, he was persuaded to give Hidcote to the Trust by Lady Colefax, who, with John Fowler, was to have such a lasting influence on the decoration of country houses and the design of their gardens.

Lawrence Johnston also had financial reasons for involving the Trust. His mother had, on her death in 1926, left him only a life interest in her estate, which meant that he was not in a position to give the Trust an endowment adequate to maintain Hidcote. Without the National Gardens Scheme the Trust would almost certainly have had to refuse his offer. In 1949, when the garden was open to the public three days a week, on a typical autumn afternoon there were seven visitors. At that time four gardeners were employed, paid £4 a week, with the Head Gardener, Albert Hawkins, receiving £4 10s. By 1950, on a glorious day in May a hundred people came. In 1993 there were 140,000 visitors to Hidcote.

Lawrence Johnston left no family, so that Hidcote's acquisition by the Trust marked a complete break. This was not so at Nymans in Sussex, where the Messel family continued to be involved with the development of the garden after it passed to the Trust in 1954. Many of the finest plants at Nymans had been brought there by Ludwig Messel, who gathered exotics from all over the world and was determined to prove that these often tender plants would thrive outdoors in Sussex. When Nymans was bequeathed to the Trust, Ludwig's granddaughter, Anne, Countess of Rosse, continued to supervise the garden, which benefited greatly from the knowledge and flair which she and her husband Michael could provide.

Both had a brilliant sense of design and colour, as their garden at Birr Castle in Ireland testifies, and a wide circle of friends with whom they exchanged plants. Their involvement ensured that the charge of sameness, sometimes levelled at the Trust for the way it cares for its gardens, never applied at Nymans. Sadly, the income from the estate of 1,500 acres intended as an endowment proved insufficient, and the very extravagance that had made Nymans so rewarding to visit began to put a disproportionate burden on the finances of the Trust. The way a garden is run relates inescapably to the number of staff employed and so

(*Overleaf*) The Fuchsia Garden at Hidcote Manor, Gloucestershire.

to its annual costs, and that cannot be overlooked for long. What may have seemed regrettable economies have been necessary to prevent Nymans becoming too great a drain on the Trust's General Fund.

Bodnant was not the only great garden to come to the Trust with a dynasty of gardeners. There has been a member of the Ayres family at Anglesey Abbey in Cambridgeshire since 1921, when Noel Ayres joined the staff. He contributed to its transformation from a modest and very ordinary small garden into a series of interlinking compartments spread over 90 acres, each area designed to make its own particular contribution at a given time of year. His son, Richard Ayres, did his best to escape, joining the Navy at sixteen. Eventually, in the mid-winter of 1959 and in front of a blazing fire in the Abbey, Lord Fairhaven persuaded Richard to accept a job at Anglesey. Noel Ayres stayed on as Head Gardener after 1966, when on Lord Fairhaven's death Anglesey Abbey passed to the Trust. By a cruel turn of events Richard succeeded his father as Head Gardener in 1974, at just the time that the garden was devastated by Dutch Elm disease. Over 4,500 elms in the garden alone had to be felled by the Anglesey staff. As Noel Ayres had contributed to the creation of the garden, so Richard oversaw its re-creation, under the guidance of both the 3rd Lord Fairhaven and the Trust's Chief Gardens Adviser, John Sales. Richard's son Christopher joined the Anglesey Abbey staff in 1987, after serving an apprenticeship in the gardens of Christ's College, Cambridge.

The Trust's relationship with the families of donors is necessarily complex. Very often it is not the donors themselves who find arrangements with the Trust hard to swallow, but their immediate successors. There are many notable exceptions. Time and again potential rifts are bridged by a shared commitment to a property which, thanks both to the donor and the Trust, will be there for the enjoyment of future generations.

To recognise that donors have often been influenced by a variety of motives is not to diminish their generosity. At times a gift of property may have served a political purpose. In one case, at Ickworth in Suffolk, the Trust has been a convenient way for a family to protect a great inheritance from the irresponsibility of an unsuitable heir. Victor Hervey, the future 6th Marquess of Bristol, lost vast sums of money as a bungling arms dealer, attempting to supply General Franco. He was associated with the Mayfair Gang who very nearly killed a New Bond Street jeweller by hitting him over the head with a mallet. In 1939 he was sentenced to three years' penal servitude for an unscrupulous theft from a female companion at the Nest Club off Regent Street. His uncle, the 4th Marquess, had no great enthusiasm for the National Trust, but it did at least provide a way of securing the future of Ickworth, which was transferred in lieu of death duties in 1956. With less picaresque families chronic financial problems may have influenced the decision to pass an estate over to the Trust.

Many have given to the Trust for the simple and overriding reason that they

Harry Stuart Goodhart-Rendel (left), the architect
who remodelled Plas Newydd and gave Hatchlands
in Surrey to the Trust in 1945, with R. C. Norman,
Vice-Chairman of the National Trust from 1923 to 1947.

want to ensure the preservation of a place they have cherished. Never has this been clearer than with the gift of Plas Newydd, Gwynedd, by Henry Anglesey, the 7th Marquess. Military historian, friend of Rex and Laurence Whistler, Trustee of the National Heritage Memorial Fund and Chairman of the Historic Buildings Council for Wales, Lord Anglesey guided and inspired the Trust's work in Wales for over thirty years. His overriding wish was to ensure that Plas Newydd, which he greatly loved, should not be broken up, and in 1976 he gave it to the Trust. The decision is one that he never regretted.

The process of offering a property to the Trust, and the subsequent procedures

Henry, 7th Marquess of Anglesey holding the
artificial leg made for his ancestor, the
1st Marquess, after the Battle of Waterloo.

for establishing its importance and calculating an endowment, can test the
patience of both parties. In the case of Plas Newydd, Lord Anglesey ensured that
the business was conducted with something of the dash and verve displayed by
his distinguished military ancestor, the 1st Marquess, during the retreat through
Genappe and at the Battle of Waterloo, where he was struck by grape shot and
earned his sobriquet of 'One-Leg'. In letters with the crispness of a military
dispatch the 7th Marquess sometimes underlined the words *Sine Mora* twice.
Members of the Trust's Properties Committee were treated with all the courtesy

Rex Whistler's sketch of Plas Newydd, painted in 1939,
shows the artist with his box of paints, and the
future 7th Marquess of Anglesey on his bicycle.

due to the officers of a much valued ally. They agreed that the position of the
house was exceptional and were influenced by John Cornforth's suggestion that
the decoration of the 1930s by Lady Colefax and Rex Whistler would in time
be regarded as an important episode in the history of taste. A major obstacle was
the size of endowment required for future upkeep, even though the methods of
calculating the capital sum necessary were then far less rigorous. Georgian silver
had to be sold and so were two Nicholas Hilliard miniatures which, much to
Lord Anglesey's relief, were acquired by the National Museum of Wales.

The transfer provided the opportunity to ask the ninety-three-year-old Sir Clough Williams-Ellis to be the principal speaker on the day when Plas Newydd was formally opened to the public in 1976: within a week of the invitation the drafts of three alternative, full-length speeches had been submitted, each showing that his zest was in no way diminished by his years. A cavalry museum was created at Plas Newydd for the display of the relics of the 1st Marquess's exploits at Waterloo. Lord Anglesey enlisted Laurence Whistler's help with mounting a permanent exhibition of the work of his brother, Rex, whose wall painting in the Dining Room is such a breathtaking display of technical virtuosity. There are continuing enrichments to the garden, its superb collections of flowering shrubs and specimen rhododendrons poised above the Menai Strait.

The family now occupies the top floor of the house, which Lord Anglesey likens to 'living in the howdah on top of a white elephant which somebody else feeds'.

CHAPTER SEVEN

AMATEURS

T O DESCRIBE THE National Trust's staff in the middle years of this century as amateurs or dilettanti usually implies criticism. Today, the assumption would be that their approach was superficial, even frivolous. This is a pity: there was a time when the words were applied to those who delighted in the arts, assembled great libraries and amassed picture and plant collections. The Trust tried to continue the tradition of the dilettante, with admirable results at some properties and occasional mistakes at others. The professionalism on which the Trust now sometimes prides itself can also be a mixed blessing.

Many of those who have helped the Trust did so because they believed fervently in what it was trying to do. Very often they brought immense knowledge and expertise to its affairs, given without thought of payment. The Director of the National Gallery, Sir Kenneth Clark, wrote a guide to the Turner paintings at Petworth and the Director of the Courtauld Institute and Keeper of the Queen's Pictures, Professor Anthony Blunt, assisted with their hanging. At least as authoritative was the Trust's own Chairman, Lord Crawford. His father had as a young man published studies of Donatello and *The Evolution of Italian Sculpture*. As First Commissioner of Works and Public Buildings in 1921, he relished the task of administering his Ancient Monuments Act of 1900, which had been drafted by Sir Robert Hunter. He was Chairman of the Royal Fine Arts Commission and of the Council for the Preservation of Rural England, President of the Society of Antiquaries and a Trustee of the British Museum, National Gallery and National Portrait Gallery. He is described by the 1st Lord Chorley, who knew him well through the CPRE, as 'moving effortlessly in the spheres where he expected his leadership to be accepted, dominating but not domineering, affable without condescension, ready to listen while making it clear that he was sure you were wrong'. It was as President of both the London Society and of the London Survey Committee that he made an important contribution to the National Trust's work. In 1936 he sponsored an appeal to purchase Sutton House in Hackney, a building of around 1535 and the oldest surviving house in the East End of London. His co-sponsors were Lord Esher, then Chairman of SPAB, and George Lansbury, Vice-President of the National Trust and Labour MP for Poplar. Sutton House came to the Trust in 1938, and back into the limelight fifty years later (see p. 244).

Like his father, David Crawford was president, chairman or trustee of most of the great national artistic institutions of this country. When the Royal Academy decided in 1962 that the Leonardo Cartoon should be sold, Crawford deplored the President's 'consistently outrageous conduct', resigned from the Academy and made it his personal mission, as Chairman of the National Art Collections Fund, to raise the money for its acquisition by the National Gallery. He organised a makeshift appeal office, drummed up volunteers and made most of the approaches to potential contributors himself, accepting discourtesy with humility and patience. His doctors had told him that he needed a serious operation, but at considerable risk it was postponed until the appeal was concluded. At the appropriate moment he had direct access to the Prime Minister. The way he conducted the campaign was characteristic of the qualities he brought to all his public work, including his chairmanship of the Trust. He once confided in a friend: 'I always worked on the principle of doing what I thought was right; and I usually found it was right. Common sense will tell you what is the right thing to do.'

Beneath the gentle courtesy, the humour and refinement there was a deep current of feeling for civilised values. It surfaced when he saved the Leonardo Cartoon, and earlier when advisers to the Treasury were proposing that the Petworth Collections should be dismantled on the death of Charles Wyndham, 3rd Lord Leconfield in 1952. The Victoria and Albert Museum and the National Gallery had valued the contents of Petworth, including incomparable master-pieces such as the Head of Aphrodite by the Greek sculptor Praxiteles and all the Turners, at £500,000. Moreover they had advised the Treasury to accept only the outstanding pictures *in lieu* of tax. On 10 February 1956 Sir Edward Bridges, then Permanent Secretary at the Treasury and, as Chairman of the Box Hill Committee in Surrey, sympathetic to the Trust's interests, received a letter from Crawford:

> Long experience has shown me that few gallery officials have any knowledge of market prices of pictures: the V & A valuation of furniture at Petworth was made by an expert on Sculpture . . . the N G advises against accepting a number of pictures which Wyndham and the NT had agreed were appropriate for inclusion. These are the pictures we want: not all good pictures, but for one

The Long Gallery at Hardwick Hall in Derbyshire. This watercolour,
painted by David Cox in the mid-nineteenth century, shows
paintings hung on top of the sixteenth-century tapestries.

reason or another appropriate to Petworth. They are all hanging in the show rooms: they have all been placed there by Blunt.

The suggestion that they should not be included would absolutely wreck the house, leaving a series of spaces on the walls. The suggestion is quite lunatic, quite indefensible: quite exasperating.

No reasons are given. One can only assume that a 'Gallery' point of view has dominated – though even so the exclusions are wildly inconsistent. But we have all agreed that the 'Gallery' point of view was precisely what we wished to avoid: totally different criteria, we agreed, were applicable to country house collections. . . . Owners won't face these obstacles and the years (three, I think in this case) of uncertainty and misery. The game is not worth the candle. If owners refuse to play – and if Wyndham sells – no-one can blame them or the NT.

The Treasury was unmoved by Crawford's letter. After much heart-searching, John Wyndham decided to accept the Treasury's paltry valuation and the contents of Petworth were ultimately transferred to the Trust. The preservation of Petworth, its collections and park was put before his family's financial interests.

To many involved with the Trust Lord Crawford seemed remote. Certainly he believed that the day-to-day running of the organisation could and should be left to Lord Esher and the Trust's staff. The business of the Council could usually be dealt with in twenty-five minutes, although its members were invited to stay on for the meeting of the Executive Committee which followed. The feeling of remoteness was exacerbated by his letters, written in a hand which was elegant but indecipherable to all but a few specialists. The Secretary, Jack Rathbone, longed to be praised by Lord Crawford, but rarely was, and at times left his deputy, Joshua Rowley, to deal with much of the Chairman's correspondence. The Trust's agents found that Crawford looked at landscape through the eyes of an artist, not through those of a land manager.

The depth of Lord Crawford's feelings for the Trust was evident when he visited its finest houses. Standing in the Elizabethan long gallery of Hardwick Hall in Derbyshire, he was acutely aware of the rarity and importance of its sixteenth-century textiles. He insisted that the historical interest of the house was enormously enhanced by the evidence of later taste, such as the hanging of pictures on top of Bess of Hardwick's tapestries by her descendant, the 6th Duke of Devonshire, in the mid-nineteenth century. Only Crawford had the authority to tell the Director of the Victoria and Albert Museum or the Keeper of the Department of Textiles that the pictures should remain there. 'Not one person of the next generation will have a clue how country houses were really lived in before the war', he confessed to James Lees-Milne and the Historic Buildings Representative, Christopher Wall. If Turner's watercolours of Petworth were needed for a small exhibition it was Crawford who secured permission from the British Museum (again, he was a Trustee) and ensured that any catalogue produced was of appropriately high quality.

One of those in whom Lord Crawford confided was St John ('Bobby') Gore who was appointed the Trust's first Adviser on Paintings in 1956 on Anthony Blunt's recommendation. Gore had studied for two years at the Courtauld Institute and had then worked for Sotheby's. His knowledge of Italian pictures was gained in conditions which, even by the standards of the Grand Tour, were of considerable discomfort. During the Second World War he fought his way up Italy until a shoulder wound separated him from his regiment. The lorry that took him back to the front line dropped him off at a deserted roadside not far from Arezzo. One of the few books that Gore had with him, Vasari's *Lives of the*

Painters, confirmed that he was a stone's throw away from Piero della Francesca's masterpiece, the fresco cycle illustrating the legend of the True Cross. Gore made his way to the church of S. Francesco, only to find that the frescoes in the choir had been bricked up for protection. Disappointment and frustration were only beginning to sink in when he heard the sound of heavy military vehicles. Gore popped his head out for long enough to discover that Arezzo was still occupied by the Germans. Not a man to want the honour of capturing Arezzo single-handed, he made his way back to the lines waving his handkerchief and convinced that he was going to be shot by his own troops.

Gore's accounts of mounting rickety step ladders to prepare notes on the Trust's pictures suggest that they were sometimes as inaccessible as the Pieros, and the task of reaching them at least as hazardous. The ladders at Attingham involved two related perils. One was the chance of a fall from what Gore described as an 'insecure contrivance like a medieval siege-engine'. He proposed an insurance policy: 'not for myself, my injuries were never serious – but for the objects: the furniture, the china and the lamps, on which I was liable to fall.' Far more worrying was the risk of incurring the displeasure of the housekeeper, Mrs Durwood, which would be expressed in a litany of mutterings sometimes culminating in the appearance of Lady Berwick herself. The daughter of the painter William Hulton, brought up in Venice and the friend of the artists Walter Sickert and John Singer Sargent, Lady Berwick knew and loved Attingham's Italian pictures and furniture intimately. She never complained or rebuked anyone: just conveyed in the gentlest, kindest way that someone else's carelessness caused her infinite pain. As Gore was no less sensitive to the vulnerability of fragile objects, cataloguing the Trust's collections, arranging for the conservation of damaged pictures and supervising their re-hanging was at times emotionally and physically draining.

Occasionally there were generous rewards. On one of Gore's first visits to Dunham Massey in Cheshire he took a preliminary look at the pictures muddled in with heaps of discarded furniture and lumber in the gallery, a room that had not been used for most of this century. A dark oval in an ugly frame caught his eye. He identified it as an early work by Guercino, traced the painting to a Dunham inventory of 1769 and thence to Guercino's account book of 1656, where an earlier painting of the same subject, described as 'Una Venere con Marte, Amore ed il Tempo', was noted, as being commissioned by the Duke of Württemberg. Gore observed at the time how refreshing it was to find 'a really well-painted picture'. There was similar satisfaction when a drawing by William

Blake, *The Sea of Time and Place*, was discovered by Eardley Knollys among a stack of prints on top of a bedroom cupboard at Arlington Court in Devon.

Gore's views on the Trust's responsibilities differed significantly from those of Robin Fedden, who in 1951 succeeded James Lees-Milne as Secretary to the Historic Buildings Committee. Fedden, like Esher, believed that the Trust's responsibilities for conservation did not extend beyond those of the enlightened

St John (Bobby) Gore, Historic Buildings Secretary
from 1973 to 1981, painted by John Ward, 1987.

private owner, referred to whenever necessary as the EPO. In *The Continuing Purpose* Fedden wrote that 'the best curator of a house is normally the donor who knows and cherishes it'. The Trust was on dangerous ground when it found itself acting 'in loco parentis'. What a private owner may do to a house will always have some historical significance. If the 3rd Earl's Irish wolfhound is allowed to chew the Aubusson carpet in the saloon, that is interesting documentary evidence of the family's likes and dislikes; all part of the rich fabric of country house life, at least for a time. But if the National Trust allows the same Aubusson to rot because of too much sunlight or to be shredded by visitors' feet, then it is failing in its statutory duties and is being negligent. Again, Fedden was skating over complex responsibilities when he maintained that the Trust 'has no wish to create museums in the countryside, and is not particularly equipped to

The Society of Dilettanti by John Ward, 1976. Among the members involved
with the Trust were (left half) Robin Fedden (extreme left), Viscount Norwich
(red cloak), Sir Brinsley Ford (standing with a red book under his arm),
Lord Clark (seated), (right half) The Duke of Grafton (extreme left, seated),
Sir George Labouchere (with glass below the Reynolds self-portrait), the
Earl of Rosse (centre, facing, seated), and Charles Brocklehurst (at the window).

run them'. That line was sometimes used to excuse a cavalier disregard for the
conservation of precious objects.

Whatever reservations Fedden felt about museum attitudes to research,
conservation and display, he had a connoisseur's eye for fine or unusual objects
and missed very little. One moment he would delight in an antique Caucasian
rug, the next in the latest exhibition of the American painter Mark Rothko.
Shortly after he arrived at Polesden Lacey in 1946 to take up his post of curator,
he gave a talk on the wireless about his approach to showing a house which had
been shut up for much of the war:

> It soon became plain that the whole point of a house such as Polesden Lacey,
> with its Edwardian background and furnishings, must be its informality. The
> objective that the Trust kept before them therefore in setting out the varied
> contents was to create not only the appearance of a large country house of
> 1910, but the illusion of a house still lived in. No red cords or barriers, no
> notices: but, on the other hand, photographs in characteristically elaborate

frames on the tables; on the writing desks the telegraph forms, the embossed notepaper, the ink and the silver pen; in the vases, flowers from the garden.

... We had, it was to be hoped, created an Edwardian interior and atmosphere, but how were they to be kept alive? I became painfully aware that the life of a house tends all too surely to depart with the owner, and that 'museum' and 'mausoleum' might not only *sound* alike.

Fedden encouraged local societies to meet at Polesden Lacey, leaving the arrangements for concerts to a local society, as music seemed to be the only art form that left him completely unmoved.

In practice, the Trust's honorary Historic Buildings Representatives brought considerable knowledge and diversity to the care of its houses. Sir Gyles Isham

Sir Gyles Isham in Rostand's *The Fantasticks* at the Lyric Theatre, Hammersmith, 1933. Sir Gyles was the Trust's honorary Representative for Northamptonshire in the 1960s.

was an authority on the buildings of Northamptonshire, had researched the history of his own house, Lamport, with meticulous scholarship, and as a young man had been a fine Shakespearean actor. Peter Fleetwood-Hesketh, responsible for houses in Lancashire, was as knowledgeable about Victorian architects as his friend John Betjeman, whose poems he corrected and whose *Ghastly Good Taste* he illustrated. Their enthusiasm for the best nineteenth-century architecture was shared by Myles Hildyard, the honorary Representative in Nottinghamshire. Charlie Brocklehurst, the Representative for Cheshire and Shropshire, had been a Director of Christie's before the war, specialising in eighteenth-century silver, making him admirably qualified to arrange an exhibition of Attingham's ambassadorial service. Hugh Euston, who looked after houses in Suffolk, came from the SPAB and was later, as the Duke of Grafton, to be the first Chairman of the East Anglia Regional Committee. Wyndham Ketton-Cremer, honorary Representative in Norfolk, was an accomplished forester and the author of outstanding studies of Horace Walpole and Thomas Gray. His book *Felbrigg, The Story of a House* – he left the estate to the Trust in 1969 – is a masterly synthesis of local history and an outstanding biography of a country house. The Trust could refer to the taste of the EPO with some justification, given the level of care and scholarship which its houses received from these honorary Representatives. More strictly professional curatorship was anyway out of the question. The Trust simply could not have afforded it.

One of the first paid Representatives was Eardley Knollys, who joined the Trust in 1942 to assist Matheson and then assumed responsibility for the Trust's properties in the south west. Knollys worked particularly closely with James Lees-Milne, was a friend of the painters Duncan Grant, Vanessa Bell and Graham Sutherland, and shared a house with the music critic Edward Sackville-West and the writer Raymond Mortimer. The area covered by Knollys was a vast one and it became increasingly clear that professionally qualified land agents needed to be appointed when resources allowed. A system of regional offices, with regional agents reporting to the Chief Agent at head office, began to take shape after 1945.

The arrangements for the supervision of the Trust's gardens also developed slowly. Graham Stuart Thomas, appointed Gardens Adviser in 1955, continued to work part-time for a plant nursery and to supplement his very modest salary from the Trust by writing a succession of books that have become classics. *The Old Shrub Roses*, published in 1955, contained an evocative foreword by Vita Sackville-West, who knew his work well from her many years on the Trust's

Gardens Committee. She captured a vivid, if slightly improbable picture of them both when she wrote:

> Mr Thomas swept me quite unexpectedly back to those dark mysterious hours in an oriental storehouse when the rugs and carpets of Isfahan and Bokhara and Samarcand were unrolled in their dim but sumptuous colouring and richness for our slow delight. Rich they were, rich as a fig broken open, soft as a ripened peach, freckled as an apricot, coral as a pomegranate, bloomy as a bunch of grapes. It is of these that the old roses remind me.

Watercolour of *Gentiana Asclepiaedea 'Knightshayes'*
by Graham Stuart Thomas, Gardens Adviser to the
National Trust from 1955 to 1974.

(*Opposite*) *The Artist at Work*, painted by
Duncan Grant, 1956. As well as being a painter,
Eardley Knollys was the Trust's Representative
for south-west England from 1942 to 1957.

Thomas's style was never so fruity. The most fastidious of bachelors, he would arrive at Trust properties wearing a perfectly chosen button hole to meet a donor or the agent. Punctilious reports on the garden would be written up that evening. His books are models of precise observation and description, illustrated with his own drawings and his sensitive, botanically accurate watercolours of plants. Most of the Trust's increasing number of gardens benefited from his unrivalled knowledge as a plantsman. The herbaceous borders he designed at Powis Castle in mid-Wales and Peckover in Wisbech, Cambridgeshire continue to amaze and delight. Perhaps his greatest achievement was the establishment in 1971 of his collection of old shrub roses in the kitchen garden at Mottisfont Abbey, in Hampshire.

The one feature that Fedden found to criticise at Mottisfont was a small stone putto, reminiscent of the type of statue found in suburban gardens. This was characteristic. Fedden approved of old roses, as an alternative to the fashionable Hybrid Tea, the very name of which would occasion a contemptuous stutter. He would latch on to the one feature that was out of scale, that was inappropriate historically or had the slightest hint of vulgarity. When he saw the Trust's standards being compromised or let down he would respond with ruthlessness and to devastating effect. The breadth of his historical knowledge was astonishing – two of his best books are *Syria* and *Crusader Castles* – and he could write a letter or a memorandum that seemed unanswerable. He was a master of understatement and made light of the experience, in his sixties, of being stung by a scorpion while on a white water canoeing expedition on the upper waters of the Euphrates. Just occasionally he resorted to an explosive outburst of temper. On a climbing expedition in the high Andes of Peru, when staying at a hotel on Lake Titicaca, he was repeatedly served with an inadequately boiled egg; until, as the writer Patrick Leigh Fermor reported, he 'let out a scarcely audible gasp of "O G-god"' and with his blue eyes ablaze, hurled the offending object the length of the dining-room. In matters of taste he usually had the last word.

Fedden was not invincible, however. One afternoon in 1968 the receptionist reported that there was a woman downstairs who insisted on seeing him and who was so cross that she was 'bursting out all over'. Reluctantly, Fedden asked for her to be shown in. Whereupon the large and formidable Phyllis Ireland delivered a tirade of criticism on the way the Trust was neglecting its holding of archaeological sites. She had come armed with quite enough information to flatten any defences Fedden might try to muster, so instead he appointed her honorary Archaeologist. In this position she proceeded to shame the Trust's agents into respecting the archaeological sites in their care. They were supplied with carefully annotated plans and notes in her precise handwriting. Although the names of Sir Cyril Fox and Sir Mortimer Wheeler appeared in the Trust's publications as honorary Advisers on Archaeology, it was Phyllis Ireland who trekked around the country, compiling her card indexes and passing the information on to the agents, who increasingly respected and admired her.

The first full survey of the Trust's woods was carried out in a similar way. John Workman helped initially as a volunteer, travelling the length and breadth of the country on his motorbike, carrying maps, gumboots and a suit if he was going to have to meet a local committee in the evening. He was an amateur in the sense that he had loved woods ever since he had worked in his father's superb beech plantations on the Cotswold Edge; but he had also read forestry at Oxford and had studied planting practice in Sweden. His work was so highly regarded within the Trust in 1953 that he was eventually taken on full time as Forestry Adviser, but even then his punishing regime was one that only he could have set himself. Half the time he was in gumboots, the other half battering away at Ministry doors in London; and for twenty-five years he lived out of a suitcase. Workman's value to the Trust was not just in his skill as a forester. His radical streak was never far below the surface and he would always be at pains to ensure that the public derived pleasure and benefit from the Trust's woods. He was also strongly critical if the Trust failed to live up to its social obligations and he would always be ready to remind agents or committees of the need to provide decent housing for its estate workers and tenants.

The great estates that came with Wallington, Penrhyn, Felbrigg and other properties imposed on the Trust responsibility for whole communities. The gift of Blickling, for instance, included over a hundred houses and cottages. The transfer of Penrhyn Castle through the National Land Fund in 1951 brought with it, supposedly as an endowment, the Carneddau and Ysbyty Ifan estates of over 36,000 acres in the heart of Snowdonia. The survival not just of the hill farms, but of the village school, the local post office and the chapel depended on the policies adopted by the Trust. A scheme to amalgamate farms would have been financially beneficial, but socially damaging. To maintain those communities meant heavy expenditure on the provision of decent sanitation and a programme of cottage and farm improvements.

Esher and Fedden felt the Trust's limited funds could be better spent. But had the Trust shirked its responsibilities, it would in effect have been acting as a landlord of rural slums; and that would have been a betrayal of the Trust's founders. Ultimately, it would also have had to pay a high political price. The argument about whether these obligations should be allowed to absorb so much of the Trust's financial resources was won by Earl De La Warr, Trevelyan's successor as Chairman of the Estates Committee, supported by the Chief Agent, Hubert Smith and by land agents such as Nicolas Corbin in Norfolk and John Tetley in north Wales. A bridge between the Chief Agent and the Historic Buildings staff was provided by Christopher Gibbs, employed initially as Deputy Secretary, in due course to succeed Smith as Chief Agent, and widely respected for his fairness, humour, persistence and hard work. Because money was so short, choices were difficult. To the casual visitor at Wallington or Attingham, there was little outward sign of the thousands of pounds spent on cottage improvements. For John Tetley it was satisfaction enough to see the playground at Ysbyty Ifan village thronged with children when a few years earlier the school was facing closure. When he died in 1991, long after retirement, a list of the names of the farms and tenants on the Ysbyty estate was at his bedside.

At Ysbyty it was essential for the Trust to be seen to be responsive to what Tetley called 'the truly Welsh ways of the estate'. Respect for local feeling was even more important in Northern Ireland, where the management of properties called for exceptional sensitivity. The first Regional Committee for Northern Ireland was set up in 1936, five years after the Scots decided to go their own way with the formation of the National Trust for Scotland: a wholly independent organisation but with similar powers to the National Trust and, when appropriate, ready to act in unison with it. In 1943 there were renewed murmurings that Northern Ireland might want to follow the Scots' example, but this was financially unrealistic and not what most of the committee wanted. After the appointment of the Earl of Antrim as Chairman of the Northern Ireland Committee in 1947, the links with the rest of the Trust became steadily stronger. Antrim's own enthusiasm for the Trust was one factor, the setting up of the Ulster Land Fund was another.

In his budget of 1946 Hugh Dalton, the Labour Chancellor of the Exchequer, announced that he was putting aside a sum of £50 million from the sale of surplus military equipment, to set up a National Land Fund as a memorial to those who had given their lives in the war. It was to be used for the creation of national parks and the acquisition for public enjoyment of stretches of coast and countryside. Undoubtedly he had the National Trust's interests in mind, and in fact the Trust was the principal beneficiary of his own Will. When the following year the Northern Ireland budget was debated at Stormont, and in response to a question from the Independent member for Queen's University, Belfast, Irene Calvert, a comparable fund was established there in 1948. The question had been drafted for her by Dick Rogers, a senior civil servant who also served as honorary Secretary of the Trust's Northern Ireland Regional Committee from 1943 to 1951. At Stormont, Rogers helped to ensure that the Ulster Land Fund was used in the most creative ways possible. This was in marked contrast to the way the Treasury so inhibited the use of the National Land Fund that its accumulated capital could eventually be looted to meet routine budget deficits. As the Fund had been established to commemorate the war dead, this was revealing of the morality of the Treasury. In Northern Ireland the purposes of the Ulster Land Fund were far more clearly defined in the Ulster Land Fund Act of 1949, allowing it to be used for the repair and maintenance of houses and their contents, and for grants or loans towards the acquisition of land and buildings. As a result a string of major acquisitions by the Trust, including Florence Court (Co. Fermanagh), Castle Ward (Co. Down) and Derrymore House (Co. Armagh), was made possible by imaginative use of the Fund.

The Committee for Northern Ireland used its independence from London to the full. Instead of the standard, staid guides, all with dark green covers, produced at Queen Anne's Gate, designs were commissioned from leading Ulster artists. The Committee put up the money for a booklet about Trust properties, with drawings and maps by James MacIntyre. In 1958 there was an exhibition at Queen's University of his drawings and of Trust photographs, opened by Tyrone Guthrie. Always ready to help the Trust, John Betjeman was invited to lecture, and delighted his Belfast audience by his accounts of the splendours of the city's Great Northern Railway station and its gas works. A scheme was established called HEARTH, modelled on the National Trust for Scotland's Little Houses Scheme and using a revolving fund to repair small buildings.

Until 1964 the Northern Ireland Committee continued to be financially independent. When Lord Antrim told John Lewis-Crosby, appointed Regional Secretary in 1960, to begin acquiring stretches of the Ulster coast, most of the funds were to be found from within Northern Ireland. The Giant's Causeway came to the Trust through the Ulster Land Fund in 1962, the year that the Ulster Coastline Appeal was launched. There was wholehearted support from Christopher Gibbs, who on a walk along the North Antrim Coast path remarked that the time had come for the Trust to embark on a national campaign to protect the coast, thus reviving the idea that G.M. Trevelyan had put forward in 1930 and which was to become Enterprise Neptune (see p.165).

Only a committee thoroughly in tune with the history and traditions of Northern Ireland could have worked effectively there. Some of the buildings that came to the Trust did so because they represented important aspects of Ulster life. One traditional process was beetling, which gives a sheen to linen by hammering it. Since the eighteenth century, the Wellbrook Beetling Mill at Cookstown, Co. Tyrone, had been used for finishing linen, once Ulster's principal manufacturing industry, making its acquisition by the Trust in 1968 entirely appropriate.

Encouragement to become involved in the industrial archaeology of Northern Ireland, as well as generous funding, came early on from John Smith and the Landmark Trust. A letter of 12 June 1952 from Harold Nicolson to Vita Sackville-West describes John Smith's introduction to the Historic Buildings Committee of the National Trust: 'We had a new member, the Earl of Euston. You know I am always rather worried that this committee, which actually decides whether we take a house, is composed almost entirely of peers. Well, we are now to have a man called Mr John Smith. When his name was put up Esher said, "Well it's a good thing to have a proletarian name on the committee – anybody know the man?" "Yes" said Lord Euston, "he is my brother-in-law".'

John Smith's contribution to the Trust's work could be summarised by listing the many properties which, through his initiative or through the generosity of the Landmark and Manifold Trusts, were given a secure future. He also helped to revise the Trust's interpretation of what it meant by 'historic interest', so taking its work into new areas and broadening its appeal. His original mind identified new challenges with bewildering speed, while his energy and resourcefulness found solutions almost as readily. Apparently insuperable problems were made to look trivial. Accommodating such a man was not easy.

The feats of engineering which in the nineteenth century helped to make Britain the most powerful nation on earth had fascinated Smith since his schooldays. He was intrigued not just by why things were constructed and when, but exactly how they worked, how new techniques were developed and why at a particular time they had such impact. During five years in the Fleet Air Arm he became increasingly interested in ships, particularly battleships. That interest had to be translated into action. It led him to the Falkland Islands – 'before they became fashionable' – where the hulks of the tall ships damaged while rounding the Horn were laid up. He threw himself into the successful campaign to preserve HMS *Belfast*. When the Landmark Trust accepted a lease of Lundy, in the Bristol Channel, from the Trust, one of the discoveries that gave him most excitement was that in calm weather the wreck of HMS *Montagu*, which went down in 1906, was clearly visible on its south-west side. Who but John Smith would have sought out the hull of Britain's first and last iron-clad, wooden hulled battleship, HMS *Warrior*, then being used as a floating jetty near Milford Haven, and arranged for her complete restoration through his Manifold Trust? HMS *Warrior* is now moored near the *Mary Rose* and HMS *Victory* at Portsmouth.

In 1961 Lord Esher retired from the chairmanship of the General Purposes Committee. He had lost none of his wit, nor his sense of timing. When he was

HM Queen Elizabeth The Queen Mother and the
28th Earl of Crawford & Balcarres at the opening of
the Stratford Canal on 11 July 1964. Lord Crawford was
Chairman of the National Trust from 1945 to 1965.

being wheeled into the operating theatre during his last illness, a large nurse leant over the trolley. 'I hope I don't wake up in Abraham's bosom', a scarcely audible Esher was heard to say.

The choice of John Smith as successor was thought likely to bring a new dynamism to the work of the Trust. One of his first major re-examinations of policy was to argue in a long and detailed report to Lord Crawford that the Trust should involve itself in the preservation of canals. Kenneth Robinson, a Labour MP recruited to the Executive Committee, Rathbone and De La Warr were press ganged into canal trips. They found Smith's enthusiasm for this 'manifestation of the English genius' irresistible but were deeply worried by the financial

implications of taking on canals. In 1960 the Trust took a lease of the Stratford Canal in Warwickshire with an option to purchase. There was to be an appeal and Smith himself found some of the funds to pay the salary of the canal manager. Almost single-handed John Smith had pushed the Trust into industrial archaeology.

Steam engines and the Cornish tin industry became another preoccupation. The Regional Secretary for Devon and Cornwall, Michael Trinick, was at that time uninterested in steam engines and had more than enough on his hands with the preservation of the coast. His defences crumbled when Smith explained the importance of the Cornish engines at the Levant mine, and how every part of the winding engine in the South Crofty mine was curved and shaped for its precise function. Alarmed by its own ignorance, the Trust appointed an honorary Adviser on Industrial Monuments, Rex Wailes, in 1964, the same year that the Stratford Canal was opened, and fifteen miles of the River Wey Navigation in Surrey were acquired. The Conwy Suspension Bridge in Gwynedd, designed by Thomas Telford in 1826, was transferred to the Trust in 1965.

Those who were concerned about the financial commitments involved with these properties were often disarmed by Smith's own generosity. Sometimes this came from his Manifold Trust, which was funded from investments of Smith's own devising, with an equity of five pounds provided by Pat Gibson, a close friend with whom he had served on the board of the *Financial Times*. Smith worked methodically at the scheme over the next twenty-five years. By 1987 Gibson's magic fiver and the Manifold Trust had produced around £41.5 million, of which rather more than half had been distributed amongst 813 different charities.

Many of Smith's interests related in some way to the preservation of the coast. Running the campaign which Gibbs was now advocating needed more time and resources than were available within the Chief Agent's Department. In November 1962 Smith urged the Executive Committee to take on an appeals director. The appointment in March 1963 of Commander Conrad Rawnsley, grandson of Hardwicke Rawnsley, was made with Smith's endorsement and against the advice of Gibbs and Rathbone. By that time relations between the

(*Previous page*) Conwy Suspension Bridge, Gwynedd, built
in 1826 by Thomas Telford and acquired
by the National Trust in 1965.

General Purposes Committee and the staff had become so strained that changes were clearly necessary. John Smith decided to stand down as Chairman, but remained a member of the Committee. He now channelled his energies into his own creation, the immensely successful Landmark Trust, which rescues interesting but often derelict buildings, repairs them and then rents them to those who want a holiday somewhere eccentric or unusual. He continued to challenge, provoke, amuse and inspire the Trust's committees for the next thirty years, in due course providing the perfect foil as Deputy-Chairman to Pat, now Lord Gibson.

By the mid-1960s the Trust had reached a point of administrative crisis. One symptom was that the Secretary, Rathbone, himself suffered a nervous breakdown. This was not just the result of conflict with John Smith. There were friends like Pat Gibson, devoted to both men, who tried to help but who found Lord Crawford distant and uncommunicative. At the root of the problem was the wholly inadequate support on which the Secretary could draw when trying to respond to Smith's dazzling array of ideas. An administration which had worked well in the late 1940s and early 1950s was simply inadequate to deal with the challenges of the 1960s. Attempts had been made to put this right, but neither Crawford nor Rathbone saw how vital it was to equip the Trust to cope with these new demands and expectations.

With hindsight, it is clear that a crucial opportunity to reform was missed in 1958 when the Executive Committee considered a report on the administration of the Trust, produced by a committee under the chairmanship of Sir Philip Nichols. As early as 1941, in a paper to the Chairmen of committees on 'The Work and Organisation of the Trust', Matheson had suggested the setting up of Regional Advisory Committees. Now Nichols put forward a fully worked-out proposal for Regional Committees, supported by Regional Secretaries. The administrative structure that he advocated was remarkably close to one finally adopted by the Trust in the mid-1970s and which since then has served the Trust well. The principal recommendation was for 'increased decentralisation of the work of the Trust from Head Office to people in the country'.

The Executive Committee accepted the findings of the Nichols Report. It was left to the Secretary to implement the change to a more devolved administration, with far more responsibility exercised by the regions. For the change to have worked, the strategy needed vigorous pursuit, so that increased activity helped to generate the funds for what would inevitably be greater administrative costs. In practice only three Regional Secretaries were appointed in the late

1950s: Carew Wallace in a region covering several of the southern counties, Michael Trinick in Devon and Cornwall, and John Lewis-Crosby in Northern Ireland. Wallace rapidly found that staff from head office, particularly the Chief Agent's Department, had no intention of respecting his position and on visits to his region would give instructions without bothering to consult him. In Trinick's Celtic fastness west of the Tamar, the region's independence was relished, with impressive benefits to the Trust. But devolution was not allowed to progress much further than that.

In November 1964 the Secretary reported to the General Purposes Committee on the implementation of the Nichols recommendations. He concluded that, in Wallace's region, 'through no fault of his, it has proved impossible for him to act in the truly regional sense contemplated by Sir Philip Nichols' Committee or to be the Trust's figurehead in the enormous region over which he has been given jurisdiction'. Other staff suitable for the post of Regional Secretary had been impossible to find, it was maintained. The Secretary had earlier written that 'regional committees are not desirable and local committees are often a doubtful asset', although he did eventually propose the setting up of eleven regional committees. The Executive Committee rejected the recommendation: even though the success of the regional committees in the Lake District and Northern Ireland suggested otherwise, they concluded that suitable people would not come forward.

It would be unfair to lay the blame for this half-hearted effort at reform entirely at Jack Rathbone's door. He had already served the Trust with dedication for twenty years and had handled its affairs with tact and efficiency. John Smith wanted the administration to work more effectively, but he was temperamentally unsuited either to much loosening of the reins, or to seeing that different staff were appointed. When Lord Antrim succeeded to the Chairmanship in 1965 the state of the Trust was far more precarious than its committees realised. A high price had to be paid for the Trust's failure to change its ways of working, and equip itself to deal with rapidly increasing responsibilities.

CHAPTER EIGHT

A Chapter of Disasters

In the early hours of the morning of 18 November 1967, Michael Trinick received a telephone call from the son of the caretaker of Dunsland House: 'We've just got out in our nightclothes, the fire brigade have arrived and the place is burning like a torch.' Trinick immediately rang the estate staff at Lanhydrock in Cornwall to tell them to bring over lorries and tarpaulins in the hope of being able to salvage some of the contents, then set out for that empty corner of Devon to the north of Dartmoor. By the time he arrived at Dunsland most of the house was ablaze. Only the back wing appeared not to be burning, but within minutes three rooms had exploded into flames.

Dunsland, a Tudor house altered and enlarged in the seventeenth century, had been bought by the Trust in 1954, using a legacy which also made possible the purchase of the sixteenth-century manor house of Trerice in Cornwall. During the ensuing thirteen years Trinick had bought or borrowed furniture and there had been extensive repairs to this remote, romantic house. To mark the completion of the restoration a concert was given on the evening of 14 November to a packed audience in the Justice Room. On the morning of 18 November Trinick was showing the smoking ruins to the last of the hereditary family to live there, the Rev. Bickford Dickinson. All he could find to take away as a relic of the house were a few lumps of melted lead, from the roof which he had repaired with his own hands years before.

The loss of Dunsland came at the end of two traumatic years for the Trust. The dispute which nearly tore the organisation apart arose from the way Enterprise Neptune was being run, and in particular the proposals of its Appeal Director, Commander Conrad Rawnsley.

The National Trust rather prides itself on not being a slave to fashion, but in 1967 it was caught up in a powerful process of change. In the late 1960s revolution was very much in vogue: students were tearing up the streets of Paris, the American Embassy in Grosvenor Square was besieged, national institutions were being challenged and university buildings occupied. In many cases the reforms

Dunsland House in Devon in 1967, just after the
completion of extensive repairs and restoration.

which followed were long overdue. That a crisis in the Trust coincided with
upheavals in many other organisations should not detract from Rawnsley's
achievement in actually getting disaffected Trust members to the barricades.
This was all the more remarkable because, as Rawnsley pointed out at the time,
the Trust had done very little to encourage young people to take an interest in
its affairs: 'education is not our business' Fedden would say, 'it should be left to
the professionals'. Nevertheless, in a very English way the Trust embarked on a
revolution that was acrimonious and at moments unedifying, from which it
emerged bruised and ultimately invigorated.

In his correspondence Commander Rawnsley referred to the devastating
effect of his broadsides. Certainly, controversy followed in his wake from the
moment that he applied for the appeal director's post in October 1962. When
notified by Rathbone that he was not to be included in the short list, he wrote
a long letter pressing his qualifications and playing the card of his relationship, as
grandson, with one of the founders. Persistence was one of the qualities he
brought to the Trust. Those who supported his appointment were also right to

Firemen attending the devastating fire at
Dunsland House on 18 November 1967.

recognise his restless energy and the sense of missionary zeal that he promised to
bring to the Trust. He may well have seemed the man to galvanize other staff: the
case for more involvement by the ordinary public in the work of the Trust had
been advocated when the preservation of canals was being urged. Rawnsley was
convinced, rightly as it turned out, that a reinvigorated campaign to save the
coast, to be called Enterprise Neptune, had the potential to attract support from a
wider public still, and he painted an impressive picture of how this might be done.

A survey had been conducted by the Trust in 1963 to examine the 3,000 miles
that make up the coastline of England, Wales and Northern Ireland, and to
identify the areas that were of outstanding beauty and worthy of preservation. It
was found that approximately one-third was already ruined; one-third was of
little interest; leaving one-third – 900 miles – that Enterprise Neptune should
campaign to acquire.

Given his reservation about the appointment, it is surprising that Rathbone
never set out clearly what Rawnsley's responsibilities and obligations were and
to whom he was reporting. The very title 'Appeal Director' encouraged

Rawnsley to think that he was entitled to be his own master, guided more by his interpretation of the wishes of the founders than by the policy decisions of the Executive Committee. Within a year of his appointment, Crawford was expressing concern to Rathbone about Rawnsley's radical ideas and his capacity to upset the Committee. Antrim urged that if the appointment was proving unsatisfactory, Rawnsley should go immediately. Perhaps too generously, Rathbone's response, given in a letter of December 1963, was to urge patience and restraint: 'I think it would be a pity now to stop the appeal and an even greater pity to get rid of Rawnsley, although he has worried not only members of the Committee but some of the Area Agents. The Wind of Change which he has produced is, I am sure, a good thing for the Trust; so are many of his ideas and the boisterous and enthusiastic sea breeze which he blows over us. His optimism and efficiency are excellent things.' In January Rathbone reported to Antrim that Lady Dalton and Sir Gerald Templer, members of the Executive Committee, were strongly critical of the way the appeal was being run, but added that he hoped 'so much that you will be able to persuade Crawford not to worry too much about this.'

One of Rawnsley's first initiatives was to set up an Enterprise Neptune 'field force', under the control of six regional directors, with teams of volunteers reporting to them. There was no serious attempt to integrate those working for Enterprise Neptune with the existing regional staff. This was particularly ill-advised, because several of the Trust's Agents had for years been successfully acquiring coastal properties and had scores of local contacts. The dangers of this independence became all the more apparent when Rawnsley began to press for greater emphasis on entertaining the public. He wanted to see the Trust's houses 'play a more active part in the life of the community' and suggested that because 'there is little merit in some of the furniture and pictures', all but the best houses could be used for public assemblies and dances. The facilities at the Trust's coastal properties were, he maintained, thoroughly inadequate. 'Where are the dinghy parks, the launching facilities for pleasure craft, the camping sites, the car parks, the access roads and paths, the lavatories?' he asked. While Rawnsley appealed to the crusading spirit of his grandfather, the Publicity Committee insisted that the Trust's prime duty was to preserve and not to entertain. They were on collision course.

In an attempt to resolve these differences and reintegrate the Appeal, an Enterprise Neptune Committee was formed in the summer of 1964, chaired by Lord Antrim and including Edward Holland-Martin, Pat Gibson, Mark Norman (the future Chairman of the Finance Committee) and Brigadier Maurice Lush. Many of Rawnsley's proposals were excellent and there were encouraging signs that Enterprise Neptune could be a resounding success. Hardwicke Rawnsley's enthusiasm for jubilee bonfires gave his grandson the idea of a chain of Armada beacons to be lit on St George's Day, 23 April 1965. The following May there was a luncheon in the Mansion House in London, at which as Patron, HRH Prince Philip, Duke of Edinburgh, launched Enterprise Neptune. £64,000 was pledged and shortly afterwards the Trust was able to announce that the government would be contributing £250,000.

The success of Enterprise Neptune, much of it due to the personal involvement of Crawford and the members of the Appeal Committee, encouraged Rawnsley to launch a crusade. He wanted a root and branch reform of the Trust and, without consulting other staff or any of the committees, began to share his ideas with those he encountered outside the organisation. One of these was Richard Dimbleby, who was making a television programme about the appeal. On 9 July 1965, Rawnsley wrote to him saying: 'Neptune is really and truly for the man in the street and so is the National Trust. It is a thousand pities that this has not been the public image of the Trust since before the war when the Stately Home Scheme bedevilled it but I'm sure Neptune will in time redress the damage.'

When Rathbone instructed him not to air his criticisms of the policies of the Trust's committees so publicly, Rawnsley's answer was to tell the Secretary that the 'stifling of criticism of any institution whatever by any person whatever and in any circumstance whatever is undemocratic and therefore cannot be right except in face of the enemy in wartime'. Antrim received a similar broadside when he had the temerity to ask for a brief for a speech and then, at the time of the meeting, departed from it: 'If you know it all', Rawnsley wrote to his Chairman, 'please don't ask for a brief. If you don't, then ask for one by all means, but have the courtesy to read it.' By December 1965 Rawnsley was writing of the need to reform 'the whole system of government of the Trust'.

At the same time the Neptune Appeal Committee was becoming increasingly concerned about the autocratic way Rawnsley was running his own office. He took it upon himself to issue a Christmas bonus of £500, the equivalent of the annual salary of some property staff, to one of his Neptune recruits without the authority of any committee. A few days later, in what was described as a 'spring clean', he summarily dismissed three of his female staff, including his deputy, with no real explanation and with one month's pay in lieu of notice. The Vice-

Chairman of the Appeal Committee, Maurice Lush, told Rawnsley that he deplored the way he had behaved, nor could he believe that 'the efficiency achieved is likely to outweigh the sense of distaste among the staff of the Trust or the personal trauma inflicted'. Lush warned Rawnsley that both he and Enterprise Neptune were in danger of losing respect inside and outside the Trust.

The first year of Neptune had produced encouraging results, but while the amounts raised were large, so too were expenses of the appeal. The Executive Committee took the view that after the successful launch of the campaign, the costs for 1966 should be kept at the 1965 level. Rawnsley pressed, unsuccessfully, for twice that allocation. In October he told the Neptune Committee that he saw his field force as vital to the whole future life and vigour of the Trust. He urged that its terms of reference 'should be wider and embrace all aspects of the work of the Trust and that its members should be vested with a suitable measure of authority, power of decision and representation in the government of the Trust'.

Experience during the previous year had convinced Lord Antrim, now Chairman of both the Neptune Committee and, in succession to Lord Crawford, of the National Trust, that this was likely to lead not to greater vigour but to a duplication of effort and expense. Already over 21 per cent of the money raised by the appeal was going to meet its running costs. Nor was it any secret that many staff were alarmed by the way Rawnsley directed his field force and by his tendency to present himself as some sort of oracle, because of his relationship with one of the Trust's founders. The Executive Committee wanted to see a more cohesive Trust, in which Enterprise Neptune was integrated into a properly constituted regional organisation, dealing with both fundraising and properties. This integration was planned to take place in March 1967. On 17 October 1966 Antrim wrote to Rawnsley telling him that the 'Executive Committee have decided to end the Neptune campaign as a separate enterprise on 31 March 1967 and to manage it as part of the ordinary organisation of the Trust'. Rawnsley's employment as appeal director was to be terminated at the end of March. Rawnsley asked for, and received, a testimonial from Antrim who rightly attributed much of the success of the Neptune campaign to him and who praised Rawnsley's 'originality and intensity of purpose'.

On 25 October 1966, the day that Antrim wrote his testimonial, there was a press conference and lunch at Saltram, on the outskirts of Plymouth, at which Rawnsley was to be the principal speaker. Trinick had asked him to stay the preceding night but Rawnsley preferred to be at a nearby hotel, saying he would arrive by taxi half an hour before the conference was due to start. In the event he was very late. There were anxious telephone calls and much offering of coffee to the waiting journalists. When Rawnsley finally appeared he was so pale that those who knew him assumed he must be ill. He immediately launched into a bitter attack on the Trust.

Rawnsley spoke from a written statement which he issued at the conference.

Randal McDonnell, 13th Earl of Antrim, Chairman of
the National Trust from 1965 to 1977.

It accused the Trust of moral bankruptcy, 'of being bankrupt in ideas, bankrupt in leadership, bankrupt in the common touch'. The Trust had become 'a part of the Establishment, an inert and amorphous organisation proceeding by the sheer momentum given to it by those who continued to bequeath their wealth and property to it, as often as not to escape death duties'. The committees of the Trust were, he maintained, 'run on the old boy net' which he wanted to replace with 'a proper system of representation'. He was fighting to 'get the government of this Trust on to a proper democratic footing', to put 'new heart and vigour into it'. He told his audience of journalists, by this time itching to get to a telephone, that the gathering they were attending was:

> . . . the counterpart of the famous game of bowls upon the Hoe 400 years ago. The Armada of mediocrity, of inertia, of incompetence, is sailing now upon the shores of England. Only you, through the weapon of the pen, can repell [sic] it as Drake and Hawkins did with their handful of gallant sailors and their canon, so long ago. . . . I have done all I can. It is up to you now, if you believe in Enterprise Neptune, to save it from obscurity and finally extinction.

The immediate consequence of Rawnsley's speech was that there were a lot of uneaten lunches at Saltram. Eventually Trinick got hold of Antrim on the telephone and was asked to tell Rawnsley, then still a paid member of staff, that he was suspended. 'Wouldn't you like to talk to him yourself?' Trinick ventured. 'No, Michael, I certainly wouldn't' came the reply.

Many of those who have the Trust's best interests at heart agree on two things: they regarded Rawnsley's behaviour as deplorable; but acknowledged that the shake-up he provoked was overdue and has been greatly to the Trust's benefit. Before it could reap that benefit, the Trust had to survive a sustained and bitter assault. At the Plymouth meeting, Rawnsley had invoked 'the fire and enthusiasm of those early struggling days' of his grandfather and 'the crusading spirit of this old man and his associates'. He had probably forgotten, if he ever knew, how the Fourth Crusade ended. All his considerable administrative abilities were now directed at pummelling the Trust into the body he believed it should be. He drummed up a Reform Committee, whose first objective was to win over the membership at the next Annual General Meeting, held in Cheltenham.

The Press did not make much of the Annual General Meeting in 1966, but it was in many ways a more significant occasion than the Extraordinary General Meeting which followed it. Under the voting rules as they were then, it might well have been possible for supporters of Rawnsley to gain control of the Council and force the resignation of the Chairman. In the event Rawnsley's supporters were not elected to places on the Council. Undeterred, the Reform Group then concentrated their efforts on winning a series of resolutions at an Extraordinary General Meeting, which under the National Trust Act of 1907 could be requisitioned by 30 or more members. Out of a membership of 160,000 Rawnsley had no difficulty in securing 150 signatures.

Rawnsley's propositions were set out in an eight-page leaflet entitled 'A case for the Reform of the Trust'. Some of the sections would have struck a chord with any reasonable member. It was true that the opening times of certain historic houses, some agreed with donor families during or immediately after the war, were unduly restrictive. So too were the provisions for campers in the Lake District, although Cubby Acland was already acting to put this right. Some of the Agents had not pressed as hard as they should have done for public access to the Trust's countryside properties. Rawnsley was also right that the public image of the Trust and the composition of its committees had become unduly aristocratic. Some of the staff agreed with him: Lees-Milne reminded Antrim that when he first came into contact with the Trust, its moving spirits included distinguished academics and writers such as John Bailey, Professor Trevelyan and Sir Harold Nicolson. Unwisely, but with typical candour, Antrim confessed that the Trust was a 'a self-perpetuating oligarchy' – a phrase seized on by Rawnsley.

Less convincing was the last page of Rawnsley's pamphlet, almost entirely devoted to an account of his own appointment and dismissal. To justify his statement at the Saltram press conference he wrote: 'I had to decide between loyalty to the Trust as an institution and loyalty to its ideals. I settled for the ideals.' Similar words, before and since, have been used to justify similar behaviour. Rawnsley's pamphlet ended by urging support for two proposals: the setting-up of an independent committee of enquiry, and the resolute prosecution of Enterprise Neptune on its former lines.

Some 4,000 members attended the Extraordinary General Meeting on 11 February 1967, at the Central Hall, Westminster. Many of those who came to support the Council and the Chairman arrived early and filled most of the ground floor. Sections of the balconies were largely occupied by supporters of Rawnsley. Never at his best at large and potentially hostile meetings, Antrim struggled to keep a semblance of dignity in the proceedings. Two members of the Council, John Barrett and Maurice Lush, spoke well in its defence, and Lord Chorley insisted that, from his own long experience, the Trust had not lost touch with its earlier ideals. For those who had worked hard for the Trust or had given generously, it was a miserable occasion.

Of the ten motions considered at the EGM, two struck a note that was reasonable and positive. Len Clark, the representative of the Youth Hostels Association on the Council, proposed: 'That this meeting expresses its confidence in the general work of the Trust's Committees but feels that their contact with members of the public who enjoy and value its properties should be improved. The meeting therefore calls on the Council to examine ways in which this may be achieved.' This was followed by a motion proposed by John Betjeman: 'That, recognizing the achievements of the Trust, this meeting gives its full support to the Council and is satisfied that the Council will give due consideration to the views expressed by members at this meeting.' Both motions were carried overwhelmingly.

Rawnsley's main success at the meeting was to gain the necessary support for a poll of all members of the Trust on a motion similar to Len Clark's but in certain key respects subtly different. It was by implication critical of the Council, stipulating that the review committee should include representatives of those who had requisitioned the Extraordinary General Meeting. Even when the membership stood at barely 160,000 this poll and the Extraordinary General Meeting were an expensive exercise, costing the general funds of the Trust £6,400. Wisely the Council made no attempt to influence the voting of members, who at moments of crisis have consistently shown themselves far better informed and more perceptive than their normally rather lax voting habits might suggest. In May the Trust announced that the motion had been rejected by a majority of over two to one. Antrim and the Council were now free to carry out the review advocated by Clark and were ready to move quickly. In July an Advisory Committee was set up, to be chaired by Sir Henry Benson, a leading chartered accountant, who agreed to take on the task without remuneration. To help him he chose Sir William Hayter, Warden of New College Oxford; Len Clark; and Pat Gibson who had served on several Trust committees. What they had in common were incisive intellects and devotion to the work of the Trust. The Assistant Secretary, Jack Boles, was to service the committee. Always ready to put the interests of the Trust first, Jack Rathbone offered his resignation. What had happened, and particularly the scathing attacks on the Trust in the press, had been a shattering personal experience and his health had again broken down. However, Antrim asked him to stay until a successor could be found. The Benson Committee held its first meeting in September 1967 and its report was published in December 1968.

One of the most vociferous critics at the EGM was Peter Grundy, a resident of Styal in Cheshire, who complained of the gross neglect of Quarry Bank Mill and the mismanagement of the Trust's many houses and cottages in the village. Quarry Bank Mill, Styal village and the hanging beechwoods, on the banks of the River Bollin, had been given to the Trust in 1939 by Alec Greg, the direct descendant of Samuel Greg, who had established a cotton mill at Styal in 1784. The factory colony established by the Gregs at Styal had combined entrepreneurship, industrial innovation and enlightened philanthropy so successfully that it merited a lengthy description in Frederick Engels's *The Condition of the Working Class in England*, the book that directly inspired Karl Marx and gave him the source material for *Das Kapital*. Styal is not just important historically. Although so close to Manchester, the river valley is tranquil and the mill buildings are an intriguing blend of industrial functionalism and Georgian detail.

Antrim wanted to be able to judge for himself whether Grundy's criticisms were valid. He took the opportunity to visit Styal when returning home to Northern Ireland just before Christmas. Gerard Noel, the Agent who had recently taken over responsibility for the West Midlands region, was asked to arrange a meeting with the Trust's tenants, to hear their grievances. They gathered in the Oak School, built in 1823 for the Gregs' 'half-timers', the children whose eight-hour working day had to be divided equally between school work and mill work. Antrim's humour, his willingness to listen, his obvious decency and his humanity disarmed his critics.

Thereafter Antrim always took a particularly close interest in Styal. He supported Noel's efforts to get an unsatisfactory and obstructive tenant out of the mill so that dry rot could be treated. The Finance Committee were gently steered towards providing the funding needed to set up a museum to the cotton industry. Under an inspired Director, David Sekers, Styal went on to win the Sandford Award for Heritage Education, to become the second Trust property to be given the Museum of the Year Award (Erddig was the first), and by 1993 it was attracting over 200,000 visitors a year. Late one night in 1986 the two mill engineers, Fred Madders and Donald Hatch, gave a cautious trial to the iron suspension water wheel, 24 feet in diameter, which they had reinstated in the pit beneath the Mill and which had come to symbolise its return to industrial life. Many of the cotton goods now sold in the Trust's shops are manufactured at Styal.

In a way the transformation which Antrim helped to bring about at Styal achieved what Rawnsley advocated. The Mill appeals to the young, who are given a vivid insight into what factory life was like for the children living at the Apprentice House. The history with which it deals is at times tough and unpalatable: the Trust is associated with that, not with the snobbery which Rawnsley rightly deplored. The river walks and the beechwoods at Styal are heavily used by vast numbers from the conurbations of Manchester. All this might have come about had there been no Rawnsley row; but perhaps the problems at Styal would not have been addressed with quite such urgency, nor would the committees have been so willing to allocate funds had they not been stung into action.

The 1970s were a period of unprecedented growth in properties and mem-

Paupers from Liverpool and Manchester were employed as child apprentices
in Greg's cotton mill at Quarry Bank in Cheshire from the 1830s, and
were housed and fed in the Apprentice House. Children in appropriate
historic costume learn about the life of the apprentices.

bership. Whether it was Rawnsley's criticisms or the Benson Report which
brought this about is a moot point. In a sense it was both, because one led to
the other. Certainly the Benson Committee was the most capable ever called
upon to review the workings of the Trust, which was now thoroughly prepared
for major changes. The most immediately significant of these was a new Act of
Parliament which altered voting procedures for AGMs and EGMs to reflect the
Trust's vastly increased membership. The preparations for this legislation were
handled with exceptional skill by the Trust's Solicitor, Robert Latham, and the
Act received Royal Assent in February 1971.

Lancashire overpick looms in the restored
weaving shed at Quarry Bank Mill, Styal.
Former workers from the cotton industry
demonstrate the various machines to visitors.

The Benson Report dealt particularly clearly with the need for greater decentralisation. It concluded that the difficulties in finding suitable members for regional committees had been over-emphasised. Fourteen committees were proposed, served by a regional agent and a regional custodian of equal status. The long-running issue of aesthetes versus agents – the confrontation of the lily and the hobnailed boot as John Smith called it – was intended to be resolved by allowing the agent to be regarded as *primus inter pares*. This was one of the very few recommendations which did not stand the test of time. The need to have a single member of staff clearly responsible for the running of a region was recognised in 1977, when the post of Regional Director was created. In practice this meant, without exception, giving the title Director to the regional agent. The appointment of a Director from another discipline was tried in 1981 and signalled the revival of what had been advocated by Sir Philip Nichols over twenty years earlier.

What the Benson Committee did not accept were Rawnsley's submissions on how the Trust's historic buildings should be looked after. Arbiters of taste were not, Rawnsley believed, equipped to deal with management responsibilities and he thought their role should be purely advisory. In his evidence to the Committee he then hinted darkly at what he suspected was sexual ambiguity amongst some of the Trust's historic buildings staff. Not unduly shocked, the Committee suggested to Rawnsley that this was not unknown in creative artists and would not be surprising among those responsible for decorating the Trust's houses. 'Woman's work, woman's work' was Rawnsley's reply. The Committee chose not to adopt Rawnsley's proposal that 'everyone, from the Chairman downwards should, in future, be carefully screened'. The Benson Report went out of its way to stress that 'aesthetic considerations should not be sacrificed for reasons of expediency' and advocated clear, executive responsibilities for the Trust's regional custodians.

On the question of access, many of the criticisms of the reformers were accepted. The report, however, drew clear distinctions between the Trust's obligation on the one hand to provide for public enjoyment and on the other its duty 'to preserve its inalienable properties, so far as possible, in their natural and traditional state'.

The Benson Report proved so formative partly because those responsible for directing the Trust for the ensuing eighteen years were totally identified with its findings. The Director-General appointed in 1968, Sir John Winnifrith, regarded its implementation as his prime responsibility. His successor, Frederick Bishop, had worked at one time with Winnifrith and later with Pat Gibson. When Antrim died in 1977, Lord Gibson became Chairman of the Trust. For most of his Chairmanship the Director-General was Jack Boles, who had been such an outstanding Secretary to the Benson Committee. The 'old boy net' so deplored by Rawnsley is undeniably evident in these relationships, and no less evident are the achievements of those years.

Antrim had an extraordinary capacity for picking those who would make an outstanding contribution to the Trust. Simon Hornby, a future President of the Royal Horticultural Society, of the W.H. Smith Group and of the Design

Council, was brought on to the Finance Committee, as was Nicholas Baring, who became one of its shrewdest, least obtrusive members and, in succession to Mark Norman, the Chairman who ensured that its funds were wisely used during the rapid expansion of the 1980s. The motives, interests and qualities of those he met rarely failed to arouse Antrim's amused fascination, which may explain why his staff appointments were so successful. A new post, that of Chief Finance Officer, was given to Jimmy Wheeler, who began to provide the Finance Committee with the information needed to run its increasingly complex activities.

When Edward Fawcett was appointed as the first Director of Public Relations in 1969, there were 170,000 members of the Trust. When he retired in 1981 there were 1,046,000 members. Initially there was a less than enthusiastic reaction when he suggested to custodians that they might consider actually welcoming and recruiting members at the Trust's houses. At the proposition that the Trust might also consider offering for sale a few well-designed tea towels, there was downright hostility, at almost every level. A committee was set up to ensure that any merchandise offered for sale was up to Trust standards. After three years this Committee of Taste had not approved a single article, as there was always some grounds for objection. At this point Antrim backed Fawcett decisively, encouraging Simon Hornby to give the Trust the benefit of his immense experience of retailing and then using him to reassure the Executive Committee that the establishment of shops at properties was both a wise and necessary development. The image of the Trust presented at properties and by the Press Secretary, Warren Davies, was increasingly of an organisation that was not aloof, but was approachable and open.

The relationship between Antrim and the new Director-General, Winnifrith, proved to be a particularly close one, not least because they both combined a schoolboy's humour with a well-developed sense of the ridiculous. Winnifrith was quite capable of warning a new and nervous member of staff about a particularly volatile donor and would then offer him a pound if he could get on Christian name terms. Beneath his easy, friendly manner was a capacity for hard, rapid and immensely disciplined work. His experience of government and of the Civil Service, as a former Permanent Secretary at the Ministry of Agriculture, Fisheries and Food, meant that Winnifrith was well-equipped to reorganise the Trust's ways of working and to deal with the increasingly complex and potentially damaging issues now confronting it.

The most serious threat was to the Trust's unique power to hold land inalienably, conferred on it under the Act of Parliament of 1907. This meant

(*Above*) Fire-engines battling with the fire at Uppark
on 30 August 1989.

(*Right*) The Saloon at Uppark after restoration.

that, for inalienable land to be taken away from the Trust without its consent, the approval of Parliament was required. In practice this procedure was not invoked until 1968 when a proposal for a new road to serve Plymouth involved the compulsory purchase of inalienable land at Saltram. The issue hung on whether the Trust had been aware of the road proposal when the land had been declared inalienable eleven years earlier. At that time the road was intended to be 80 feet wide and the Executive Committee concluded that its impact on Saltram would not be disastrous. By 1968 the specification for trunk roads had changed radically, and the proposals involved a scheme three times larger than originally indicated, with a total of eight lanes instead of four. Under pressure from the Charity Commissioners, it was decided to take the issue to Parliament and in November 1968 the Joint Select Committee of both Houses found against the Trust.

This would have been an extremely serious weakening of the Trust's position and powers, had the principle of inalienability not been put to the test again,

An aerial photograph of Saltram in Devon, showing
the Plymouth by-pass bisecting the park.

almost immediately. Rainbow Wood Farm, a relatively small and not particularly
distinguished property on the outskirts of Bath, had been owned by the Trust
since 1959 and it had been declared inalienable. In 1968 Bath City Council,
which at that time had an appalling record of vandalism to its Georgian houses,
wanted the land for new playing fields. Winnifrith was satisfied that the Trust
had followed with scrupulous correctness all the procedures for declaring land
inalienable and he himself gave evidence on behalf of the Trust at the enquiry.
The decision of the Minister for Housing and Local Government, in March
1969, was to support the Trust against the City Council. This success was all the
more valuable to the Trust, because a vigorous campaign had been conducted
in its support. The public was now far better informed about the meaning and
significance of the Trust's ability to declare land inalienable.

Antrim and Winnifrith were single-minded in the way that the policy of
devolution was pursued. In some regions the agent and representative argued

that setting up a regional committee could be delayed, but Antrim would have none of that. If suitable names for a chairman were not put forward by the region, he took it upon himself to make the appointment without further consultation. If head office staff or committee members did not respect the authority of one of his regional chairmen, he personally issued a blunt rebuke.

The one committee which Antrim would sometimes take for granted was the Council, as had his predecessor, Lord Crawford. The problem went back a long way. Writing of the Trust in the 1920s, Lord Chorley described meetings of the Council as 'purely formal' and lasting 'only a few minutes while it listened to a report on what had been done in its name by its Executive'. Attendance by members was then patchy and irregular. In 1949 the Secretary, Admiral Bevir, suggested that perhaps it was only necessary to hold one meeting a year. Writing to the Chairman, Matheson confirmed that 'the Council has ceased to exist for all practical purposes and has become little more than a legal fiction'. The Benson Committee recommended that meetings should be at least quarterly and that there should be a review every six years of the bodies able to nominate members to the Council. Although the report re-emphasised the central role of the Council in reviewing policy, Antrim failed to impress on its members sufficient awareness of their responsibilities as trustees. The first Chairman in recent years to work hard at making meetings of the Council an adequate reflection of its statutory position was Lord Gibson. His successor, Dame Jennifer Jenkins, was even more committed to the principle that the Council has ultimate responsibility for the direction of the Trust.

One of the saddest decisions which Antrim and his committees had to face was what to do with the shell of Dunsland. When Coleshill, in Berkshire, an even more important house designed by the seventeenth-century architect Sir Roger Pratt, was burnt out in 1952, it had been demolished, although this happened four years before the gift of the Coleshill estate to the Trust. In 1989, within a few days of the remarkable eighteenth-century interior of Uppark in Sussex being reduced to smouldering ruins, an announcement was made that the house would be rebuilt. By that time the Trust knew that it could call on conservation staff of unrivalled experience, and its insurance policies provided for full reinstatement. At Dunsland, however, the fire had proved so intense that none of the contents could be saved. Only a few exquisite rainwater heads and a couple of relatively undamaged door-surrounds had survived. An architect's report also showed that the heat of the fire had shattered the brick core and its bonding with the stone casing of the house. To rebuild it would at that time have involved taking most of the walls down to ground level and little original fabric would have remained. Rather than attempting such wholesale renewal, the walls were pushed over into the cellars. A simple plaque shows where the house stood.

During the 1970s one of the Trust's least known properties narrowly escaped destruction no less than six times. Derrymore is an eighteenth-century house in remote countryside in County Armagh. At first glance it might be mistaken for a cottage or even a folly. The three single-storey wings are grouped around a courtyard, with the Treaty Room occupying the central pavilion. Here the builder of Derrymore, Isaac Corry, is reputed to have assisted with the drafting of the Act of Union of 1801 between England and Ireland. When the Trust accepted the gift of the house in 1953, it was some sixteen years before 'the troubles' resurfaced in Northern Ireland. Political considerations would anyway not have dissuaded the committees from protecting a building of such clear architectural merit. No Trust property has had to be looked after in quite the way that Edmund Baillie and his two sisters have cared for Derrymore. It escaped devastation one night in 1972, when the Baillie family were woken by bright lights in the garden. They were told by republican terrorists that a large bomb had been placed against one of the doors and they had to leave the building immediately. Edmund Baillie did so. He picked up the bomb and carried it out into the garden, away from the house. Derrymore was damaged, but not irreparably; and the Baillies insisted on continuing as caretakers.

CHAPTER NINE

PATCHWORK

T HE FIRST REACTION to the gale early in the morning of 16 October 1987 was one of shock and dismay. The Great Storm as it came to be called struck south-east England, particularly Sussex, Kent and Surrey, before blowing itself out over Norfolk. Where a few hours before had been majestic stands of beech or immaculately tended formal gardens, there was complete disorder, a chaos of uprooted and shattered trees. Gardeners and woodmen saw the work of a lifetime devastated in a night. A few years on, what is most striking is the way destruction can be revivifying. In several areas of woodland the gale

After the Hurricane, Nymans, West Sussex, painted by Cherryl Fountain
for the National Trust's Foundation for Art, 1987.

broke open a dense canopy of foliage and, where the light flooded in, a dormant seed source was released. The result has been vigorous natural regeneration: a metaphor, perhaps, for other forms of renewal.

Many of the most significant developments in the history of the Trust have emerged like wild flowers in recently coppiced woodland. This sudden germination can surprise and disconcert those who like everything to be planned, ordered and predictable. There is a sense of the Trust being caught unaware in its response to the acquisition of Great Gable in 1923. The Trust appreciated the educational potential of country houses only because of what John Hodgson achieved, entirely on his own initiative, at the Museum of Childhood which he created at Sudbury Hall in Derbyshire in the 1970s. Many of the Trust's most significant acquisitions have been set in train by a chance encounter or an opportunity presenting itself without warning.

For many years the Trust saw this feature of its work as a sign of strength and wanted to be judged on the way it responded to a challenge, however unexpected. 'Our policy on that issue is not to have a policy', Antrim would sometimes tell the committees. To him it seemed more important to nurture and support creativity in the regions than to give the central administration of the Trust a spurious sense of importance by producing all sorts of policy and planning documents that nobody would read.

One of the most significant, least premeditated, acquisitions in the history of the Trust was pieced together, like a patchwork, over forty years. When the Trust was eventually told that it was to become custodian of one of the finest stretches of limestone scenery in the north of England, it was delighted and surprised. Vision, opportunism and great generosity all combined to make David and Graham Watson's gift of Upper Wharfedale in North Yorkshire remarkable, even by the standards of the Trust. 'It was not intended to be generous', Graham Watson later explained, 'it was selfish: we wanted to protect Upper Wharfedale and we knew of no other way of doing so.'

Graham Watson's first contact with the Trust was through the Trevelyan family: he was a particularly close friend of John Dower, who was married to one of Sir Charles's daughters. During vacations from Cambridge in the 1920s, Watson would join Trevelyan's hunt, organised while they were staying at Seatoller in Borrowdale, Cumbria. Professor G.M. Trevelyan was coming to the end of his years of enthusiastic participation in the Man Hunt: he last exercised his prowess at 'running and leaping downhill over very broken ground' in 1926, when he was fifty. At Cambridge Watson had taken his running seriously and he knew he could catch or evade any Trevelyan in the chase across the fells. Watson later introduced Sir Charles's son, George, to potholing and together they explored the limestone caves of the Clapham area of the Pennines.

David and Graham Watson were employed by Listers, the textile business in Bradford where their father and grandfather had also worked. At weekends they would escape on motorbikes to Upper Wharfedale, walking the moors around Buckden and Yockenthwaite. They also continued to visit the Lake District, which by this time Graham Watson knew intimately. He had been introduced by Dower to the Rev. H.H. Symonds who in 1934 formed the Friends of the Lake District. The following year Watson was recruited and asked to form a branch in Leeds. It was Dower who was the driving force behind the National Parks Act of 1949, and not surprisingly Watson found himself involved from the start, first through the Yorkshire Dales National Park Committee and then as a member of the Lake District Planning Board. Serving on these committees reinforced his belief in the value of the role of the Trust as land owner and manager. As a member of the Trust's North West Regional Committee, he was not particularly vocal, but when he did contribute it immediately became apparent that he had prepared himself meticulously and had thought deeply about whatever issue was being discussed. He often left the Trust's Regional Director, Laurence Harwood, musing: 'I wish I'd said that'. On contentious subjects such as whether to allow boating on Wastwater, Watson was able to articulate the Trust's principles and obligations in a clear, compelling way, and then give unwavering support to the staff who had to carry out sometimes unpopular decisions.

The Watsons bought their first property in Upper Wharfedale, Beckermonds Farm, in 1943, a year after David was wounded at El Alamein. In 1945 they were able to buy Redmire Farm, always their favourite property, its 1,333 acres stretching from the valley bottom to Birk's Tarn. Parts of the woodland on the lower slopes were planted in the last century with ornamental trees which exploit the glimpses of natural waterfalls, but at 2,000 feet Birk's Fell and Firth Fell are wild and open. Thereafter the patchwork began to come together: Cowside Farm, New House Farm and 753 acres of Moor End Farm in 1947; Manor House

(*Overleaf*) Farmland near Cray on the Upper Wharfedale
estate in North Yorkshire. The estate was
given to the National Trust by Graham Watson
and his brother David in 1989.

Farm, Mount Pleasant Farm and parts of Kettlewell in 1949; Yockenthwaite Farm with its fine Neo-classical farmhouse in 1963; Scar House Farm in 1971; Raisgill in 1983; and Langer Ings, Buckden, bought in 1985. David and Graham Watson had assembled an estate of 5,590 acres, bringing most of Upper Wharfedale between Kettlewell in the south to the dale head at Langstrothdale in the north under one protective ownership.

Before David died in 1988, the brothers had decided that the Trust was the body best equipped to continue the consistent management and protection they had worked for. They were worried about the possibility of inappropriate alterations to farm buildings and what would happen if there were inadequate checks on the excessive demands of tourism. Rather than risk complications after his death, Graham decided that he would prefer to see the whole property pass to the Trust in his lifetime, when he could deal with people he already knew. Even with someone as long involved with the Trust as Graham, the

(*Above*) Graham Watson and Dame Jennifer Jenkins at Upper Wharfedale, in December 1988, on the day that the gift of the estate was announced. Dame Jennifer Jenkins was Chairman of the National Trust from 1986 to 1991.

(*Right*) The 1st Lord Chorley, President of Lake District Farm Estates Ltd, handing over the deeds of eight farms to Mark Norman, Deputy Chairman of the National Trust, on 17 June 1977. Cubby Acland, Area Agent in the north west from 1949 to 1973, is standing between them.

requirement of an endowment to meet future wardening costs came as a surprise and might have been a setback had the Chairman, Dame Jennifer Jenkins, and the Director-General, Angus Stirling, not visited Upper Wharfedale in 1988. Both were determined that negotiations should be concluded successfully. When the estate was finally transferred to the Trust on 31 January 1989, Graham Watson commented that he and his brother felt that the Trust had 'the commitment and the necessary conservation and management skills to care for such an unspoilt landscape' and added that he knew the Trust would respect the rights of access enjoyed by the public, as well as the interests of those living and farming in Upper Wharfedale. At eighty Watson was still walking the higher fells.

Many of the Trust's most important properties have, like Upper Wharfedale, been assembled piece by piece, often from small beginnings. The first foothold in the Buttermere Valley in Cumbria was secured in 1935 and scarcely a year has gone by without the addition of a few acres here or a farm there. Borrowdale

Ashes Hollow, the Long Mynd, Shropshire.

and Derwentwater have an even longer and more complex history of piecemeal acquisition. Between 1937 and 1971 a society registered under the Provident Societies Act, called Lake District Farm Estates Ltd, acquired a succession of farms around Langdale Pikes and in the Duddon Valley, to secure their preservation. Their object achieved, the President of the Society, Lord Chorley, handed over the title deeds of eight farms to the Deputy Chairman of the Trust, Mark Norman, at a simple ceremony in 1977 at Yew Tree Farm in Borrowdale. In Shropshire the area agent, John Cripwell, acquired the first, central area of the Long Mynd in 1965. Over twenty-five years later the Shropshire Hills Appeal was still very active and extending its remit to Housman's Wenlock Edge, where 'the wood's in trouble'.

The launch of Enterprise Neptune meant that a similar strategy could be increasingly applied to coastal acquisitions. The protection of the Gower Peninsula in south Wales preoccupied Hugh Griffith for over thirty years. He was resourceful both with those prepared to sell coastal property to the Trust and with its committees. Just once, when they were baulking at a proposed acquisition, he had to confess with his irresistible Welsh smile, 'Oh dear, you see I've bought it already'. It was entirely in character that Enterprise Neptune, the campaign that had caused Antrim such personal anguish, should have been pursued with such total commitment. During his years as Chairman, from 1965 to 1977, the Trust's coastal properties were extended from 187 to 386 miles, often with large areas of hinterland to give protection back as far as the eye could see. Whenever Trinick appeared before the Committee with a proposal to add another piece to one of his Cornish coastal jigsaws, Antrim would say with relish, 'Ah, I see King Neptune is here, let's hear what he has got to say'. Trinick would then be solemnly accused of producing the same evocative photographs of Atlantic rollers breaking on Cornish granite that he had shown at previous meetings.

During the 1960s the agent for Dorset and the Isle of Wight, John Gaze, assembled an estate of unrivalled richness and variety around Golden Cap, the highest cliff in the south of England. The undulating meadows leading to the cliffs have been relatively unchanged and unimproved for centuries, and are exceptionally rich botanically. Sometimes there were substantial additions, such as 405 acres of Chardown Hill and Upcot Farm in 1966 or the 252 acres that came with Filcombe and Norchard Farms in 1972. Occasionally there were the messy little patches, which if unprotected might detract from the adjoining property and were an important element in the broader strategy. Convincing the committees of the value of unprepossessing smaller properties sometimes taxed even John Gaze's powers of persuasion. 'You mean it is a white-wash job', challenged Lord Antrim. 'Yes, white-washing you, Chairman' countered Gaze; and the acquisition was approved. The summit of Golden Cap was not finally purchased until 1978, when the 26 acres were bought as a memorial to Lord Antrim. He had aroused greater antagonism, and more warmth of affection, than any Chairman in the Trust's history.

Because property was being acquired at such a pace, the Finance Committee and its Chairman, Mark Norman, became increasingly concerned about the Trust's long-term liabilities. During the 1970s it had become all too clear that

with inflation running at over 10 per cent and with wages rising far faster than investment income and rents, the basis of assessing endowments needed to be radically revised. In 1976 Roger Chorley, a member of the Finance Committee, was asked to re-examine the method of calculating what the future costs of maintaining and running new acquisitions would be, so that over a fifty-year period they could be expected to be financially self-supporting. To deal with these concerns, he proposed that allowance should be made for falling rental income, higher standards of conservation and, most important of all, the likely future costs of wages. A contingency figure of 12 per cent was also included in the final calculations. Once adopted, this became known as the Chorley formula. It has been applied to open space properties such as the Upper Wharfedale estate, but has been of particular significance when the Trust has had to decide whether or not to take on major country houses.

Without the ability to assess in a systematic, consistent way the financial implications of new acquisitions, there would not have been the confidence to take on the houses that in the 1970s and 1980s came in disturbing numbers, and which might well have bankrupted the Trust. With country houses – in contrast to its policy for the protection of the coast – the Trust does not seek to be acquisitive. It has never wanted to do more than act as a safety net for houses at risk. In several cases, the buildings acquired have been on the verge of destruction, with their contents about to be dispersed.

Clandon Park in Surrey was a much depleted house when it came to the Trust in 1956. The opportunity to bring interest and colour back to its bleak eighteenth-century state rooms occurred in 1969, when the Trust received a substantial legacy from Mrs Hannah Gubbay and with it the eighteenth-century lacquer furniture, needlework and porcelain which she had collected throughout her life. The successful integration of these often small and delicate objects into Clandon's great rooms of state posed decorative problems which, at the time, the Trust was not equipped to resolve. With Fedden's support, Gore turned to John Fowler, for many years a close friend of both Lord Rosse, the Chairman of the Properties Committee, and Lees-Milne.

The inevitable cycle of taste means that John Fowler's work as a decorator is now frequently disparaged. His detractors accuse him, among other things, of being unscientific. They rarely understand, as he did, that a room can be a many-

John Fowler, photographed at his bedroom
window at the Hunting Lodge, Odiham.

layered work of art; nor would they accept Kenneth Clark's assertion that 'a work of art can survive anything, except perhaps scientific restoration'. Certainly after his involvement at Clandon, Fowler tended to be over-used by the Trust, sometimes at houses where his particular talents were not needed, and where he was not given clear enough guidance on what was historically appropriate. What is not always understood by his critics is that Fowler's approach to decoration involved gathering together every fragment of evidence that might contribute to a better understanding of the house: scraps of eighteenth-century wallpaper would be taken to the Victoria and Albert Museum to be dated; attics would be searched for discarded curtain material or lengths of fringe, which Fowler would then establish were part of a decorative scheme of a particular date; filthy pieces of Brussels carpet would be carried off so that their designs could be copied. Although not scientific by today's standards, Fowler's use of 'scrapes' enabled him, by removing successive layers of paint, to establish how the decoration of a room had changed during its history. At Clandon Fowler's work was as much to do with the archaeology of decoration as it was with subtle variations of colour and tone.

Another house which helped to change perceptions and move the Trust's work in new directions was Erddig, an eighteenth-century house on the outskirts of Wrexham, Clwyd. Those who visited Erddig in the 1960s were left in no doubt of its perilous condition. Undermined by the Coal Board, with water cascading through the roof into the state rooms and the garden an impenetrable jungle, the house had every appearance of being in the final stages of collapse. When Norman visited the house to see for himself what the Finance Committee was being asked to consider, he was prepared to be convinced of the value of saving the house, but was appalled at the idea of spending money on the roofless and derelict outbuildings. 'You're not serious about wanting to repair these?' he brutally asked the Agent, Gordon Hall. Having heard a carefully reasoned case for why they represented an essential element in the social history of the house, Norman then sat down with Hall to help him rewrite his report and so make it more acceptable to the Finance Committee.

When Erddig was opened to the public in 1977, it was the outbuildings, restored to working order, which aroused as much interest as the house. The Trust had been guided by Elisabeth Beazley, an architect, planner and a member of its committees, who had made a particular study of how historic sites and countryside properties could be made comprehensible and enjoyable for visitors. The emphasis on the social history of Erddig also owed much to what Trinick

The nineteenth-century kitchen at Cragside, Northumberland, with its
hydraulic spit and 'dumb waiter' lift connected to the basement scullery below.

had been doing at Cornish houses such as Lanhydrock and at Cotehele, where not
only the domestic quarters, but the mill, quay and workshops were painstakingly
repaired. In Northumberland the honorary Representative, Sheila Pettit, was
about to embark on a still more ambitious project, the restoration of Cragside,
where as much trouble would be taken over preserving the fascinating technology
of the house as would be lavished on the conservation of its wallpapers.

Another significant move, helped forward by acquisitions such as Erddig, was
towards a more rigorous approach to conservation. Fowler's ability to identify
early textiles and wallpapers was influential – he was the first to appreciate that

there were at Erddig extremely rare early eighteenth-century textiles such as moreen and caffoy needing particularly restrained and skilled repair – and so too were the studies of original documents carried out by John Cornforth and the Trust's Architectural Adviser, Gervase Jackson-Stops.

Clearly these curatorial responsibilities called for more than an enlightened private owner would have contemplated in similar circumstances. Wholesale renewal and replacement was no longer an option for the Trust. Solutions were found by two advisers, Sheila Stainton and Hermione Sandwith. A textile conservation workshop was set up at Erddig, where Stainton and a team of over a hundred volunteers repaired, strengthened and lined the curtains and chair covers that were among the most important elements in the decoration of Erddig's largely panelled rooms. When Dunham Massey, on the outskirts of Manchester, was given to the Trust in 1976, its historic textiles posed similar problems. Again, Stainton established a conservation workshop, enlisting some of the volunteers who had helped her at Erddig. In 1977 Stainton became the Trust's first Housekeeper and with Hermione Sandwith was author of *The National Trust Manual of Housekeeping* (1984), an influential work both inside and outside the Trust.

Throughout the 1970s and 1980s the Trust found itself being offered one great house after another. There were ritual protestations that the financial burden would ultimately prove too much, that the balance of the Trust's work would be upset and that too rapid growth would put intolerable administrative strains on the organisation. In spite of these reservations, the Trust found itself repeatedly used as a safety net. One explanation for this is that during the years that Frederick Bishop was Director-General, from 1971 to 1975, the Trust rapidly grew in competence and confidence. Another is the decisive shift in public and government attitudes towards the country house and its place in Britain's cultural history.

Two events coincided to turn public opinion. One was the exhibition in 1974 on *The Destruction of the Country House*, at the Victoria and Albert Museum. Leading authorities on aspects of the country house lent their support. Sir Oliver Millar wrote about the breaking up of picture collections; A.N.L. Munby about lost libraries; Miles Hadfield on the destruction of gardens; Peter Thornton on the dispersal of contents; and James Lees-Milne put their contributions into a broad historical context. The whole exhibition and the book that was published with it were imbued with the passionate commitment and powers of com-munication that Marcus Binney and John Harris brought to their writing about country houses. The exhibition provided not just 'a melancholy record of the frailty of bricks and mortar and the vanity of ostentation', as a leader in *The Times* described the catalogue of neglect and loss; it also offered prescriptions. There were accounts of the role of the preservation societies, of the Historic Buildings Councils and an essay by Robin Fedden on the contribution of the National Trust. The case for preservation was reinforced by a simultaneous, independent report by John Cornforth, *Country Houses in Britain: Can they survive?* The report was commissioned by the British Tourist Authority and published by Country Life, throughout its history concerned with the preservation of great houses and a magazine sympathetic to the Trust's work. None of these writers proposed that the Trust should do more than continue to act as a refuge of last resort. What was made abundantly clear was that, had the Trust not been prepared to play its part, there would have been a still more shameful inventory of loss.

Three years later the fiasco of Mentmore, in Buckinghamshire, rammed the message home. The idiotic and negligent behaviour of the Treasury and the government that allowed the disposal of this exceptionally important country house collection did more to change attitudes than any amount of discreet lobbying and reasoned argument. Not everyone enthused about the architecture of Mentmore, although it was designed by Joseph Paxton, who had been responsible for an undisputed Victorian masterpiece, the Crystal Palace. But there was no doubt about the quite exceptional quality of the contents, particularly the pictures, which were offered to the nation at what turned out to be a knock-down price. The Treasury had learnt nothing from the strictures of Lord Crawford about the way they and the national museums had behaved over the acceptance of the contents of Petworth in lieu of tax twenty years before. Day after day Hansard and the press were full of detailed reports on how the Treasury and the government had been both incompetent and dishonest about the use of the National Land Fund. Because the National Gallery finished up buying pictures from Mentmore, the country was seen to have paid a high price for the vacillation and mean-mindedness of ministers. The Trust was not even given the opportunity to mount a rescue campaign.

Some good came from the sad and unnecessary sale at Mentmore. There was an overwhelming public and parliamentary call for a re-examination of the use of the National Land Fund and for its removal from the suffocating grip of the

(*Overleaf*) The Library at Dunham Massey, Cheshire, with
the carving of 'The Crucifixion', attributed to
Grinling Gibbons, over the fireplace.

Treasury. A particularly clear explanation of how a new heritage fund could assist the work of the Trust was submitted to the government by Jack Boles, who had succeeded Sir Frederick Bishop as Director-General in 1975. The result, of immense significance to the Trust, was the setting up of the National Heritage Memorial Fund in 1980. From the start the Fund responded with speed,

Lord Gibson, Chairman of the
National Trust from 1977 to 1986.

imagination and unerring judgement to requests for help. That it has been so generous to the Trust was a reflection of the position that the Trust now occupied in national life; and that in turn is a measure of what was achieved during the years 1977 to 1986, when Lord Gibson was Chairman.

Those who only saw Gibson conducting an Annual General Meeting or chairing committees might have concluded that his courtesy and infinite patience were integral to his personality. He seemed actually to enjoy accommodating the tiresome or wrong-headed in any discussion and would explain privately that he valued such contributions as the committee equivalent of a nicely placed dissonance in a Mozart string quartet. But appearances were misleading.

Although a small man, he was physically and mentally extremely tough, as he had shown as a young prisoner of war, escaping into the Abruzzi mountains.

In the early years of Antrim's chairmanship Gibson had been spoken of as an obvious successor. When he was appointed Chairman of the Arts Council in 1972 it seemed that the chance had gone. During his time at the Arts Council Gibson was always ready to listen to those whose tastes were not identical to his own, including those of the Prime Minister. Harold Wilson had particularly strong views on the staging of *The Mikado*. That did not cause serious problems; but when one of his ministers tried to make appointments to the Arts Council without consulting its Chairman, it was rapidly made clear that that was not acceptable. If there was a steely side to Gibson, there was also an exceptionally generous and considerate one. His wife Dione usually went with him on visits to properties and had an ability to communicate quickly and informally with staff. Their close friendship with John Smith ensured that his highly idiosyncratic knowledge and interests were at hand to protect the Trust from sameness.

As it turned out, Gibson was able to return to a major role in the affairs of the Trust because Antrim did not stand down as Chairman when might have been expected: he was determined to battle on against ill-health and the effects of major transplant surgery. This allowed Gibson to complete a five-year term at the Arts Council and then take up the reins of the Trust. He returned in 1977 with valuable experience of dealing with the civil service and government ministers.

There were still periodic grumbles while Gibson was Chairman that the Trust ought never to have become so involved with country houses. Those complaints could be countered by reminding critics of the Trust's statutory duty, from its inception, to preserve historic buildings. The arguments were complex, however. The spectacularly successful drive to enlist more members depended to a large extent on recruitment at the Trust's country houses. Another important initiative, the Young National Trust Theatre, was again largely country-house based. So too were most of the increasingly profitable National Trust shops. The outbuildings of several houses provided simple accommodation for Acorn Camps, which by 1993 were involving over 3,922 young people in practical conservation work. All these activities brought undoubted benefits to the Trust. Many of them helped to pay for the Trust's work in the countryside.

Gibson had no qualms about the Trust's increasing preoccupation with houses. He supported Gore's efforts to bring greater professionalism to the conservation of their contents and took a special interest in the replanting of

historic gardens under the supervision of John Sales and Jim Marshall, the Trust's Gardens Advisers. If the Trust's Chairman could be accused of having a bias towards the work of the Trust's aesthetes, the Director-General, Boles, was much more the countryman, who wanted one day to be allowed to slip into the role of a Devon yeoman farmer. They complemented each other.

The buildings which came to the Trust with the support of the National Heritage Memorial Fund included some of the best, and least known names in English architecture: Fountains Abbey and the early eighteenth-century gardens at Studley Royal in Yorkshire in 1983; Belton House, Lincolnshire, in 1984; Calke Abbey, Derbyshire, in 1985; Robert Adam's masterpiece, Kedleston Hall, also in Derbyshire, in 1987; the park monuments at Stowe Landscape Gardens in Buckinghamshire in 1990; and Chastleton, a wonderfully romantic Jacobean house in Oxfordshire, in 1991. The successful conclusion of negotiations often depended on the promise of repair grants from the Historic Buildings Council; and under the chairmanship of Jennifer Jenkins the response was prompt and almost always generous. Dame Jennifer had already played a crucial part in the repair of Cragside and of the stable block at Wimpole Hall, as well as in the transfer of Fountains and Calke Abbey, before she joined the Trust's committees.

In Northern Ireland the National Heritage Memorial Fund's role was no less crucial. Grants made possible the renewal in Portland stone of the façade of James Wyatt's sumptuous Castle Coole, near Enniskillen, Co. Fermanagh. In 1987 the Crom estate of 1,633 acres, also in Co. Fermanagh, with its lakes, wooded islands and historic parkland, was bought and endowed with grants provided by the Fund and the Department of the Environment, Northern Ireland. Another important acquisition, completed in 1979, was The Argory in Co. Armagh, a house which has remained virtually unchanged since its completion in 1820, and where gas light was still in use in 1983. The property was the gift of W.A.N. MacGeough Bond and an endowment was provided by the Northern Ireland Department of Finance. Of all the repairs to historic houses completed by the Trust during the 1980s, the restoration of The Argory, under the direction of the Historic Buildings Representative, Peter Marlow, was probably the best researched, least obtrusive and ultimately most restrained. It provides a wholly convincing answer to those who assert that the Trust cannot resist

The staircase hall at The Argory
in County Armagh, Northern Ireland.

imposing its own taste on historic houses. The secret of its success lay in Marlow's decision to spend months living in the house, often in conditions of considerable discomfort, and in his willingness to be guided by the donor.

For a period of around twelve years, from 1980 to 1992, an extraordinarily effective alliance was formed between the National Heritage Memorial Fund, the Historic Buildings Council (later renamed the Historic Buildings and Monuments Commission), and the National Trust. When smaller buildings were at risk, as at Stowe Landscape Gardens, the Landmark Trust joined the alliance. So too did the Countryside Commission if important landscapes were involved. As a way of saving precious buildings and countryside it was a complicated set of relationships, but a remarkably fruitful one. The failure in 1992 to preserve Pitchford Hall in Shropshire as an entity showed that for the partnership to work, government ministers had to resist the temptation to interfere. All might have been well had the Secretary of State for National Heritage, David Mellor, not prevented English Heritage and the National Heritage Memorial Fund from implementing their plans to secure the future of Pitchford.

One of the most hopeless cases ever contemplated by the Trust was Canons Ashby in Northamptonshire. In a county rich in old houses, Canons Ashby had lapsed into obscurity and dereliction. The Dryden family who had owned it since the sixteenth century could claim kinship with a Poet Laureate, but were otherwise surprising only for their recurring antiquarian interests. With the motto 'Ancient as the Druids', they did not need to improve themselves socially or their house architecturally. When Gervase Jackson-Stops first visited Canons Ashby as a schoolboy on a bicycle, the Drydens were living in Rhodesia and it was occupied by tenants, two faith healers, Dr Christopher Woodward and his brother Peter. Whether levitations pose a threat to the structure of an ancient and decaying building can never be scientifically proved. The next tenant disappeared in a hurry to Ireland, leaving behind angry creditors and a house riddled with dry rot so fecund as to be almost asphyxiating. The Drydens were advised it was time to sell off the furniture, tarmac the courtyard and turn the house into an antiques market.

The sale of the furniture, to take place in July 1980, was announced in the local press. John Dryden, one of the three brothers who owned the house, let it be known that he was coming over for the sale. This galvanised Jackson-Stops. On 20 June he arranged a visit to the house by John Smith, as there was a possibility that the Landmark Trust might be willing to help with repairs to the tower on the west side of the courtyard. The Trust's Adviser on Furniture,

Martin Drury, and a member of the Arts Panel, Christopher Gibbs, also came to assess the contents. Provided they were convinced of their importance, Simon Sainsbury, a frequent benefactor, was prepared to purchase them. If the Trust's efforts to acquire the house failed, Gibbs would sell them on. The whole scheme had an air of wild improbability about it.

In late June John Dryden flew in from Zimbabwe and was due to stay nearby. When invited to lunch at The Menagerie, Jackson-Stops's Baroque folly also in Northamptonshire, John Dryden was told why this was probably the last chance to save the house as an historic entity, while retaining the link with the family. He responded by saying that the family would rather see the house burnt down than leave Dryden hands. After lunch Jackson-Stops took the risk and spoke frankly: 'There is a completely new institution, only founded a few months ago, called the National Heritage Memorial Fund. Goodness knows whether they will be interested, but it's worth a try.'

The sale of the contents duly took place the following week. It was agreed that Drury, Gibbs and Jackson-Stops would sit well apart and each would bid for separate items. All went to plan and between them they secured all the really important lots. There was one awful moment when Jackson-Stops and Drury realised that they were bidding against each other for a very plain set of library steps, which consequently was perhaps a little more expensive than it need have been. By a strange chance, within a few days of the sale, a set of early eighteenth-century seat furniture covered in continental needlework – sold years before but identifiable in early photographs of Canons Ashby – turned up in a saleroom in Bath. Before Drury could run it to earth the suite had been bought by a London dealer; but by this time Simon Sainsbury's enthusiasm for the quest was fired and it too was secured.

Canons Ashby immediately caught the imagination of the National Heritage Memorial Fund Trustees. Lord Charteris, the Chairman, and Lady Airey made a late summer visit and appreciated what an extraordinary survival the house was. On 14 August another of the Trustees, Lord Anglesey, received a begging letter, interspersed with sketches of gate-piers, mullion windows and newel posts, pleading with him to visit the house. He drove from Plas Newydd, collected Jackson-Stops from The Menagerie, spent several hours at Canons Ashby, then returned to Anglesey that night. Not long afterwards Gore put his head round the door of Jackson-Stops's office and remarked casually: 'You've got Canons Ashby, by the way. The Heritage Fund has given you a million pounds.' It was the first property to be endowed by the Fund.

(*Above*) The Green Court and west front of Canons Ashby
in Northamptonshire. (*Right*) The Tapestry Room at Canons Ashby.
The early eighteenth-century needlework chairs, settee and
firescreen were sold to pay death duties before the Second World War,
but were re-acquired for the house in 1984.

The Dryden family's gift of Canons Ashby to the Trust was announced on
a bitterly cold day in January 1981. Braziers had been lit in the courtyard and
had filled the Great Hall with acrid smoke. The Secretary of State for the
Environment, Michael Heseltine, was able to explain how several different bodies
had worked together to find a joint solution. The National Heritage Memorial
Fund would be contributing £1.5 million for an endowment and towards the
cost of repairs, which were also to be grant-aided by the Historic Buildings

Council. The Landmark Trust had agreed to repair the tower, at a cost of £100,000 and rent it to those who wanted to stay at Canons Ashby for a holiday. The Victoria and Albert Museum had contributed towards the cost of some of the contents, many were donated by Simon Sainsbury, while others were loaned back by the Drydens. A public appeal was expected to raise £100,000.

Reassembling Canons Ashby took several years. The family papers had been brought back from Zimbabwe, where termites had been devouring them, by Joan Wake, the Northamptonshire County Archivist. The Drydens returned a sundial which had originally stood in the middle of the early eighteenth-century garden: on the wrong side of the Equator it had proved a misleading time-keeper. Most of the contents are original to the house, with a notable exception. The cast-iron fireback in the Dining Room is a replica, modelled and cast by

Lord Charteris and incorporating the symbols of the National Trust and the National Heritage Memorial Fund. The Dryden family continue to stay at Canons Ashby from time to time and have more contact with the house now than at any time since their move to Rhodesia in the 1920s.

The art of patchwork is still being practised. At Gibside, near Gateshead in Tyne & Wear, James Paine's exquisite eighteenth-century chapel was given to the Trust in 1974. Nearly twenty years later the Trust bought the park and the ruins of the house and orangery, accepting calculated financial risks not otherwise taken since the 1960s. Again, the NHMF is contributing. The Landmark Trust has restored the Banqueting House. Many of the key elements are now secure but the remaining pieces will not come together easily, nor is there the money to do more than persist with a holding operation, carrying out only such repairs as are absolutely necessary.

The protection of the countryside around Flatford in Suffolk has also been extended gradually and over a long period. In recent years parts of the landscape near Dedham have changed so totally that John Constable would have difficulty even recognising the subjects of some of his greatest paintings. A visit to Stratford Mill is now a dispiriting experience: the A12 dual carriageway thunders within a few yards of what Constable knew as an idyllic spot, where children fished, and horses on the journey from Ipswich to London could be watered. Not only has the peace been shattered, but so has the scale of this gentle landscape. Constable repeatedly used the view from the woods above Stratford Mill, looking towards the Stour estuary. He sketched there in 1802 and happily returned in the late 1820s to capture the transient effects of scudding clouds and racing shadows for his *Dedham Vale*, now owned by the National Galleries of Scotland. Today that view is blocked by the concrete bridges of the highway. Fortunately there is still much worth protecting.

Flatford Mill itself was bought in 1943, and leased two years later to the newly formed Field Studies Council. An educational use seemed appropriate for the Mill, particularly as the courses included painting classes by John Nash and botanical drawing taught by Mary Grierson. The partnership with the Council has proved a useful one and shortly afterwards similar arrangements were made at Malham Tarn in North Yorkshire and Juniper Hall in Surrey. Valley Farm, Flatford, was acquired by the Trust in 1959; then there was a long pause.

The purchase of Bridge Cottage heralded a new, more urgent phase in the preservation of Flatford. In the early 1980s a Bergholt farmer was given permission to create an irrigation pond on land immediately behind Willy Lott's

House. Throughout the summer of 1981 several gravel lorries a day shook the sixteenth- and seventeenth-century mill buildings and cut into the banks of Flatford Lane so that large sections collapsed. In the mid-1980s the Trust bought both Gibbonsgate Field, to ensure there was no more gravel extraction, and Bridge Cottage, which features in several Constable masterpieces. Unknown to the Trust, the dry dock painted by Constable in 1814 still survived, although silted up and grown over.

Constable's biographer C.R. Leslie records that *Boat Building* was the only picture, as opposed to sketch, 'which I have heard him say he painted completely outdoors'. The finished painting, now in the Victoria and Albert Museum, and the several pencil sketches which preceded it, provided the Trust's architect with all the detailed information needed for the reconstruction of the dry dock and its timber gates. An extraordinary survival was the pipe which allowed water to drain from the dock, under the river and out into a ditch on the far side of the opposite bank. This simple, effective device is again in use.

In 1991 the Trust was approached by the owner of water-meadows between Flatford and Dedham. It would be hard to exaggerate the importance of these fields in any scheme to protect the landscape painted by Constable: they are the scene of haymaking in the National Gallery's *The Hay-wain* of 1820, and they were repeatedly painted early in his career, for instance in *The Stour Valley and Dedham Village* (now in the Museum of Fine Arts, Boston). Constable used sketches taken from these water-meadows, looking north east, for *The Leaping Horse* of 1825 (in the Royal Academy); and he returned to them again in *The Cornfield* of 1826, now in the National Gallery.

The description 'Constable Country' is often applied loosely to a large area of Essex and Suffolk. The stretch of river which Constable insisted 'made me a painter' is barely five miles long – from Brantham Mill to Stratford Mill – with far and away the most significant section being the two miles between Flatford and Dedham. Much of this landscape remains very much as Constable knew it: a landscape of subtle beauties, but one which could easily be suburbanised by the introduction of pony paddocks and inappropriate tree planting. It is these threats, as well as the more obvious damage caused by new roads and commercial exploitation, that persuaded the Trust to buy the meadows with the help of a grant from the Countryside Commission and a bequest from the Dedham architect Marshall Sisson.

Writing to his friend John Fisher in 1824, Constable explained why, throughout his career, he kept returning to the same stretch of the Stour for subject

(*Above*) Constable's *Boat Building* of 1814, 'painted completely outdoors'. (*Right*) The dry-dock at Flatford in Suffolk, restored by the Trust in 1988, using John Constable's sketches as evidence of its original features.

matter. Because he knew every detail of this landscape, had studied in hundreds of sketches almost every tree, bank and rotten post, he was free to concentrate on the patterns of light and shade that gave him the subject matter for a new and revolutionary way of painting. 'Change of weather and effect will always afford variety', he wrote, and went on to describe the persistence needed in his own approach to making pictures: 'I imagine myself driving a nail; I have driven it some way, and by persevering I may drive it home.' His example is one which the Trust has tried to follow at Flatford.

CHAPTER TEN

BINDING TOGETHER

A T THE NATIONAL TRUST'S inaugural meeting in 1894 the Duke of Westminster told Octavia Hill that he expected it to be 'a very big thing'. Neither of them can have imagined for a moment that the Trust would become the most widely respected conservation organisation in Europe. A hundred years later the Trust owned over 590,000 acres of land and 547 miles of coastline. It opened 162 gardens to the public, protected 24 National Nature Reserves and 396 Sites of Special Scientific Interest in England, a further 70 SSSIs in Wales and 5 Areas of Special Scientific Interest in Northern Ireland. Over 200 historic houses were open to the public. Its membership far exceeded that of any political party in the country. The growth of the Trust had been at an uneven pace, but since the early 1970s its responsibilities increased at a rate that in turn surprised, encouraged and alarmed even its most committed supporters.

The Trust was never intended to be an organisation of big battalions. It was founded on principles of flexibility, enthusiasm and the absence of formal rules. Writing in 1968, Robin Fedden believed that the Trust had somehow managed to retain these qualities in what was by then already a large corporate body: 'There can be few organisations of comparable size which remain, after a life of seventy years, so human, so little rigid, and with so many valuable illusions. The Trust's informality may sometimes exact a price in terms of strict efficiency, but it brings its own rewards.' In 1992 another major influence on the Trust, Len Clark, summed up what have seemed to many to be its greatest strengths: 'Of all the voluntary bodies concerned with conservation and enjoyment of the countryside and its heritage, the National Trust – now with 3,000 paid staff – is the most professional. Looking down the opposite end of the telescope, of all the professional bodies in the world of conservation it is the most amateur, in the best sense of the word.'

By continuing to depend so much on volunteers the Trust has managed to resist the image of a blundering bureaucracy. Immediately there is a paradox: organising many thousands of volunteers calls for considerable professionalism.

In the 1970s, liaison with the Trust's Centres and Associations – local groups formed and run by members to meet and share common interests – was the responsibility of Arthur Foss, who was already past the normal retirement age. As well as travelling around the country to attend evening meetings, Foss needed to spend a good deal of time at head office, because he also edited the Trust's magazine. He would travel up by train after 10 o'clock, on an off-peak ticket, and then leave before 4 o'clock to get the cheap fare back. What he achieved, both as editor and with the Centres, was remarkable, and far more than could reasonably be expected.

With such very limited resources for organising voluntary help there was an inevitable tendency always to turn to the same sources of support. Octavia Hill had appreciated this in the Trust's early years and was always concerned to look for contributions not just from a wealthy élite: 'I feel about gifts of time even more than about gifts of money, that they are such a good thing they ought to be a joy to the giver.' It was that principle that encouraged Foss's successor, Leslie McCracken, to approach the recruitment of volunteers from new directions. First of all he carried out surveys to discover more about the sort of people who were already assisting the Trust, why they wanted to help and what were the obstacles to greater involvement.

A startling fact emerged. More than half the volunteers who worked for the Trust were not members. No one in the organisation had imagined for a moment that there was a vast reservoir of support from people who were not interested in having the benefits of membership, but who wanted to be involved through giving their time. What this meant in practice was that when the Trust appealed for help, it tended to look to its own members, and in doing so ignored over half its potential volunteers. It was also frequently appealing to the wrong social groups.

One of the most influential reports in the history of the Trust, 'Gifts of Time', was produced by McCracken in 1985. He identified that, in a rapidly changing society, there were people who could bring to the Trust skills in management and information technology, as well as more traditional professional experience. They were people who might have retired early or who were not tied to a conventional job. But very often they could not give their time if it also meant making a financial sacrifice as well. What was needed was a fair and consistent way of meeting the travelling and other expenses of volunteers. They also needed to be given recognition, to be treated as far as possible as the professionals they were in terms of skills, if not remuneration.

The benefits of the approach advocated in 'Gifts of Time' were not slow in coming. In 1992 it was calculated that 26,465 volunteers had devoted 1.38 million hours of work for the Trust, the equivalent of 822 full-time employees. The contributions of volunteers ranged from the strenuous physical tasks undertaken by groups of young people, to the stewarding of rooms open to visitors. They included qualified architects, surveyors, accountants and health and safety supervisors working in the sixteen regional offices. In some Trust gardens major schemes of restoration were undertaken because there was now confidence that volunteers would remain fully integrated with paid staff and would be a reliable and permanent source of skilled labour.

A continuing dependence on voluntary support scarcely accords with the image of the Trust suggested by its critics, of an organisation stultified and paralysed by bureaucracy. At times, that criticism has been levelled at the Trust when it has appeared to respond to issues in a way which the more politically minded could have warned would provoke hostility. The National Trust has occasionally walked, apparently blindfold, into furious controversy.

This naivety was particularly evident in the way the Trust dealt with an application by the Ministry of Defence to use part of the Bradenham estate, near High Wycombe in Buckinghamshire, for a command centre for the adjoining headquarters of RAF Strike Command. As had happened at Saltram over the bypass proposals, the Trust was initially asked to release a relatively small area of land for what was made to appear a modest proposal. Once the principle that inalienable land might be used had been established, the government department concerned progressively increased its demands. In 1979 the regional committee responsible for Bradenham took the view that the site was inconspicuous and that if the Ministry of Defence was determined to build an underground bunker, build they would. By granting a lease, the Trust would secure a legal right to be consulted over landscaping and could insist that the road to take heavy duty traffic away from the nearby village would revert to a cart track once construction work was finished. Such an approach apparently offered the best hope of limiting damage to Trust property and seemed preferable to engaging in token resistance which might ultimately lead to conflict with the government and a weakening of the principle of inalienability. It was the Director-General, Jack Boles, who first sensed that this response might appear to ordinary members to be sacrificing the Trust's principles for political expediency and who insisted that the matter was considered not just at a regional level but also by the Properties and Executive Committees. They endorsed the policy advocated by the region, and in doing so totally misjudged the sense of outrage that would be felt not just locally but nationally.

The Press was presented with perfect copy: the membership of the Trust divided over an issue involving national defence. The resulting furore should not have surprised the committees; nor should the relative ease with which peace movement activists gained the support needed for the second Extraordinary General Meeting in the Trust's history. To save expense this was held on the morning of the Annual General Meeting, in November 1982. Far and away the most impressive speech was made by Sir Richard Acland, for thirty years an outspoken opponent of nuclear weapons. But both the motions critical of the Council were decisively defeated.

The reasons for the Council's decision at Bradenham were complex and far more easily misrepresented than explained. The Council might well have been unable to convince sufficient supporters if the Centres and Associations of the Trust had not provided a channel of communication to ordinary members. By 1981 there were 131 groups of these members and, although their support has never been uncritical, in the last resort they were reluctant to see the Trust deflected from its central and urgent task of conservation. Moreover, many of their members had come to recognise in Lord Gibson an outstanding and fair-minded Chairman, with no interest in ingratiating either himself or the Trust with the government. Ultimately they backed the Council, because they were satisfied that it had been guided by what were perceived to be the best interests of the Trust's properties.

The issue of hunting on land owned by the Trust has proved even more divisive. Again, Sir Richard Acland was much involved, on this question supporting the Council's policy as it applied on the Holnicote estate, although he did not himself hunt. The Council has consistently refused to allow political expediency to dictate the management of its properties.

As early as the 1930s the Council of the Trust found itself having to decide how to respond to members opposed to blood sports. A motion put forward in 1934 required the Executive Committee to ban hunting on Trust property on moral grounds. Those speaking against the motion put forward two fundamental reasons why the recommendation was unacceptable. In the first instance the Council believed that the work of the Trust would be weakened if it alienated the local communities on which it depended for labour, co-operation and goodwill. This particularly applied in the Lake District where, as Professor Chorley pointed out, hunting on foot is one of the favourite sports of the fell farmers and a ban would be impossible to enforce. He told the Executive Committee that the Trust 'would have to bring in the local battalion of the Territorials' to impose the ban. The second and more fundamental objection to such a ban was that it would involve the Trust in becoming a moral arbiter on issues which went well beyond the statutory purposes set out in its Acts of Parliament. The Trust had not been founded to improve the whole moral welfare of the nation. Its purpose was to protect places of natural beauty and historic interest, for public benefit. This very clear sense of the Trust's purposes was easier to communicate in the 1930s, when membership stood at less than 7,000. At that time the motion to ban field sports was defeated by a large majority. In the 1990s, with membership at more than two million, the precise nature of the Trust's obligations could be more widely misunderstood. Motions on hunting have been put to the Annual General Meetings in 1988 and 1990, with the League Against Cruel Sports more and more actively involved in efforts to influence the voting of members.

One weakness in the Trust's position was that it was inadequately informed about both the frequency of hunting on its property and about the conduct of the various hunts involved. By instituting, in 1990, a system of licensing of hunts, the Trust ensured that the necessary information was to hand. It could also withdraw licences if, as happened in 1993 with the Quorn in Leicestershire, a hunt was found not to be following agreed codes of practice. Still more serious was the lack of accurate information about the management of deer in the West Country, and how hunting with stag hounds might or might not be contributing to a healthy, viable deer population on Exmoor. In 1993 a working party under the chairmanship of Professor Savage produced a report which revealed the full extent of previous ignorance. For the first time reasonably accurate figures were collated for the size of deer herds on Exmoor, with estimates of the numbers killed through road accidents and poaching. The main conclusion to be drawn from the report was that it would be irresponsible for a ban to be considered until a properly researched and co-ordinated policy for deer management had been agreed.

The Annual General Meeting of November 1993 may come to be regarded as one of the most significant in the history of the Trust. There was to have been a members' resolution proposing that the Council should set up another working party to examine the issue of the cruelty involved in deer hunting, which had deliberately not been addressed in Professor Savage's report. Consideration of this resolution was postponed because the League Against Cruel Sports successfully took out an injunction against the Trust, on the grounds that the wording of the Council's recommendations in the papers sent to members was unclear. This did not prevent consideration of another resolution, put forward by a member, Peter Afia, and two former Trust Chairmen, Lord Gibson and Dame Jennifer Jenkins, supported by a former editor of *The Times*, Simon Jenkins, and the mountaineer Chris Bonington. Their resolution was a reaffirmation of the principle that the Trust should adhere to its own statutory purposes, while leaving ethical or moral considerations to be determined by Parliament. 'I have never hunted, and I have not been on a horse for forty years', was how another member, Ben Glazebrook, introduced the resolution, and in a speech that was cogent, restrained and courteous he argued that:

> the issue is whether the Trust, entirely against its constitution, should be put in
> the invidious position of having to take sides on a matter which so deeply stirs
> the feelings of many people in the country. If it were forced to do so, by a
> powerful pressure group believing passionately, let it be said, in their cause, one
> does not have to have much imagination to see what seeds of bitterness and
> animosity would be sown in many parts of the country.

Speaker after speaker warned of the dangers of the Trust being used as a convenient source of publicity for all those wanting to pursue their own moral crusades, from anti-hunting to vegetarianism, from objections to factory farming to nuclear disarmament.

At the annual meeting the previous year there had been a motion put forward by those who wanted the Trust to take a stand against nudity and what is absurdly called naturism. On Studland beach in Dorset, for instance, the Trust has set aside an area for nudists to avoid embarrassment. For some, this is not sufficient; they would like a total ban on nude sunbathing. Having gained publicity at considerable expense to the Trust, the proposers of the motion failed to attend the meeting to speak in its support.

The majority of Trust members were fed up with seeing their organisation being used to promote causes which seemed to have very little to do with the Trust's real objectives. The resolution that the Trust should devote its resources to its primary, statutory purposes and that moral issues should be left to Parliament received overwhelming support, with 100,723 members voting in favour of it, and 29,722 against.

One feature that many of these single-issue campaigners seemed to have in common was a failure to see that it is the Trust's ability to take a broad view of conservation, to integrate a wide variety of management skills, that has been its greatest strength. They demand that the Trust should concentrate its resources on the area of its work that they happen to think is most valuable. Sometimes this amounts to a plea that the Trust should forget its commitment to places of historic interest and think of itself as only the 'National Trust for Natural Beauty'. A separation of what have always been twin obligations, to buildings and to landscape, would be a betrayal of the Trust's founders and would deny some of the Trust's greatest achievements. The case for integrating different strands of management has strengthened throughout the life of the Trust. So too has its awareness that appreciation of natural beauty and an understanding of history usually go hand in hand.

The periodic calls for the Trust to turn its back on country houses often reveal a surprising ignorance about the history of nature conservation. What is generally regarded as the first Nature Reserve in England was established by Charles Waterton, the grandson of Sir Henry Bedingfeld, whose descendants still live at Oxburgh Hall, a Trust property in Norfolk. Between 1821 and 1826 Waterton enclosed the park of his Yorkshire estate with a nine foot wall, allowed no gun to be fired within it, and proceeded to study the extraordinary variety of waterfowl that gathered there. Eccentric he may have been, but he was no recluse, and his journeys to the jungles of Brazil and the forests of Demerara were among the most enterprising scientific expeditions of the nineteenth century. From May to September his park was specially opened for the benefit of local schools and associations.

Although the word 'holistic' is now so fashionable, the ideas which lie behind it are nothing new. The word derives from the Greek *holos*, meaning 'whole', so that the noun 'holism' refers to the tendency in nature to form wholes that are more than the sum of their parts. All this may sound academic and unimportant, until someone incapable of seeing the value of that whole proposes breaking things down to the bits they think are significant, jettisoning the rest. Waterton might not have heard of holistic or integrated management, but that is certainly what he practised. The same is true of the Harpur-Crewe family at Calke Abbey in Derbyshire.

In 1984 when the Trust was trying to decide whether or not to take on the immense and costly task of rescuing Calke Abbey, it had to acknowledge that the house, built at the beginning of the eighteenth century, was architecturally

Gnarled and stag-headed trees,
relics of ancient woodland, in the
park at Calke Abbey in Derbyshire.

undistinguished. What made Calke of outstanding national importance was its value as a document of social and natural history; and it was these qualities that led the Trust's President, H.M. Queen Elizabeth, The Queen Mother, to take a close personal interest in its rescue. To the north and west of the house lies a park with an unbroken history of open woodland reaching back to the ancient forests of Britain and Europe. There are around a thousand mature English oaks, some over 400 years old: decaying, stag-headed and providing an ideal habitat for deadwood beetles. It is only sites of this antiquity which can sustain such a range of invertebrates, and over 250 beetle species have been recorded at Calke. This essential task of assessing the nature conservation value of the park was carried out by the Trust's Biological Survey team shortly after the transfer of the property, and provides the information needed on just one aspect of the care of Calke, to be integrated with a number of other specialist reports into the estate management plan. What emerged at Calke was that, while most of the contents of the house may be second rate, many of the butterflies and beetles in the park are of great rarity.

Sir Vauncey Harpur Crewe, whose grandson Henry ensured Calke's transfer to the Trust, was far more concerned about the protection of its wildlife than he was about repairs to the roof. Motor vehicles were banned from the park and visitors were instead picked up at the gates in a horse-drawn carriage. Even the local postboy was instructed to look straight ahead on his way to the Abbey, lest he be tempted to disturb any living creature. The Trust's management of the park can be a little less severe, but cars have to be restricted to areas where they will not damage botanically rich grassland, and grazing by deer has to be carefully monitored and if necessary controlled.

With estates of this diversity, it is vital that the Trust should not allow itself to be influenced by prejudice against country houses, which sometimes seems to derive from personal preoccupations to do with class. Social exclusiveness can cut both ways. Whatever may be felt about the architecture and picture collection at Kingston Lacy in Dorset, Ralph Bankes's gift of the estate in 1982 brought to the Trust the 1,216 acre National Nature Reserve of Holt Heath, and one of its most important archaeological sites, the Iron Age fort and Bronze Age burial mounds at Badbury Rings. Just as at Calke Abbey a biological survey was essential, so at Kingston Lacy the Trust's archaeologists spent several years recording, appraising and surveying, before management prescriptions could be agreed. As it happens, the house at Kingston Lacy acts as a display cabinet for the archaeological collections amassed in the 1830s by W.J. Bankes, whose interest in ancient Egypt is reflected in an obelisk from the Island of Philae that has pride of place in the garden. The house and estate were acquired because they are a composite work of art of supreme value, not just because of one particular area of interest, such as the Venetian pictures; although it would be a dull soul who was unmoved by the paintings by Titian and Sebastiano del Piombo.

The variety of responsibilities undertaken by the Trust's archaeological staff on an estate such as Kingston Lacy may surprise those who think that the subject is largely concerned with digging holes in the ground. A site as heavily visited as Badbury Rings clearly needs protection from the compaction and erosion that can rapidly wear away sections of its earthworks. The preservation of the Roman fort at Crab Farm, to the south west of Badbury, will be dependent on negotiation between the Trust's land agent, guided by the Archaeological Adviser, and the farm tenant. That there was a medieval manor at Kingston Lacy became clear when in 1990 gales uprooted numerous trees in the park. Stone, tile and mortar fragments were revealed to the north of the present house, and this material needs to be properly recorded. Groups of volunteers have sifted through medieval deposits at nearby Corfe Castle, under the supervision of professional, trained staff. The same archaeologists may then turn their attention to the industrial remains on the estate. They might one moment be expected to compile evidence to date a feature in the garden, and the next be advising on how to slow down the decay of a Second World War pillbox.

Where a garden or landscape park is of sufficient beauty or importance, the Trust has sometimes intervened even when there was no chance of acquiring the related house. At Biddulph Grange in Staffordshire, the house was not outstanding and there was little prospect of the local health authority relinquishing its use. The garden, however, was exceptional: a mid-nineteenth-century evocation in plants, hedges and rock of different parts of the world, including Egypt and China. With the help of the National Heritage Memorial Fund and with money donated through the National Gardens Scheme, Biddulph was acquired in 1988. There followed a period of careful restoration, drawing on the Trust's growing experience of the repair of historic gardens.

Several outstanding parks have been acquired by the Trust on account of their landscape importance, and without the intention of regularly opening the principal house to the public. Sheringham in Norfolk was purchased in 1987, again with NHMF help, because the park, with its undulating oak woodlands and dramatic views of the sea, was with good reason described by Humphry Repton as his 'most favourite work'. In 1990 care of the great landscape gardens

A view of Sheringham Park
in Norfolk, from Humphry
Repton's Red Book, 1812.

at Stowe was transferred to the National Trust, while the school retained the mansion. This has made possible the restoration of the park and its unrivalled collection of follies, monuments, bridges and temples. The Dinefwr Park estate in Dyfed will take many years to reassemble, but the Trust now owns 480 acres of wild and romantic parkland, associated for centuries with the medieval Princes of Wales.

At Dinefwr the return of its ancient breed of Dinefwr White Park cattle is as significant historically as the repair of buildings or the replanting of trees. At several other properties the Trust is working with the Rare Breeds Survival Trust, notably at Wimpole Home Farm in Cambridgeshire. Sir John Soane's magnificent early nineteenth-century farm buildings house over thirty rare breeds, including at one time half of the world's breeding population of Bagot goats, a breed which would seem to have no commercial value whatsoever. With only sixty recorded females, the Bagot was endangered, but very far from extinct. Quite apart from the genetic importance of this aspect of conservation, properties

The Bagot Goat, painted by James Lynch, 1993. The
building in the background is the Gothic Tower at Wimpole,
Cambridgeshire, designed by Sanderson Miller, *c.*1749–51.

with rare breeds are popular with visitors, and there is considerable scope for
educational work.

Stackpole in Dyfed is another great estate that has given the Trust opportunities to diversify. Although Stackpole Court was architecturally rather dreary,
its position above a long sea inlet was unrivalled. In the late 1950s its owner, Earl
Cawdor, offered it for some institutional use. When this came to nothing, and
aware of the steady deterioration of the building, Lord Cawdor's agent, Hugh
Griffith, organised its demolition in 1962, with accustomed thoroughness.
Griffith found himself working first part-time, then full-time for the Trust, but
maintained friendly relations with the Cawdor family. In 1976 he persuaded the
trustees to offer 2,000 acres of the finest parts of the estate to the Treasury in lieu
of tax, so that it could then be transferred to the National Trust. The property
includes two beaches, a series of large freshwater lakes that are Sites of Special
Scientific Interest, and eight miles of cliffs.

Since acquiring Stackpole in 1976, the Trust has set about finding new uses

for the redundant farm buildings. The Stackpole for Schools Project uses part of the Home Farm, while other buildings provide workshops and a base for the Stackpole Trust for the Less Able. Over a thousand children a year, many from urban homes, stay at Stackpole. Special care is taken to ensure that the cost per child is kept at an affordable level. Under the supervision of three resident teachers the children are taught geography and science field studies, canoeing, abseiling and orienteering. None of this would have happened if Griffith had not carefully steered the estate in the Trust's direction. He had even ensured through the judicious use of high explosives that the Trust was not frightened off by the daunting prospect of taking on another semi-derelict country house.

The care of the Trust's smaller buildings calls for ingenuity in finding appropriate uses and increasing resourcefulness in maintaining traditional techniques. In the Lake District this has involved reopening lime kilns and reviving the skills needed to slake lime. The use of hard cement mortars and rendering can do irreparable damage to otherwise well-preserved vernacular buildings, and if the Trust is to insist on traditional lime mortar, it must ensure that the necessary materials are available. At Townend, in the village of Troutbeck in Cumbria, the Trust reintroduced the practice of splitting, rather than sawing, rafters and purlins to give its roofs the slight undulations that reveal the hand of man and not the lifelessness of the machine. The restoration of the Fen Cottage at Wicken in Cambridgeshire has similarly involved the revival of local building techniques such as using bundles of reed as laths and clay lump for bricks. These skills provide a vivid demonstration of what local materials were available and how they could be used. The Fen Cottage has much to teach the school parties who come to Wicken, not only about the harsh, unforgiving lives of fenworkers, but indirectly about the changing ecology of the Fen.

There is no significant distinction between the principles of conservation as they apply to these modest vernacular buildings, and the approach needed for the care of the grandest country houses. The Browne family's books, papers and

(*Left*) Cowman with young Dinefwr White Park cattle,
photographed as part of a survey of
the Dinefwr Park estate in 1921.

(*Overleaf*) The Fen Cottage at Wicken Fen in Cambridgeshire
has been restored using materials from the Fen.

furniture at Townend, so revealing of the interests and aspirations of yeoman farmers over three centuries, need very much the same preventive conservation as the contents of the library at Kingston Lacy. They must be protected from too much ultra-violet light and from dust. Above all they need to be kept in an environment with a reasonably constant relative humidity, neither too damp nor too dry. Very often it is the humbler object that is the rarer survival: far more eighteenth- and nineteenth-century ball-gowns have been preserved than farmworkers' smocks.

The range of the Trust's activities, as well as the sheer number of its properties, can reinforce the impression that its management structure has become unwieldy and would benefit from being broken down into smaller units. In 1990 an editorial in the *Independent* went so far as to suggest that the Trust needed a new Act of Parliament to divide it up into smaller bodies, permitting its properties to revert to private ownership. This prescription produced such a storm of protest that the editor rapidly dropped the issue. He would have done better to have advocated a renewed commitment to the regional structure of the Trust, which has served it so well during the last quarter century. Maintaining a creative tension between the central administration of the Trust and the regions has never been easy. If the ties are allowed to slacken too much, consistency, and the Trust's national role, could suffer. If the Trust were to revert, as in the 1960s, to a highly centralised form of administration, it would almost certainly make it harder to respond to the full range of opportunities continually presented to it and the vast diversity of its properties might be eroded. Mutual respect, understanding and the confidence to delegate responsibilities are needed to maintain an effective, devolved administration of the Trust.

The extent to which real responsibility was to be exercised by regional committees was an issue that exercised the Benson Committee. In fact it very nearly brought the future Chairman of the Trust, Lord Gibson, and the future Secretary of State for the Environment, Nicholas Ridley, to blows. Ridley had served on the Trust's Council and at one time had been thought of as a possible honorary Historic Buildings Representative. As an increasingly influential politician he veered between admiration for the Trust and exasperation at its increasing authority: he was once heard to remark that 'it was high time the National Trust was privatised'. When there was discussion of these issues at one of the Trust's meetings in 1968, Ridley disagreed violently with Gibson over the role and authority of regional committees, which he insisted could not be treated 'like little boys'. Gibson countered by warning that if too much authority was devolved to the regions, the Trust's role nationally would be diminished and it would be far more difficult to maintain standards. Antrim, who had been observing the temperature rise alarmingly and felt that Gibson was winning the argument, turned to Ridley and with his mischievous grin asked 'Why don't you give in?' Ridley, by now incensed, thought Antrim had said 'Why don't you hit him?' He could only reply: 'I can't – he's sitting too far away.'

In a sense both Ridley and Gibson have been proved right. The Trust benefited enormously by having strong regional committees. Thanks to the wisdom of Mark Norman, the Benson Report's recommendation that regional chairmen should not sit on the Trust's Executive Committee was not followed, even though their inclusion made it unwieldy. That was a price worth paying for cohesion. Norman also persuaded the Trust of the benefits of allowing the regional chairmen to behave like 'feudal barons in their respective regions', provided that policy and financial decisions continued to be taken by the Executive Committee. He recalled the first regional chairmen as 'a splendid lot' and although 'one or two were embryo brigands . . . we never had a Bolingbroke rebellion'.

Many of the issues that increasingly preoccupied the Trust in the 1980s needed that consistent, national view that the central committees and the staff at head office could bring. One such issue is the government's roads-building programme, which may seem to present only very local threats to Trust property, but which nationally is a strategy for devastation on a huge scale. The Trust has to try to protect its own properties with all the powers available to it, but it must also address the wider conservation issues raised by government transport policy.

The difficulty of finding any common ground became increasingly evident when Nicholas Ridley was Minister for Transport, and again it brought him into conflict with Lord Gibson. One of the proposals that caused particular concern was the preferred route for the future M40, which had apparently been planned without a thought for the impact on the views from the terraces at Farnborough Hall in Warwickshire. The battle to change the route was lost and on this issue the Trust had to accept defeat. However, it requested a meeting with Ridley to discuss ways of limiting the damage to Farnborough. This gave Ridley the opportunity to lecture Gibson and the other representatives of the Trust on the need for the Trust to 'learn to live with motorways'. Gibson replied that learning to live with the M40 by trying to lessen its impact on Farnborough was the purpose of the interview. Ridley was unyielding and eventually Gibson took an opportunity to say, 'I can see I am wasting your time and mine'. Finally, Ridley decided to leave. His civil servants, perhaps embarrassed by this display, then went out of their way to see whether the potential damage to Farnborough could be mitigated. Successive ministers for transport have shown greater courtesy, but little apparent understanding of why the Trust believes government policy to be destructive and shortsighted.

There are moments during the negotiations for major properties when a successful outcome depends on a neatly executed *pas de deux*, shared by regional and head office staff. Without local knowledge and contacts, the Trust would very often not even be aware of what opportunities existed. To find the necessary resources for an important acquisition and secure the support of government departments and agencies, the Trust needs to use all the influence and expertise available centrally. Just how well the partnership can work was demonstrated when, in July 1982, the Hayfield estate in Derbyshire, including Kinder Scout, came unexpectedly on the market.

The wild and dramatic plateau of Kinder Scout, crossed by the Pennine Way, is the most visited part of the high moors of the Peak District. The enjoyment that it gives to walkers was not secured without a fight. In 1932 there was a mass trespass, organised to support the campaign for access to the mountains. This peaceful demonstration resulted in five people being sent to prison for riotous assembly, assault and incitement to riot. As at other moments in English history, the brutal misuse of the law offended all reasonable people. The same principles were at stake as those that had inspired Robert Hunter to devote so much of his life to the protection of common land, and had driven Octavia Hill and Hardwicke Rawnsley to fight for public access in the Lake District. The mass trespass of Kinder Scout marked a turning point in the campaigns both for access to open country and for the designation of National Parks. For its own qualities – the whole plateau is a Site of Special Scientific Interest – and for its symbolic significance, the sale of Kinder Scout in 1982 called for a quite exceptional response from the Trust.

If it had been intended to test whether the Trust was committee-bound, slow moving and bureaucratic, the timing and conditions of the sale could scarcely have been better devised. News first came to the Trust that it was on the market in late July. None of the head office committees was due to meet before mid September. Lord Gibson and James Turner, the Regional Director, were about to go on holiday. There was also an extremely difficult diplomatic issue that needed to be resolved, in that for very understandable reasons the Peak Park Joint Planning Board was extremely keen to become the owner of Kinder.

The vendors, who were looking for a sum of £1.5 million for the whole estate, were insistent that the sale should be completed by the second week in September.

The Director-General, Jack Boles, went to see Kinder for himself at the beginning of August, on the same day meeting the Director of the Peak Park Joint Planning Board. Boles concluded that its protection by a conservation body was so important that he spoke to the Director of the National Heritage Memorial Fund, Brian Lang, from a telephone in the house of the Trust's Warden in Edale. On his return to London, Boles then made special arrangements to deal with the negotiations and the preparation of reports for the Trust's own committees and the grant-aiding bodies. The former Chief Agent, John Gaze, had just retired but was still being used as a consultant. Having worked in the Peak District as Regional Agent for six years, he knew the property and all the people involved extremely well. Within a fortnight he had drafted a full assessment and financial report.

Boles also entrusted a lot of the detailed negotiations to Angus Stirling, who had recently joined the Trust as Deputy Director-General. He had been recruited by Mark Norman, who had known him years before as a young man in Lazards. Stirling had subsequently worked for the Mellon Foundation and then as Deputy Secretary-General of the Arts Council. Because Lord Gibson, as a former Chairman of the Arts Council, felt inhibited from luring away a senior member of its staff, Norman was left to conduct the courtship. Much to his relief, Boles and Stirling immediately found they could work together. Kinder Scout gave Stirling the opportunity to develop the skills he had recently shown over the acquisition of Canons Ashby, which had prompted Gibson to remark to Boles: 'You had better get Angus directly involved in the negotiations; he will have many more of these to do in future.'

From its first discussions with the Peak Park Joint Planning Board, the Trust made clear that it wanted above all to avoid a situation in which the two bodies would be bidding against each other. If necessary, the Trust was prepared to stand aside, and would have done so if the National Heritage Memorial Fund and the Countryside Commission had not insisted that they wanted to throw their full support behind its bid. There were no secrets about this preference: the Commission explained that they were anxious to give Kinder the full protection of the Trust's inalienable powers and they appreciated the advantages of management by an organisation which already owned adjoining property. There was also concern that government policy at that time was against extending the ownership of land by public bodies and local authorities. If the Trust had ever allowed its powers to be diluted or had abdicated its role as a national body, that decision might well have gone the other way.

Before leaving for their holidays, Gibson and the Chairman of the Finance Committee, Nicholas Baring, had approved the principle of acquisition and had authorised expenditure from the Trust's own funds of up to £200,000, even though the Derbyshire and Peak District Appeal was at the time overdrawn as a result of other land purchases. The Deputy Chairman, Sir Marcus Worsley, managed to fit in a visit, and so too did Len Clark, who wrote subsequently about the importance of Kinder Scout: 'It now seems to me possibly the most important open space acquisition ever to confront the Trust' and he went on to predict that 'it could be an essential breakthrough in the Trust's relationship with the great visiting public from the northern cities'. By late August the National Heritage Memorial Fund and the Countryside Commission had offered grants of £315,000 and £75,000 respectively. To complete the package Boles rang up a benefactor of the Trust to ask whether the bequest left by his father, Maurice Fry, could be used to bridge the remaining gap of £50,000 and received an enthusiastic reply. The Peak Park Joint Planning Board agreed to support the Trust's bid, provided it was fully consulted over the preparation of a management plan.

By 6 September, Turner was able to put in an offer for those parts of the Hayfield estate that were of interest to the Trust, and it was accepted. On 16 September 1982, the Executive Committee was presented with a *fait accompli*. The response was a unanimous expression of pleasure and, by implication, approval that the Chairman and the Director-General had broken every rule, in order to seize an opportunity that might not recur.

The conclusion of negotiations for a major property such as Kinder Scout mark the end of one phase of acquisition and the beginning of another. Although the site was recognised to be of exceptional interest because of the extent of high-altitude blanket peat, it was also acknowledged to be one of the most degraded and eroded upland areas in Europe. Acid rain, the tramping of vast numbers of visitors, accidental fires and chronic overgrazing had combined to prevent natural processes of recovery. Only a carefully researched and monitored policy of repair and protection could arrest its decay.

One of the first and most controversial decisions was to ban all sheep from the Kinder moors. It had been estimated that in 1914 there were 17,000 sheep in the Kinder and Bleaklow area. By the mid-1970s that number had increased to over 60,000, as a result of government subsidies paid on the basis of the total number of sheep kept, which encouraged ever larger flocks. In the preceding hundred years the area of heather in the Peak District had been reduced by 30 per cent, largely as a result of this overgrazing. By bringing in lime, where necessary by helicopter, to encourage regeneration, and by planting native species such as cotton grasses around boggy areas, degeneration has been halted. When recovery seems secure, sheep will return to graze on Kinder.

On some of the lower slopes where the land is more robust, there is a Share Farming Scheme, in which Trust and farmer divide both the costs and the profits of the enterprise. This arrangement gives more direct control to the Trust than its normal tenant farming agreements, enabling levels of stocking and grazing to be adjusted from year to year. The Trust has provided new farm buildings and improved sheep-handling pens to assist the farmer. Volunteers have helped with the rebuilding of dry-stone walls. At higher levels, where bare peat has been mashed into a semi-liquid by walkers' boots, the Trust's wardens have repaired paths using pitching, a traditional method of construction which involves bedding blocks of local gritstone into the ground to provide a durable walking surface. Mountain bikers have been restricted to the bridleways which are recognised routes for cycling. Like restrictions on grazing, such decisions are unpopular, at least until there is evidence that vegetation is gradually being re-established.

Exactly how the Trust reconciles the need for decisive action with the obligation to nurture and retain the loyalty of a vast membership has become an increasingly delicate and exacting exercise. In 1993 the former law Lord, Lord Oliver, produced a report on the workings of the Trust's constitution and on the role of members in the running of the organisation. The report explained very clearly that members were subscribers to a great charitable work and that the Trust's Acts of Parliament put responsibility for all major policy decisions into the hands of the Council. In view of the increasing disruption caused by minority interests, this clarification was immensely valuable, spelling out the fiduciary role of the Council and its authority to act in whatever way best served the Trust's statutory purposes. Given the immense responsibilities that the Council now exercises, the future of the Trust will depend on whether it can attract those of sufficient ability to guide it through the next century. The related organisations and other bodies that continue to nominate half its members must continue to

(*Overleaf*) The Hayfield estate
in Derbyshire, with the plateau
of Kinder Scout on the horizon.

put forward for appointment those who will serve the Council loyally and with distinction.

The scale of the Council's responsibilities is now such that it will need to rely increasingly on highly effective Executive, Properties and Finance Committees and on vigorous regional committees. The strength of the Trust's regional administration can underpin the foundations of its national role. What is certain is that the demands on the Trust will go on increasing, while the responsibilities for managing its existing estates become ever more onerous. The need for it to take on new properties shows no sign of becoming less urgent. Certainly the continued confidence of its benefactors and the support of a large membership will be essential. The suggestion that the Trust should be split up and its different areas of responsibility parcelled out to different bodies needs to be resolutely resisted. It would destroy the cohesive, integrated approach to conservation which will remain the Trust's greatest strength. Octavia Hill shared with Ruskin the perception that things 'bind and blend themselves together'. She never lost that conviction; and neither should the Trust.

CHAPTER ELEVEN

New Circumstances

O NLY ONCE, during her five years as Chairman, was Dame Jennifer Jenkins heard to make a wholly misleading and frivolous remark. Commenting on her succession to Lord Gibson, in March 1986, she intimated that she 'could hardly be less qualified for this new job'. That was nonsense. She had learnt the principles of enlightened planning from her father, Sir Parker Morris, who as Town Clerk of Westminster had helped to produce the 'Parker-Morris' standards for council house building after the Second World War. To her, Octavia Hill's work for the urban poor was not a remote chapter of Victorian history, but a forerunner to what her father achieved. With a group of friends she had set up the Consumers' Association, started from scratch in a garage and, in spite of frequent warnings that the libel laws would be used to drive them to bankruptcy, rapidly transformed it into a respected national institution. As Chairman of the Historic Buildings Council she had carried its work into new areas, initiating grants for churches and for conservation areas in historic towns. Her independent approach, accessibility and soundness of judgement greatly impressed those who turned to the HBC for help and who often found themselves dealing not with a civil servant but with the Chairman herself.

Aware of these qualities, Lord Gibson identified her as a possible successor and invited her to join the Executive Committee in 1984. The aspect of the Trust's work about which she knew least was the protection of the countryside, and ironically it was here that she was to be most influential. She encouraged the Trust to regard its work as the care of complete landscapes, in which nature conservation, the repair of vernacular buildings and an understanding of archaeology needed to be exercised in unison. Astringent and sceptical one moment, ready to tease the next, Dame Jennifer combined a refreshing Fabian outlook with a thoroughly practical approach to the Trust's work.

Shortly after becoming Chairman, she visited the Trust's membership department at Beckenham in Kent. Membership had reached 1.3 million by 1986, and she was doubtful that the department was capable of dealing efficiently with its immense administrative responsibilities. She concluded that a complete overhaul of the operation was needed. Her years with the Consumers' Association had shown how essential it was to develop first-rate research and efficient mailing if members were to be recruited and retained. This was vital to the survival of the Trust: by the late 1980s a faltering in subscription income would have had dire financial consequences. By the end of 1990 there were over two million members.

Because the Trust owns property on such a vast scale, it appears to be a rich organisation. But its treasures are all liabilities, the affluence they seem to imply an illusion. Most of the great estates in the Trust's ownership are held inalienably and so are assets that can never be realised. To a private owner, the paintings and furniture that are in the Trust's care would be worth millions. For the Trust they are valueless, except as consummate works of art. The Trust's greatest assets are its members, its benefactors and its voluntary supporters. During 1986, Dame Jennifer's first year as Chairman, the income from membership subscriptions amounted to £16,764,000 a year, accounting for 24.5 per cent of total income. By the time of her retirement in 1992 subscriptions brought in £37,382,000 or 33 per cent of total income. The broadening of support for the Trust has increased the number of legacies received, contributing £22.3 million in 1992 towards the acquisition and conservation of properties. The Trust's Centres and Associations by then numbered 187, with over 100,000 members taking a close interest in how the funds they raise were used at properties. Given the scale of its responsibilities the Trust will never be a rich organisation, but its continuing ability to attract and retain members has enabled it to develop skills that it could not have afforded in the past.

Her work with the HBC had convinced Dame Jennifer that conservation had reached a stage in which the protection of the individual building or parcels of countryside sometimes achieved relatively little. Small may be beautiful, but if isolated can also be frighteningly vulnerable. Co-ordinated care and planning were needed if the built and natural environment were to survive the constant demands for development and the onslaught of an increasingly mobile population, wanting easy access to the countryside. The problems had been foreseen by Fougasse as early as the 1930s, when his prophetic cartoons described what has become a sad reality at many of the Trust's coastal properties.

The way in which the Trust had successfully assembled patchworks of properties meant that the integration of management on the coast and in areas like the Lake District was increasingly practicable. Subscription income enabled the Trust to employ well-qualified wardens and estate staff. There was also the means to carry out the necessary survey work to reveal what areas included botanical rarities, and where the Trust had, sometimes unknowingly, acquired archaeological sites of the greatest importance. Much of this surveying was organised from the Estates Department in Cirencester, and was greatly assisted by employment schemes such as those of the Manpower Services Commission. The fact that the work was long overdue was not simply a matter of negligence. Only in the 1980s had the Trust's more secure financial position allowed for adequate research and for the active conservation work which often followed.

"......Now, at Starfish Bay, you're miles away from anyone ——

that's what everyone likes about it. "

The need to treat the care of buildings and of landscape as interrelated was particularly evident in the Lake District, where property in Trust ownership exceeded 130,000 acres. There, in 1988, the Historic Buildings Representative, Susan Denyer, set up a landscape survey, largely financed by the Lake District Appeal. The work was undertaken by a team of two surveyors and an archivist who, beginning in Great Langdale, then moving on to Borrowdale, recorded how the landscape had evolved over many centuries, in response to changing financial and social circumstances. Having established the historical significance of the different farmsteads, including those long abandoned, of the patterns of walling around them, and the purpose behind the planting of trees in some places, but not in others, the Trust was then able to plan for maintenance on the basis of clear, accessible information. A greater understanding of why the landscape developed in earlier centuries will guide the Trust on how to respond to inevitable changes in the future. While the outlook for hill farming is so very uncertain, the uplands will have to continue to adapt to new circumstances, as they have in the past. The Trust's ability to influence these changes will be limited, but it can help to ensure that in the process what is of most significance is properly valued and where possible protected.

The buildings in the Trust's care can be as seriously threatened by too many visitors as a fragile landscape. Again, the Trust had to develop carefully researched and monitored ways of limiting and slowing down that damage. The popularity of Sir Winston Churchill's home, Chartwell in Kent, meant that a system of issuing restricted tickets which specified the time of admission was introduced as early as 1969, when there were over 163,500 visitors a year: it was found that the paths through the Golden Rose Walk – a present to Sir Winston and Lady Churchill from their children – had been reduced to a muddy shambles in a matter of days. If the number of visitors goes on increasing, members of the Trust may have to get used to the idea that advance booking will be as necessary at its most popular properties as it is at the theatre: after all, there is nothing new in the idea that country-house guests should be wary of turning up unexpectedly. Although efforts to reduce the damage caused can never be entirely effective, the techniques of preventive conservation are being constantly refined and include the careful regulation of blinds to reduce destruction by light, the use of wool floor coverings or druggets, and the control of relative humidity, which all help to slow the rate of decay. Most vulnerable of all is the sense of intimacy, the atmosphere that is unique to a particular property, and sadly that is something which at times the Trust is powerless to protect.

The Trust's experience of these problems has, in recent years, increasingly attracted the interest of conservationists overseas. Dame Jennifer inevitably became involved in European conservation when her husband, Roy Jenkins, was President of the European Commission. She was keen to encourage this international role for the Trust, without squandering its limited resources and without allowing it to be deflected from its own statutory obligations. The benefits came not just from the stimulus of such contacts: the Trust received growing recognition in Europe of the value of its work, and this in turn encouraged both the flow of grants from the European Community and the financial support of the British Council. Identifying an appropriate role for the Trust outside Europe involves similar opportunities and potential pitfalls. For many years the Trust has been sharing experiences with sister organisations abroad, many of which are also called National Trusts. Some of the most important gatherings are the periodic conferences of these Trusts, in 1986 held in the Wessex region and in 1989 hosted by Bermuda. Although representatives came from as far afield as Fiji, Malaysia and the Caribbean, the objectives and problems are similar: how to educate and influence governments, the use of volunteers, how to raise funds, and how to widen the base of support.

Involvement with the changes taking place in central Europe and Russia is in many ways more difficult. Not only are the conservation problems immense, but the framework and institutions for effective dialogue scarcely exist. If the Trust is not realistic, and if its offers of help are not carefully directed, it could waste its own precious resources. Worse, it might be seen to be assuming a role of cultural imperialism that would be unhelpful and ultimately resented. As it has only a tiny budget for developing these contacts, exchanges are possible only because of the generosity of the British Council and other grant-giving organisations. The simple experience of looking at shared problems and discussing practical solutions often offers the most constructive, practical benefits. Several important contacts were made at the conference 'Europe Preserved for Europe' which the Trust organised in York in September 1990, and which was the first of its kind to bring together the principal conservation bodies of most European countries. The Director of the Estonian Heritage Society, Mart Aru, was present and so too were representatives of the Monuments Service of Southern Bohemia. Mart Aru and the President of the Estonian Heritage Society, Jaan Taam, subsequently visited Britain and were shown how conservation area legislation works in practice and how textiles are repaired at Blickling. These exchanges were not all just earnest discussions amongst specialists. When the formalities are out of the way, a healthy scepticism often emerges about what the market economy and the international leisure industry could do for their historic monuments. There was something salutary in having it politely pointed out that in Czechoslovakia gardens began to be listed in 1957, seven years before the scheduling of gardens in this country. The blunt fact is that Prague and Tallinn have been better preserved under repressive socialist systems than have most of the great historic towns and cities of western Europe. It remains to be seen whether eastern Europe and Russia can revive their economies without the motor car wrecking their city centres and without advertising demeaning their countryside.

In 1991 came a sequel to the struggle in the 1880s to save Sayes Court (p. 25). The Trust found itself involved in the conservation of Archangel, where Peter the Great had determined to build a sea port to serve his Muscovite empire. In response to an invitation to the Director-General, a group of conservationists was invited to visit the area around Archangel, where churches were systematically destroyed after the 1917 Revolution, traditional wooden houses were swept away and even the street names changed. A pall of smoke now hangs over its vast industrial complexes. But its history has not been completely obliterated. At Malye Karely, some forty-five kilometres away from Archangel, there is an open-air museum of wooden architecture set in beautiful, rolling countryside. There the Trust's Surveyor of Conservation, Nigel Seeley, discussed how humidity could be controlled to protect the contents of buildings which experience rapid and dramatic changes of temperatures. The quality of those farmhouses, granaries, bell towers and churches could scarcely make a more telling contrast to the stark ranks of concrete, panel-constructed flats that now dominate the environs of Archangel.

Two months before the Archangel visit a conference in Tallinn was called by the Estonian Heritage Society. Few countries have experienced more determined and brutal efforts to change their cultural identity than Estonia. The mass deportation of intellectuals, the deliberate destruction of historic buildings and the wholesale burning of books were all part of a systematic policy by the Soviet Union to extinguish the memory of Estonia as an independent republic. The Estonian Heritage Society set out to show that the history of their country could not be erased and was not forgotten. They were affirming the same message that Vaclav Havel had for the people of what was then Czechoslovakia: the mark of an enlightened culture is that it 'sets our drowsy souls and lazy hearts moving'. The National Trust was regarded as a natural ally and was represented at the Tallinn conference.

Involvement in these exchanges with conservationists in the former Soviet Union and eastern Europe was an unforgettable experience. Those met had something of the zeal that characterised the founders of the Trust and some of the great benefactors that have kept their ideals alive. It was both inspiring and humbling that recent dissidents who had risked their lives for what they believed in, should look to the Trust as a model of a non-government organisation with mass support, able to present historic monuments honestly, without ideological manipulation, and capable of caring for more than half a million acres of countryside. The Trust's representatives took home far more than they had given.

If this international role is questioned, it is as well to remember that the Trust has at various decisive moments in its history been ready to learn from foreign example. The founders shared with the Trustees of Public Reservations, Massachusetts experience of how to frame a constitution. In 1899 Canon Rawnsley and C.R. Ashbee toured the United States together, 'to invite the co-operation of citizens of the States in the work of the National Trust'. Rawnsley lectured on the literary associations of the Lake District, while Ashbee spoke on 'The Country Homes of England', warning prophetically of 'the breaking up of great estates, and the work of the National Trust in the future with reference to the English country house'. By 1902 the National Trust had fifteen members in the United States, including the architect Frank Lloyd Wright and the Professor of Fine Arts at Harvard, Charles Eliot Norton. The formation in 1975 of the Royal Oak Foundation, an American public charity to encourage support for the Trust, was an extension of what Rawnsley had advocated. The willingness to take on new and wider responsibilities also had the sanction of Octavia Hill. When friends presented her portrait by Sargent, she responded by saying: 'When I am gone, I hope my friends will not try to carry out any special system, or to follow blindly in the track which I have trodden. New circumstances require various efforts, and it is the spirit not the dead form that should be perpetuated.'

The last decade has seen the Trust reacting to new circumstances in a variety of ways. Among the most significant developments is its renewed commitment to education. In this it has been doing no more than taking up the Earl of Carlisle's challenge at its inaugural meeting, and pursuing the ideals of the Kyrle Society and of Ruskin. But in the middle years of this century education was regarded by those running the Trust as not merely peripheral but *ultra vires* – beyond the narrow interpretation of its obligations as set out in the Acts of Parliament.

When Angus Stirling became Director-General in 1983, one of his main concerns was to re-define for the Trust what is referred to in these Acts as 'public benefit'. He wanted to reach a far wider audience, and one way of achieving that was to devote more resources to education.

Stirling believed that the Trust had allowed its allegiance to preservation to eclipse its other objectives, including at times that sense of compassion which guided Octavia Hill. Some of those at the heart of the Trust's work in the 1970s, such as Sir Jack Boles, question this criticism. What is significant is that the new Director-General felt there needed to be a renewed commitment to earlier ideals. He was dedicated to the principle that the purpose of preservation was to give sustenance to people, that the Trust needed to recover the quality of humanity which infused the idealism of the founders, without losing its primary allegiance to conservation. This reassessment of obligations gained encouragement from others concerned about the future of the Trust. In an influential article in the *Financial Times* in October 1990, Colin Amery called for the Trust to become 'a university of the built and natural environment' and he urged that there should be 'more teaching and learning about art, architecture and the land'.

The property which became the base for much of the Trust's educational work was Sutton House, a Tudor courtier's house in east London. That it did so was not because of any Trust initiative, but because local people in Hackney were appalled at what would otherwise have happened to the building. Between 1938, when the National Trust acquired the building, and 1953 Sutton House was occupied by a variety of societies, the objectives of which seemed to be in the spirit of St John's Institute, the charitable Church foundation that had occupied the building during the early years of the century, and which had a clear, community role. In due course the lease was assigned to the Association of Technical and Managerial Staff, which left in 1982, with a minimum of warning. Dry rot was rampant, but this did not deter squatters from moving in.

Worse was to come. In 1986 the building was broken into and sixteenth-century panelling and fireplaces were stolen. Having searched without success for a tenant capable of combining care of the building with a community role, and faced with a repair bill of over £250,000, the Trust tried to off-load its responsibility. A planning application for conversion into five residential units was submitted and advertised in the local press. The scheme involved demolishing part of the Wenlock Barn, an addition of 1904 designed to give members of the Institute a place where cultural activities could take place, as well as purely social pastimes such as billiards. This was too much for some of the highly articulate and perceptive residents of Hackney, who launched a Save Sutton House campaign.

The Trust's ability to respond quickly and positively to criticism has some-times been underestimated. In the case of Sutton House, Dame Jennifer needed little persuasion, provided that the Save Sutton House campaign turned their efforts to fundraising and support for the Trust. The Trust's Regional Director, Robin Mills, threw himself into harnessing their energies, insisting that if the project was to work, then local people would have to provide continuing creativity and commitment. He welcomed the return to the Trust's earliest system of management, a local committee, which included former critics of the Trust's original proposals. Some of the most respected people working in conservation came forward: Fiona Reynolds, the future Director of the Council for the Protection of Rural England; Peter Burman, Secretary of the Council for the Care of Churches; and the Trust's own Publisher, Margaret Willes.

Sutton House now gave expression to that renewed sense of social purpose which both the Chairman and the Director-General wished to see. The Sutton House Music Society was formed, to give concerts in the Wenlock Barn. The Foundation for Art, founded in 1985 to encourage young artists to record National Trust properties, mounted a successful exhibition. There have been lec-tures, entertainments from different cultures, and seminars on landscape and arch-itectural conservation. The cost to the Trust in purely financial terms has been high: over £1 million has been devoted to the project, at a time when there were many other calls on its resources. The campaigners from Save Sutton House now operate as the Sutton House Society and have proved invaluable in raising funds. The considerable expenditure is unlikely to be questioned by those who have visited the house and have seen how it is helping to reinvigorate the Trust.

The decision to run the Young National Trust Theatre from Sutton House meant that its productions were seen by school children in London, as well as around the regions, with sometimes unexpected reactions. The policy of the YNTT is to create Theatre-in-Education programmes which, through drama, dance, music and costume, draw children into the social and moral issues of the past. In 1993 a production entitled *Virtues and Vanities* examined the religious conflicts of the seventeenth century. The actors found that some school children in rural areas such as Shropshire and Norfolk had difficulty understanding the tensions of that period, whereas children from London schools, with mixed ethnic backgrounds, immediately became engrossed in the dilemmas and some-times agonising decisions faced by Catholics and Protestants three hundred years ago. Increasingly, those directing the Trust's educational work have confronted

(*Above*) Children in costume for
a performance of the Young National Trust
Theatre at Petworth in 1996.

(*Right*) The staircase at
No. 2 Willow Road, Hampstead.

uncomfortable issues from the past, determined to avoid a sanitised view of
history. At the Apprentice House, Styal, children re-live parts of the daily routine
of the paupers employed at Quarry Bank Mill in the early nineteenth century.
They cannot, and should not, appreciate the full horror of industrial accidents,
but they find themselves eating gruel, as unfamiliar to them as cotton looms
powered by a giant water-wheel or by steam.

The problems at Sutton House had been simmering for many years, and
finding an acceptable solution took time. With 2 Willow Road, Hampstead,
time was a luxury the Trust did not have. In January 1991 Ursula Blackwell,
widow of the architect Erno Goldfinger, died, leaving 2 Willow Road, its
furniture and important collection of surrealist and Kinetic art with an uncertain

future. There were the familiar obstacles of how to endow the property and deal with outstanding tax liabilities. But more serious was the issue of whether 2 Willow Road really was of outstanding historic importance. The Historic Buildings Secretary, Martin Drury, and his Assistant, Ed Diestelkamp, concluded that though not a first-rate building of its type, it would, if preserved with its contents, be a record of a significant aspect of the cultural life of Britain between the two World Wars. Whatever the ultimate assessment of its architectural importance may be, in the early 1990s it represented the most discredited and despised episode in the history of taste in this country. The Trust could perhaps take comfort from the fact that Wightwick Manor, the first building to be acquired under the Country Houses Scheme, was in the 1930s almost as unfashionable (p. 109)

The Trust's commitment to the protection of twentieth-century buildings has been at best patchy and scant. The gift of Castle Drogo in Devon in 1974 meant that its properties included a house built between 1910 and 1930. Sir Edwin Lutyens's design is a masterly essay in asymmetry, exploiting a superb site on a rocky outcrop high above the River Teign. His use of granite ensures a complex and intriguing relationship with the surrounding landscape. But it has nothing whatever to do with the international style of architecture that found almost universal acceptance during this period and in the middle years of the century. Anyone wanting to understand what the Modern Movement was about would do much better to start with 2 Willow Road.

Erno Goldfinger was born in Budapest, moved to Vienna in 1919 and to Paris in 1920, where he joined the circle of Braque, Brancusi and the surrealists Max Ernst and Man Ray. His terrace of three houses in Willow Road was built between 1938 and 1939, four years after his arrival in London, where he became a highly influential teacher. Goldfinger here applied the same principles of design that he brought to his major post-war commissions: an austere use of reinforced concrete relieved by brick facing, avoidance of any unnecessary mouldings and a sense of scale which, depending on one's point of view, could be called bold, assertive or simply arrogant.

The pictures and sculpture at 2 Willow Road are at least as significant as its architecture. Many of the artists were personal friends of the Goldfingers, and their work came to the house direct from the studio and not through dealers. The paintings by Roland Penrose, Bridget Riley, Max Ernst, Henry Moore and Hans Arp show how international in outlook was the Hampstead avant-garde at that time. Many of those who found its architecture unsympathetic were in no doubt of the value of its paintings, not just individually but as a collection.

The appeal for funds to acquire Willow Road had to be set a strict time limit. Drury and Diestelkamp wrote over two hundred letters to individuals who lived in Modern Movement houses or were known to collect contemporary art. But by early December 1992 it still looked as though there was no hope of meeting the required target of £750,000. Then came a message that one of the Sainsbury family charitable trusts was prepared to help. Many members will be bewildered by, or even downright hostile to this addition to the Trust's properties. They may be reassured that the National Heritage Memorial Fund and two benefactors have provided for its future preservation. There was a final twist to the story. In 1938, when Goldfinger proposed to demolish the row of eighteenth-century cottages that formerly stood on the site, he provoked a vigorous local campaign of opposition, led by the President of the Hampstead Society, Henry Brooke. Half a century later, his son, Peter Brooke, enjoyed the irony of giving his approval, as Secretary of State for the National Heritage, to the complicated tax provisions and grants needed to preserve Goldfinger's house.

The terrace of Willow Road and the semi-detached houses of Blyth Grove at Worksop in Nottinghamshire epitomise the life of two nations: the one international, innovative, outward-looking, rationalist, functional; the other introverted, reclusive, homely in its accumulation of ordinary objects and pre-occupied with an often drab and monotonous past. The Trust accepted 2 Willow Road because it was original and influential. No. 7 Blyth Grove was acquired in 1990 because it was so utterly commonplace. Or once was. Working- and middle-class housing of the early years of this century was the nation's most common form of building, filling street after street in every town and city. Because of mass-produced decoration and easy transport by rail, regional variations were minimal. What made Mr Straw's House, at No. 7 Blyth Grove, exceptional was that it had remained unaltered since the early 1930s, embalmed as an act of filial piety.

William Straw, a successful Worksop grocer and seed merchant, died in 1932, leaving No. 7 to his two sons, one also called William, the other Walter. The brothers never married, never moved any of their parents' possessions, had no radio, telephone or television and even continued to use their mother's recipes when cooking. Every letter and account book was retained. While surrounding houses and millions of others like them were improved, adapted or demolished, No. 7 remained, like the calendar of 1932 on the wall in the front room, frozen in time.

The hall of Mr Straw's House at 7 Blyth Grove, Worksop, in
Nottinghamshire. An Edwardian semi, frozen in time in the 1930s.

When in 1990 young William Straw died at the age of 93, he left nearly £1
million to the Trust. There was never any suggestion from the Straws that
No. 7 was intended for permanent preservation. It was the Historic Buildings
Representative for the East Midlands, Simon Murray, who realised just what an
extraordinary survival it was and who persuaded the Trust's committees that Mr
Straw's legacy should be used to acquire a house which, as a social document,
was as important in its own way as Erddig or Calke Abbey. The house itself

together with its neighbour, No. 5, had been left to Mr Straw's tenant, Mr Charles Hopkinson, who agreed to sell the freehold of both houses and the land opposite to the Trust. No. 7 Blyth Grove shows how the Trust's definition of what constitutes 'historic interest' needs constantly to be questioned, revised and re-evaluated.

Until the Foundation for Art began to commission work from a wide range of contemporary artists – many of whom have greatly valued the interest and encouragement given them by its Chairman, Sir Brinsley Ford, and Secretary, Dudley Dodd – the Trust had tended only to acquire important twentieth-century paintings when these were already part of a country house collection. In the former dining-room at Dudmaston in Shropshire there are major works

Towards St Ives, painted by David Bomberg
on the West Penwith coast of Cornwall in 1947.

by Ben Nicholson, Dubuffet, Sonia Delaunay and Barbara Hepworth. Perhaps the most interesting of the pictures collected by Sir George Labouchere are those acquired when he was Ambassador in Madrid and was able to visit the studio of the Catalan artist A Tapiès. But Dudmaston is unusual, not least because Sir George and Lady Labouchere have gone on collecting contemporary paintings and sculpture for the house after giving it to the Trust in 1978. This continuing enrichment gives the house a remarkable sense of vitality. The aim of the Foundation for Art is to bring this continuing creativity to other houses.

While the Trust has continued to break new ground, in new circumstances, it has also been ready to revive past practice. There have recently been painful reminders of all the vigorous hill running that G.M. Trevelyan and his friends had relished in the 1930s. The various marathons of the world each has its own special and refined form of discomfort, but for sheer physical misery none rivals the Snowdonia Marathon, first organised by the Trust in 1982 and now with its reputation firmly established as the most romantic, most punishing in the world. The course starts in the Llanberis Pass, rapidly climbs 1,000 feet; drops down to Beddgelert; crawls up another 1,000 feet, only to lose height again; and then at 21 miles inflicts on the participants a steeply rising track from Waunfawn that drives them up another 1,000 feet before plummeting down to the finish, near the start, at Llanberis. It is absurd as a marathon course, exquisitely uncomfortable even for very fit runners, and all to raise money for the Trust's Snowdonia Appeal, of which the actor Sir Anthony Hopkins has been an exceptionally active Chairman.

At West Penwith in Cornwall, more commonly known as the Land's End peninsula, falling agricultural incomes have left many of the farms looking scruffy and disfigured, while the decline of Cornish tin-mining has littered the coast with derelict and dangerous industrial sites. There should not be too much sentimentality about what remains. Many of the mine buildings are now so unstable that whole sections have been known to collapse in a single storm. The area around the Levant engine house, St Just, has been contaminated with heavy minerals, leaching sulphuric acid and arsenic; scarcely a plant is growing over half a century after the mine was abandoned.

This is natural beauty in its severest, grandest form. Much of West Penwith is still essentially an Iron Age landscape, its history written in granite. As the painter and critic Adrian Stokes remarked, it is 'the only part of Britain belonging to the geography of the Ancient World'. There are the cliff castles owned by the Trust at Bosigran, Sennen and Gurnard's Head, the ancient courtyard houses gathered in groups with walls five or six feet high and mysterious structures called Fogous, from the Cornish word 'fogo' or cave. The field systems are the most striking Iron Age survival. When areas were first cleared to create tiny fields, the stones were used to construct what are referred to locally as hedges. Like lead-work in a medieval stained-glass window, these dry-stone hedges shape and define the landscape. Their sinewy lines have been traced by the pencil of Ben Nicholson; the colours and textures have given inspiration to the palettes

The engine house and mine buildings at Levant
on the West Penwith coast of Cornwall, 1904.

of David Bomberg, Peter Lanyon and Patrick Heron. For those who farmed, fished or mined here, West Penwith was unremittingly harsh and dangerous. It took some courage to persuade the Trust's committees that what might seem irreconcilables – the waste land and the wild grandeur – were in fact essential elements of West Penwith.

When the Trust's land agent, Peter Mansfield, began to string together a succession of headlands, farms and abandoned industrial sites in the 1980s, he often found his colleagues and the committees sceptical or straightforwardly obstructive. However, he also found powerful allies in the Trust's Deputy Chairman, Sir Marcus Worsley; in Sir John Smith who was prepared to give practical and financial help; and in Len Clark, who would come down on his motorbike whenever there was the prospect of a piece in the jigsaw coming up for sale, and who could be relied on to swing any committee with an irresistible mixture of understatement, modesty and an understanding of the feelings of ordinary Trust members and supporters.

The first acquisition in West Penwith, the Mayon Cliff, came in 1935 as a gift from Ferguson's Gang (p. 84). A scattering of properties was given or bought in the 1950s, including part of Zennor Head and Rosemergy Cliff. In the 1960s covenants were accepted over several strategic stretches, and in 1967 the Cornish Engines Preservation Society, supported by the local authorities and a public appeal, gave the Levant engine house. But it was in the 1980s that Enterprise Neptune, supported at Lower Porthmeor by Sir John Smith's Landmark Trust, made possible a succession of acquisitions which in turn led to a coherent management strategy for the whole area and to the appointment of adequate full-time staff.

The Trust was now in a position to work effectively with all those who had an interest in the protection and enhancement of West Penwith. The Trust's Archaeological Adviser, David Thackray, supervised a complete and large-scale survey of the area, in sufficient detail to be able to tell tenant farmers exactly which features were significant and had to be preserved. Full use was made of West Penwith's status as an Environmentally Sensitive Area, encouraging grants to those farmers willing to respect and protect features of archaeological and botanical importance. Abandoned mining sites were to be stabilised and made safe, using Derelict Land Grants. Above all, the Trust began working increasingly closely with the very tight knit and independent-minded community around St Just. The ultimate success of the Trust's work in West Penwith will depend as much on the goodwill of that local community, as it will on the generosity of its benefactors.

On the Durham coast it was not the legacy of tin-mining that scarred the beaches, but the refuse of the collieries at Easington and Horden, tipped directly into the sea so that the surf foamed black. The surveys carried out at the time Enterprise Neptune was launched in 1965 concluded that the Durham coast was irrevocably ruined by industrial exploitation and waste. A different view was taken twenty years later. By then the collieries were facing closure, the communities which had served them had been wracked by the miners' strike and there were the first signs that as tipping ceased, so longshore drift would sweep away the cloak of coal debris from the beaches. The Regional Director, Oliver Maurice, argued that here was an opportunity to secure a property which would show how the Trust could heal wounds in both the landscape and the local community.

British Coal also saw the point. In 1988, for a nominal £1, the Trust purchased Warren House Gill and 88 acres of cliff and woodland including part of Fox Holes Dene. Its first warden was Denis Rooney, who had worked for

A coal-strewn beach near Easington Colliery in County Durham,
the 500th mile of coast acquired by Enterprise Neptune.

seventeen years at Dawdon Colliery and now relished the opportunity to help tidy up a stretch of coast he already knew intimately from walks with his dog at the end of a shift. Rooney was soon recruiting teams of volunteers from local schools. The acquisition was given wider significance because it marked the 500th mile of coastline protected through Enterprise Neptune. Since its launch in 1965 Neptune had raised £11 million and was now more than half-way to achieving its aim of safeguarding nine hundred miles of coastline.

For much of its history, the Trust has been at best passive in its relationship with those living in the great industrial cities. The rather glib assumption could always be made that its properties were there for everyone to enjoy. But for children in the inner city area of Pottery Bank on the Tyne in Newcastle those opportunities meant nothing. To meet this challenge Oliver Maurice secured the support of the Rank Foundation to fund a trainee Youth Officer whose job it was to establish links between city children and National Trust properties.

Some children have worked with the Trust's warden at Wallington. Others have adopted Manhaven Bay, a property in Tyne & Wear acquired in 1987. The task of the project leader, Liz Fisher, is to translate the ideals of Octavia Hill and Hardwicke Rawnsley into a scheme which will work for today's Tyneside.

On both the Durham coast and the West Penwith peninsula the Trust is

Denis Rooney, National Trust Warden on the Durham coast.

demonstrating how far nature's own powers of recovery can heal the scars left by industrial use. Evidence of the changing face of the landscape will remain, as just another layer of archaeological evidence. That capacity for recovery will be further tested by the acquisition, in 1993, of Orford Ness on the Suffolk coast. When first confronted with its potential problems, many committee members and senior staff were appalled. Those who urged caution may yet be proved right: an uncomfortable thought, but one which challenges those who criticise the Trust for excessive caution and complacency.

For most of this century Orford Ness had been occupied by the Ministry of Defence. There were no public rights of way and no legitimate public access. In the 1920s Professor Alfred Steers was able to carry out pioneering studies of its accreting ridges and so establish that it was physiographically one of the most

important shingle spits in Europe, as well as being exceptionally rich ornitho-
logically and botanically. Precisely because it was a great area of wilderness,
accessible only by boat or by trudging from the northern, Aldeburgh end across
miles of shingle, the Ness was an ideal site for testing ballistics and, later, parts of
nuclear weapons. In the First World War it was used by the Royal Flying Corps.
During the 1930s Sir Robert Watson Watt carried out the first experiments in
radar – a discovery which was to play a decisive part in the Battle of Britain and
throughout the Second World War. Barnes Wallis worked there, experimenting
with new types of bombs. Then, during the Cold War, huge aerials were erected
on what became known as the Cobra Mist site. This form of 'over the horizon
radar' was, at the moment of its introduction, the most advanced defence system
in the world, gathering and processing information which might at any moment
have signalled the beginning of a third world war. Like other such innovations,
it was superseded and redundant within months of its installation. In the 1960s
the Atomic Weapons Research Establishment erected vast pagoda-like structures
designed to reduce the impact of massive explosions if tests went wrong. In two
very different senses Orford Ness is a Site of Special Scientific Interest.

When in the 1970s the Ness was declared surplus to MoD requirements,
there was an assumption that it would pass to the Nature Conservancy Council,
already owners of the National Nature Reserve at the southern end. But
negotiations got hopelessly bogged down. As Louis MacNeice wrote of the
Ministry of Defence:

> Neither sense nor conscience stirred,
>
> Having been ultimately deterred.

With nothing concluded, there was talk of new defence needs. While all this
went on, the site was left derelict and vandalised, the buildings ripped apart by
scrap metal merchants and the fragile shingle ridges churned up by four wheel-
drive vehicles. The abuse of the site finally prompted the Regional Officer of
the Nature Conservancy Council, John Morley, to suggest that the National
Trust should put in a bid. A report went to the Properties Committee in January
1992.

The initial reaction was one of extreme alarm at the possible hazards to any
visiting public and the potential liability for the sea defences, not just of the Ness
itself but of the neighbouring communities of Aldeburgh and Orford. At the
moment when the mood of the Committee seemed to have swung irretrievably
against accepting these risks, Sir John Quicke reminded everyone that this stretch
of coast 'is ringing with the music of Benjamin Britten'. Long influenced by the

gentle harmonies of Wordsworth, the Trust also needed to have regard to the more brutal realities that concerned Crabbe and Britten.

The poetry of George Crabbe gave Britten the inspiration for his first opera, *Peter Grimes*. In 1941 he was in self-imposed exile in the United States and there he read in the *Listener* an article by E.M. Forster, which began, 'To talk about Crabbe is to talk about England'. Forster's article led him to the long narrative poems *The Village*, *The Borough* and *Peter Grimes* with their bleak evocations of the Suffolk coast, of Orford, Aldeburgh and The Ness, which Britten had known since childhood:

> Ah! hapless they who still remain;
>
> Who still remain to hear the ocean roar,
>
> Whose greedy waves devour the lessening shore;
>
> Till some fierce tide, with more imperious sway,
>
> Sweeps the low hut and all it holds away . . .

The harshness of Crabbe's view of nature gives his poems a power and relevance lacking in the work of some of the more celebrated Romantic poets who were his contemporaries. Nature to Crabbe was not necessarily benign and forgiving.

Because Orford Ness presented so many liabilities and such a large financial commitment, the Chairman of the Trust and the Director-General took over direct, personal responsibility for negotiations. As a former colleague of Professor Steers and President of the Royal Geographical Society, Lord Chorley was in no doubt that it merited an exceptional effort by the Trust. His years of climbing in the Alps and Himalayas had also made him acutely aware of the rarity and fragility of areas of genuine wilderness. He found that the Secretary of State for the Environment, Michael Heseltine, was sympathetic; and his department earmarked over £2 million towards an endowment. Chorley also turned to the local MP, John Gummer, then Minister for Agriculture, to try to put pressure on the MoD to help tidy up the site. A ministerial visit took place and all sorts of assurances were given. Just when the transfer seemed assured, a General Election was called for April 1992. The grant offers that had been painstakingly assembled promptly went into limbo.

Nearly a year later final approvals were given. The total cost of acquisition was to be £3.5 million. A special allocation from the Department of the Environment to the Countryside Commission enabled it to make the largest grant in its history and, for the first time, provide an endowment for an open space property. Derelict Land Grants will be used to clear up military and weapons-testing debris, so making the site safe for visitors. The National Heritage

2nd Lord Chorley, Chairman of
the National Trust from 1991 to 1996.

Memorial Fund overcame its misgivings about grant-aiding an acquisition from the MoD and it too contributed generously. The local authorities rallied round and the Trust's own Enterprise Neptune found £500,000, the largest allocation it has ever made.

The protection of Orford Ness has assumed a much wider significance. Once again it is to be an area of wilderness, valued as the habitat for the sea poppy and sea pea growing on the shingle; for its breeding avocets, marsh harriers, terns and short-eared owls. What was until recently a testing ground for weapons of mass destruction has become a symbol of what is worth conserving. The pagodas are now stark monuments to the futilities of the Cold War. The great vacant spaces within them are a chilling reminder and a symbol of hope.

CHAPTER TWELVE

A GENEROUS NET

THE NATIONAL TRUST owes its existence to a shared sense of loss. Its three founders had seen places they loved destroyed through greed or negligence. Their response was to form an organisation committed to the preservation of unspoilt landscape and fine buildings. During the last hundred years the National Trust has pursued that task, guided and served by those who, like its founders, believe that places of beauty can be a continuing source of pleasure and inspiration.

When in 1846 Octavia Hill first moved with her mother and sisters to Finchley, it was a village in open countryside. She lived to see the fields where, as a girl, she had gathered wild flowers gradually engulfed by London suburbs. Her later battles to protect Swiss Cottage Fields, Parliament Hill and parts of Hampstead Heath were influenced by what had happened to Finchley. It was these campaigns that brought her into contact with Robert Hunter and the Commons Preservation Society. Their ideals were shared by Hardwicke Rawnsley, who saw how easy it was for speculative builders, the developers of reservoirs and quarry syndicates to pursue their own commercial interests in the very heart of the Lake District. Ruskin, a major influence on both Octavia Hill and Rawnsley, had watched appalled as the urban sprawl of south London swallowed up the landscape around Camberwell which he had known from childhood. Such experiences are all too common.

In the late twentieth century there is nothing inevitable about the preservation of places of natural beauty. Historic buildings do not survive by chance. They have come to us not as a birthright, but frequently because when threats arose, a few individuals of vision were determined to intervene. Those who have helped to shape the ideals and policies of the Trust come from no particular social group, still less do they have a common political allegiance. What they share is a conviction that the needless destruction of beauty impoverishes the human spirit.

One of the most influential supporters of the Trust was the cartoonist

Kenneth Bird, who signed himself Fougasse. While he was Art Editor of *Punch* from 1937 to 1949, he designed posters and pamphlets for wildlife organisations, including a cartoon for display at Blakeney Point in Norfolk, urging visitors not to leave litter. Fougasse would never have become a cartoonist if he had not been blown up by a Turkish mine at Gallipoli in 1915. His injuries meant that his career as an engineer was over, so he turned instead to drawing. As there was already a cartoonist of the same name, Bird, he signed himself Fougasse, after a French mine that might or might not go off. One of his many cartoons to appear

1914.—MR. WILLIAM SMITH ANSWERS THE CALL TO PRESERVE HIS NATIVE SOIL INVIOLATE.   1919.—MR. WILLIAM SMITH COMES BACK AGAIN, TO SEE HOW WELL HE HAS DONE IT.

in *Punch* was used by Clough Williams-Ellis as the frontispiece of *England and the Octopus*. Fougasse's cartoon is captioned: '1914. Mr William Smith answers the call to preserve his native soil inviolate'. Its sequel is '1919. Mr William Smith comes back again to see how well he has done it'. In view of Bird's personal history, it had a poignant message.

A similar warning, in a different style, appeared in the *Fell and Rock Climbing Club Journal* of 1934. The author, Professor Chorley, predicted that Buttermere in the Lake District could go the way of Windermere and was vulnerable to a 'rash of ill-considered buildings'. Walkers on the ridge that links Blea Crag, Red Pike, High Stile and Haystacks can today look across to gently sloping pastures and a succession of farmsteads on the eastern side of the lake. If they assume that Buttermere retains its serenity by some happy accident, they are mistaken. It does so thanks to the efforts of Chorley and to those who have given generously to the Trust to ensure its protection. The neighbouring valley of Borrowdale narrowly escaped a proposal in 1883 to quarry green slate, which would have involved a railway to the dale head. This was successfully resisted by Hardwicke

Between 1932 and 1934, the Buttermere Valley in
the Lake District narrowly escaped development.

Rawnsley and is now long forgotten. Today the Trust owns over 6,300 acres in
Buttermere and Borrowdale.

Fifty years ago the Yealm Estuary, between Torbay and Plymouth Sound in
Devon, offered countless dream sites for bungalow builders. Between the World
Wars there was rapid, sporadic development around Wembury and this would
almost certainly have continued along both sides of the estuary had Mrs Sebag-
Montefiore not given the Trust Warren Point in 1938. Since then there has been
a vigorous and successful campaign to protect other unspoilt stretches of the
estuary.

Writing in the Trust's Jubilee year of 1945, G.M. Trevelyan saw 'more
widespread appreciation of natural beauty and of historic buildings than ever
before'. He also warned that 'never before was the destruction of natural beauty
going on at such a pace by uncontrolled development; and the break-up of
country houses and the grounds surrounding them is one of the social acts of
the age'. The impact of the Trust was, he admitted, 'still pitifully small'. It may

Claremont Fête Champêtre,
painted by Leslie Worth, 1993.

have seemed only a modest victory when the Trust's acquisition of Claremont Gardens in Surrey prevented the building of a housing estate in the eighteenth-century landscape created by Sir John Vanbrugh, Charles Bridgeman, William Kent and 'Capability' Brown. How many of the thousands who now come each summer to the Trust's *fêtes champêtres* at Claremont realise that in 1949 the garden had already been lotted up and plans drawn for an extension to suburban Esher?

Visitors to the imposing fifteenth-century brick gatehouse of Oxburgh Hall in Norfolk are not likely to remember that in 1950 the whole estate was sold by Sir Edmund Bedingfeld to a property development company. What happened next would today be called asset-stripping: Oxburgh was to be auctioned in seventy lots, with each element likely to attract a buyer with a different interest. All the mature trees around the house were measured for felling by a local firm of timber merchants, which intended to demolish the building and sell off any valuable architectural fragments such as fireplaces, doors and panelling. At the start of the sale on 3 October the auctioneers announced to those gathered in

the Globe Hotel, King's Lynn, that the previous night agreement had been reached on a sale of the Hall itself, but not the surrounding farmland, to the Dowager Lady Bedingfeld, mother of Sir Edmund. She and two other members of the family had sold their own homes in order to be able to buy back Oxburgh, which in 1952 they gave to the National Trust. Much of the history of the Trust is of frantic efforts to snatch things back from imminent destruction, of last ditch attempts to rescue places which, at the moment they were threatened, somehow stood for civilised life.

In the 1970s it looked as though Turner's paintings of the park at Petworth in Sussex were to become a record of a once Elysian landscape, lost irrevocably. Only the exceptional powers given to the National Trust in its Act of Parliament of 1907, by which it could hold land inalienably, prevented a major by-pass being cut through 'Capability' Brown's parkland. As part of the Trust's campaign to ensure that Parliament did not give permission for a new road through the park, the artist David Gentleman produced dramatic posters warning of the threat to shatter the tranquillity of Petworth and destroy the vista that inspired several of Turner's masterpieces.

By 1992 road schemes threatened over thirty National Trust properties, from the Devil's Punch Bowl and surrounding heathland in Surrey to Fontmell Down in Dorset, from Bellister Castle in Northumberland to the Ysbyty Estate, where there are proposals to realign Thomas Telford's Holyhead Road even though an alternative major road along the north Wales coast has already been constructed. In all these cases the Department of Transport's approach has tended to be piecemeal, with environmental factors only considered at a very late stage. With the Council for the Protection of Rural England and other bodies, the Trust has renewed the call for a national transport strategy, with the aim of looking beyond the immediate demands for ever larger, faster roads.

There is a fashionable argument that this continuing commitment to preservation is mere nostalgia, a perennial preoccupation with the past as a way of avoiding the realities of the present. But the losses are undeniable. It has always been one of the strengths of the Trust that the task it has set itself is so very specific, as defined in its Acts of Parliament and in the clearly articulated objectives of its founders. The Trust was set up to hold property for permanent preservation. It is what distinguishes the Trust from the Council for the Protection of Rural

The fifteenth-century brick gatehouse of Oxburgh Hall
in Norfolk, under threat in the 1950s.

England, Friends of the Earth and Greenpeace, which are essentially propaganda organisations, not land-owning, land-managing ones. The need for a body with very simple aims was what led its founders to shape the Trust in the way they did. Octavia Hill knew from bitter personal experience that grander schemes often promised more, but produced less. She taught the Trust to treat each property as an entity, administratively and financially, to be managed in a methodical, efficient, down-to-earth way. This piece-by-piece approach to conservation is often far from glamorous. It offers no instant global solutions. But what has been achieved empirically by the National Trust over the last hundred years still has something to teach. The fact that the Trust's methods of operating have been so specific has not diminished its wider impact. Each individual property has the potential to enrich experience and can demonstrate in a simple,

Petworth Park: Tillington Church in the Distance,
painted by J. M. W. Turner, *c.*1828.

practical way what conservation means. This was how the founders of the Trust saw it fulfilling moral and social purposes. They also envisaged the Trust's properties playing an increasingly important educational role.

As already noted, in recent years the Trust has re-examined its approach to education. One significant change is actively to discourage purposeless outings for schoolchildren who often find the state rooms of a country house utterly bewildering. Under the guidance of the Trust's Education Manager, Tricia Lankester, a relatively small number of properties are equipped to provide carefully prepared and presented programmes for children, specifically directed at parts of the National Curriculum. At properties such as Wimpole, where the Home Farm with its rare breeds has such broad appeal, there are staff who can help schools plan for a visit and arrange for children to have access to parts of the house and estate that the ordinary visitor would not normally see. In 1993 over 490,000 schoolchildren visited Trust properties, most of them taking

One of a set of four posters produced by David Gentleman as part of the
Trust's campaign to protect Petworth Park in Sussex from a major by-pass.

advantage of Schools Corporate Membership. Increasingly schools are adopting a particular site and undertaking fieldwork such as dry-stone walling, tree planting and stream clearing, guided by the wardening staff of the property.

Although the Trust has always been wary of setting itself up as some kind of teaching authority, it is increasingly sharing its experience of caring for country-side and historic buildings. Perhaps the most valuable examples of this pooling of expertise occur when conservationists from overseas visit Trust properties and meet its staff. There are also links with the Historic Houses Association, which represents the private owners of country houses. The Trust's former House-keeper, Sheila Stainton, has helped to organise the conservation of textiles at Holkham Hall in Norfolk, and the staff there have taken part in training days at Blickling. There is ample scope for similar exchanges of management skills between countryside staff. The problems of how to reconcile modern, often high-tech leisure activities such as hang-gliding and jet-skiing with the care of the countryside are the same the world over, with the key ultimately lying in John Bailey's succinct summary that preservation must come first, because 'without preservation access becomes for ever impossible'. In 1993 the local community and fishermen at Brancaster in Norfolk were initially surprised to find themselves dealing not with a familiar National Trust member of staff but with a warden from the Angahook-Lorne State Park in Victoria, Australia; but they seemed to adjust quickly.

Increasingly the conservation of the environment is seen as an international, ethical issue, because it concerns the survival of the human race. However reticent the Trust's donors may be about the reasons for their generosity, they are often influenced by moral considerations and not by their own material interests. The Trust was itself a reaction against the unbridled materialism of the late nineteenth century. Many of those who support it today do so because consciously or unconsciously, they are aware of the poverty of free market capitalism. Materialism can never entirely satisfy the appetite it feeds.

When describing the purposes of the Trust, the language used by the founders was frequently biblical, with a strong moral tone which today can seem unsympathetic and which is certainly unfashionable. In her essay *Natural Beauty as a National Asset*, Octavia Hill wrote:

> Is there one of us, poor or rich, busy or idle, philanthropist or man of the world, who does not devote something to a love of beauty? . . . we all set aside some of our money for that which does not supply creature comfort. It is the dawn of the spirit which craves for such possession. The National Trust asks that this need, which is human, shall be met by common possessions.

A similar passion infuses G.M. Trevelyan's writing about the moral issues with which the Trust was concerned. His plea for 'Spiritual Values' is central to *Must England's Beauty Perish?* and it recurs in his other books. In his *History of England* he warned that 'man's power over nature' had 'far outstripped his moral and mental development'. In an earlier essay he foresaw a world of 'ugliness, vulgarity, materialism, the inspired negation of everything that has been accounted good in the past history of man'.

An anonymous reviewer – it was probably John Bailey – of *Must England's Beauty Perish?*, writing in *The Times Literary Supplement*, was prepared to use equally emotive language, when he described the National Trust as a 'moving and spacious poem of Nature, and one which the spirit must deepen and burn more furiously as we identify our best generosities of human interest with it'. He shared Trevelyan's view that: 'All that is good in the world is threatened. . . . We are mortgaging the whole future of mankind.' The words that Geoffrey Young sent ringing across Great Gable, Green Gable and Windy Gap on a rainswept day in June 1924 identified that great mountain fastness as a symbol of the freedom of the spirit, to be held in trust for ever. There are similar echoes in Lord Lothian's essays and letters, with their references to the 'quiet and peace-giving love of spiritual things', as a true end of civilised life.

The spirit of our own time may seem to run counter to these ideals and to the way they have been expressed. The Trust's Centenary provides an opportunity for its past and future role to be assessed, for its achievements and ideals to be scrutinised. One reaction may be that these earlier values are not to be despised. An answer to those inclined to criticise or disparage what the Trust is trying to do is given in the sheer scale of public support, by the allegiance of its two million members. If enough ordinary people care about what the Trust stands for, they may ultimately have an impact on the politicians who decide what is preserved and what is sacrificed. Not surprisingly, there have throughout the Trust's history been those who wanted to widen its scope, who have urged the Trust to launch a crusade on every environmental issue. They may have been disappointed by the Trust's response. But consistency of purpose explains why its benefactors still give to it with such extraordinary generosity.

There have been moments during the last hundred years when members of the Trust have questioned whether it has lost its way. The ultimate test is whether its properties are being cared for as they deserve. If ever the Trust is deflected from protecting individual places of historic interest and natural beauty, then it will have betrayed its fundamental objectives. If it becomes preoccupied with a sense of being some great national institution, it will be in danger of making a fool of itself. If a blanket of bureaucracy ever threatens to smother the Trust, it will do well to remember that Octavia Hill described her housing work as being achieved with 'next to no printing and next to no stationery; we have no office, and we have no machinery that costs anything'. The key to the success of her housing work, as it has been to the achievements of the Trust, was to build from secure foundations, stone by stone. She worked like the medieval masons so admired by her mentor Ruskin, not to some grand inflexible design, but instead delighting in every profile and moulding, ready to alter, improvise and adapt.

One of the greatest strengths of the Trust has been its commitment to strong and authoritative local representation, initiated at the very earliest meetings of the Executive Committee and strengthened over the ensuing hundred years. Frequently it has been local initiatives that have carried its work into new areas. This is true of many of its most imaginative acquisitions, of pioneering experiments in nature conservation, of new ways of showing country houses and of efforts to develop an educational role for the Trust. A need perceived locally has frequently set a precedent to be emulated nationally. The reaction of the Trust's head office staff and committees has almost always been to encourage and nurture such initiatives, as far as resources permit. At a time when the government of Britain is rapidly becoming the most centralised in western Europe, and when the role of local authorities is being relentlessly whittled down, the Trust will need to move in the opposite direction, devolving administration and increasingly using its regional committees as both a constitutional support for the Council and as a source for new ideas, to criticise, enliven and challenge orthodoxy.

By throwing its net generously and wide, the Trust has sometimes landed an unexpected catch. This was particularly evident when in 1991 bewildered committees heard the Regional Director for Northern Ireland, Ian McQuiston, propose the acquisition of Patterson's Spade Mill, near Belfast. For most of this century the Patterson family had made every shape and size of spade found in Ireland, using water-powered punches, a guillotine and a massive trip hammer. Because so much of life in Ireland depended on the spade, there was a chance to demonstrate a history of labour that crossed the border and every divide. The educational opportunities were inspirational, and so too was the subject matter for the distinguished Irish painter Jack Crabtree.

Vision and idealism constantly recur in the story of the Trust, and in that sense its history is a romance. It is also a political tract, because as David Cannadine remarks in his biography of G.M. Trevelyan, 'The National Trust was then, as now, the pursuit of politics by other means'. Finally, it is a morality tale, because the Trust confronts greed, self-interest and short-sightedness with generosity and concern for others, including future generations. It shows how far it is possible for the individual to care for something without personally having to possess it.

The Trust has remained politically elusive, as the wisest of the founders, Sir

Patterson's Spade Mill near Belfast, Northern Ireland.

Robert Hunter, intended it should, and this continues to be a strength. To many of its benefactors the Trust is an inherently conservative organisation which happens to have enlisted prominent socialists and radicals. Others have supported it because they see its objectives as essentially socialist; but they have been happy to see conservative support turned to good use. At some moments the Trust has seemed to be a socialist organisation run by liberals; at others a conservative body infiltrated by socialists. In fact, many of its supporters would agree with Clough Williams-Ellis: 'What is wrong with the Conservative Party is that it seeks to conserve the wrong things, with the Liberals and the Radicals that they are respectively neither, with the Communists that all Marx and no Morris has made them dull boys'.

Nobody wrote more trenchant criticism of absentee landlords than that great protector of the Lake District, Mrs William Heelis (née Beatrix Potter) whose background was Unitarian and radical. But when in 1924 the *Sunday Herald* confused her with Mrs Sidney Webb (née Beatrice Potter), she fulminated that she did not want readers of her books to think they were 'of socialist origin'; nor did her husband want to be confused with 'such a little animal' as Mr Webb.

Sketch from an illustrated letter by
Mrs William Heelis (née Beatrix Potter), 1924.

The solution she proposed, illustrating it with a sketch, was 'to get photographed along with a favourite pig. ... I had lately a pig that continually stood on its hind legs leaning over the pig stye, but it's hanging up, unphotographed and cured now.'

Perhaps only a country with a social and political history as diverse as Britain's could have produced the Trust. It was a child of the Romantic Movement, with aesthetic judgements and moral purposes shaped by Coleridge and Wordsworth, Maurice and Ruskin. Reflecting their ideals, Octavia Hill described her life as an endless conflict between her passions and her search for quiet. 'She was made passionate by her earnestness', wrote one of her friends, and it was this that made her sometimes an awkward and uncomfortable companion. The other two founders of the Trust shared that zeal. Hardwicke Rawnsley was described by one of his parishioners as at times 'a peppery old swine' but another recalled that, when moved, he was 'the most active volcano in Europe'. A few weeks before his death Sir Robert Hunter trudged through pouring rain to see for

The National Trust Scolt Head Committee outside the Watcher's Hut on
20 July 1928. The Watcher, Charles Chestney, can be seen at the window.

himself where a footpath had been illegally obstructed in Torn Ghyll, near Tarn
Hows on the Monk Coniston estate.

As the decision to acquire Orford Ness demonstrated, the Trust has not, in
the course of the last hundred years, turned away from what is difficult, harsh or
unglamorous. Orford Ness was opened to the public in 1995, the year of the
Trust's Centenary. Exactly a hundred years earlier Octavia Hill had wondered
whether its first property, Dinas Oleu, would also be its last.

Few of those who explore the usually deserted beach and dunes of Scolt
Head, another early acquisition, have any idea that when this windswept island
off the Norfolk coast was given to the Trust in 1923, a cluster of holiday chalets
at the eastern end had to be removed. Today the Watcher's Hut looks out across
a great expanse of salt-marsh to Norton Creek and The Nod. Sea lavender
covers the marshes and samphire lines the creeks. Behind the sand dunes are
three miles of beach and then the North Sea. To the south, masts and pantiled
roofs cluster around Brancaster Staithe, as they did two hundred years ago. The

few changes since then are innocuous. Nothing mars the view in any direction. The beach at Brancaster, and the windmill at Burnham Overy, to the south east, are also Trust property. Beyond are Stiffkey Marshes, acquired by the Trust in 1976, Morston Marshes and Blakeney Point, just visible with the help of binoculars. The Romans ringed this coast with shore forts, the ramparts of which are clearly visible at Branodonum, again protected by the Trust. Now the enemy is commercial exploitation.

The sloping writing-desk in the Watcher's Hut has served generations of naturalists. On the wall behind is a faded photograph of the National Trust's Scolt Head Committee, taken on 20 July 1928 by Professor Oliver, who served with Octavia Hill, Hardwicke Rawnsley and Sir Robert Hunter on the Trust's Executive Committee in the early years of the century. The photograph shows the watcher, Charles Chestney, at the window.

Every year the shingle banks and sand bars along this coast accrete and shift, sometimes allowing narrow bands of vegetation to become established. Clearly the conservation of natural processes is ultimately more important than attempting to preserve a particular form of landscape, at a particular time. The thickening of the marram grass gives a misleading sense of permanence, because winter gales and storm surges can cut through the dunes in a night. These changes do not threaten the natural beauty of Scolt, nor the sense of continuity.

Orford Ness was acquired from the Ministry
of Defence in 1993 and opened to the public in
the National Trust's centenary year.

NOTES AND BIBLIOGRAPHY

As explained in the Preface, the records in the Registry at 36 Queen Anne's Gate are an indispensable but incomplete source of information about the Trust. The files held in the sixteen regional offices fill some of the obvious gaps and very often have information that was never passed on to the Trust's head office. This material has now been supplemented by the transcriptions of interviews made during the preparation of this book. Details of these interviews and of other oral evidence are given below, followed by a bibliography relating to each chapter.

GENERAL BOOKS ON THE NATIONAL TRUST

Robin Fedden, *The Continuing Purpose: A History of the National Trust, its Aims and Work*, 1968.

John Gaze, *Figures in a Landscape: A History of the National Trust*, 1988.

James Lees-Milne (ed.), *The National Trust: A Record of Fifty Years' Achievement*, 1945.

Clough Williams-Ellis, *On Trust for the Nation*, 1947.

CHAPTER 1

Some of the correspondence between Octavia Hill and Sir Robert Hunter, including their accounts of Sayes Court, are among the Hunter papers in the Surrey Record Office in Guildford. Papers on the significance of the Evelyn family's property in Deptford are in the Local History Centre, Lewisham. Information on the later history of the house was generously supplied by Mr John Coulter. For photographs and records

of Canon Hardwicke Rawnsley we are indebted to Rosalind Rawnsley. Information, much of it unpublished, on the links with the Trustees of Reservations, Massachusetts, was gathered together by Ronald Lee Fleming, assisted by Paul Rosa and Keith Morgan.

Gillian Darley, *Octavia Hill: A Life*, 1990.

E.M. Bell, *Octavia Hill: A Biography*, 1942.

William Thomson Hill, *Octavia Hill: Pioneer of the National Trust and Housing Reform*, 1956.

H.D. Rawnsley, *Sonnets at the English Lakes*, 1882.

H.D. Rawnsley, *A Coach Drive at the Lakes*, 1890.

John Bowle, *John Evelyn and His World*, 1981.

William Bray (editor), *The Diary of John Evelyn*, 1895.

Emily Southwood Maurice, *Octavia Hill*, 1928.

Graham Murphy, *Founders of the National Trust*, 1987.

Gordon Abbott Jr, *Saving Special Places: A Centennial History of the Trustees of Reservations*, 1993.

Charles W. Eliot, *Charles Eliot, Landscape Architect*, 1903.

CHAPTER 2

B.L. Thompson, *The Lake District and the National Trust*, 1946.

John Ruskin, *Praeterita*, 1899.

Anon, *The Most Active Volcano in Europe: A short Life of Canon Hardwicke Drummond Rawnsley*, no date.

Kenneth Gravett, *The Clergy House, Alfriston: a Reappraisal*, in *National Trust Studies*, 1981.

Leslie Linder, *The Journal of Beatrix Potter*, 1966.

Octavia Hill, *Natural Beauty as a National Asset*, in *Nineteenth Century*, lviii, 1905.

H.D. Rawnsley, *A Nation's Heritage*, 1920.

Beatrix Potter and Canon Hardwicke Rawnsley, *Peter Rabbit's Other Tale*, 1989.

CHAPTER 3

Detailed records of the acquisition of Great Gable are with the papers of the Fell and Rock Climbing Club in the Cumbria Record Office, Kendal. The Honorary Librarian of the Fell and Rock, G.G. Watkins, was exceptionally generous with help and advice. Lord Chorley's unpublished memoir supplements these archives.

E.L. Turner, *Bird Watching on Scolt Head*, 1928.

E.L. Turner, *Stray Leaves from Nature's Notebook*, 1929.

G.M. Trevelyan, *Must England's Beauty Perish? A plea on behalf of the National Trust*, 1929.

David Cannadine, *G.M. Trevelyan: A Life in History*, 1992.

CHAPTER 4

Dr John Harvey, Dr Max Walters and Dr Charles Turner have guided us to photographs and records of early research at Wicken Fen. The Minute Book of Ferguson's Gang is held in the Registry.

N.W. Moore, *The Bird of Time: The Science and Politics of Nature Conservation – a personal account*, 1987.

Sir Harry Godwin, *Fenland: its ancient past and uncertain future*, 1978.

Margaret Lane, *The Tale of Beatrix Potter*, 1968.

Hunter Davies, *Beatrix Potter's Lakeland*, 1988.

Ulla Hyde-Parker, *Cousin Beatie. A Memoir of Beatrix Potter*, 1981.

T.A. Rowell & H.J. Harvey, 'The Recent History of Wicken Fen, Cambridgeshire: a guide to ecological development', in *Journal of Ecology*, 76, 1988.

J. Sheail, '*From preservation to conservation: wildlife and the environment 1900–1950*', in *Biological Journal of the Linnean Society*, 32, 1987.

H.J. Harvey, '*Changing attitudes to nature conservation: The National Trust*', in *Biological Journal of the Linnean Society*, 32, 1987.

Taylor, Whalley, Hobbs and Battrick, *Beatrix Potter 1866–1943*, 1987.

CHAPTER 5

James Lees-Milne has generously allowed me to quote from his diaries and other books about the Trust, as well as providing notes, corrections and advice.

J.R.M. Butler, *Lord Lothian (Philip Kerr) 1882–1940*, 1960.

James Lees-Milne, *People and Places: Country House Donors and the National Trust*, 1992.

John Cornforth, *The Inspiration of the Past: Country House Taste in the Twentieth Century*, 1985.

James Lees-Milne, 'The Early Years of the Country Houses Scheme', in *National Trust Studies*, 1976–1977.

Clough Williams-Ellis, *England and the Octopus*, 1928.

James Lees-Milne, *Another Self*, 1970.
Lawrence, Second Marquess of Zetland,
    Essayez, 1956.

CHAPTER 6

The account of the gift of Wallington is
based on Sir Charles Trevelyan's broadcast
at the time, with comments from Mr
Geoffrey Trevelyan. Sir John Acland has
allowed me to quote from his parents'
unpublished letters, and has supplied a
mass of other information about the
transfer of Holnicote and Killerton. For
information on Bodnant, M.W.
conversation and correspondence with
Lord Aberconway; and S.W. recorded
interview with Martin Puddle. On
Anglesey Abbey, S.W. recorded interview
with Richard Ayres. On the transfer of
Ickworth, M.W. conversation with Mary
MacRae. Lord and Lady Anglesey's
contribution extends far beyond the
account of the gift of Plas Newydd.

Geoffrey Beard, *Attingham: The First Forty
    Years, 1952–1991*, 1991.
Alvilde Lees-Milne, 'Lawrence Johnston:
    Creator of Hidcote' in *National Trust
    Studies*, 1977–1978.

CHAPTER 7

On 28th Earl of Crawford, M.W.
conversation with St John Gore. On
Robin Fedden and the variegated talents
of the Trust's honorary Historic Buildings
Representatives, M.W. personal
acquaintance and conversations with Sir
Joshua Rowley and Martin Drury. Lord
Crawford's correspondence is in the
National Library of Scotland, Edinburgh.
On Graham Stuart Thomas, M.W.
personal acquaintance and conversation
with Nicolas Corbin. S.W. recorded

interview with John Workman. On Lord
Antrim and the Trust in Northern
Ireland, S.W. recorded interviews with
Dick Rogers and John Lewis-Crosby. On
Sir John Smith, M.W. personal
acquaintance, conversation and
correspondence with Lord Gibson.

Patrick Leigh Fermor, *Three Letters from
    the Andes*, 1991.
St John Gore, 'Solvitur ambulando: the
    "travels and trials" of a National Trust
    adviser', in *Apollo*, 1993.
Graham Stuart Thomas, *The Old Shrub
    Roses*, 1955.
Lyn Gallagher and Dick Rogers, *Castle,
    Coast & Cottage: The National Trust in
    Northern Ireland*, 1986.
John Wyndham, *Wyndhams and Children
    First*, 1968.

CHAPTER 8

On the loss of Dunsland, S.W. recorded
interview with Michael Trinick. On
Enterprise Neptune and the Rawnsley
row, files in the Registry and information
supplied by Commander Conrad
Rawnsley. On Styal, S.W. recorded
interviews with Gerard Noel and David
Sekers. On Benson Report, M.W.
conversation and correspondence with Sir
Jack Boles and Lord Gibson. On Lord
Antrim, written memoir provided by
Mark Norman. On recruitment of
members, S.W. recorded interview with
Ted Fawcett. On inalienability and the
Saltram bypass, contrasting written
accounts by John Gaze and Michael
Trinick. On the rescue of Derrymore,
M.W. conversation with Edmund Baillie.

CHAPTER 9

On Upper Wharfedale, M.W. conversation
with Graham Watson; S.W. recorded

interviews with John Garrett and Laurence Harwood. On Lord Gibson, M.W. personal acquaintance and correspondence. On The Argory, S.W. recorded interview with Peter Marlow. On Canons Ashby, S.W. recorded interview with Gervase Jackson-Stops, conversation with Martin Drury.

Merlin Waterson, *The Servants' Hall: A Domestic History of Erddig*, 1980.

John Harris, Marcus Binney and Roy Strong, *The Destruction of the Country House*, 1974.

John Cornforth, *Country Houses in Britain: Can they survive?*, 1974.

John Cornforth, 'John Fowler' in *National Trust Studies*, 1978.

Merlin Waterson, 'Constable's Views Under Threat', *Country Life*, 18 June 1992.

Elizabeth Battrick, *Guardian of the Lakes: A History of the National Trust in the Lake District from 1946*, 1987.

CHAPTER 10

On the changing role of volunteers, S.W. recorded interview with Leslie McCracken. On the Bradenham row, M.W. conversation with Sir Jack Boles, correspondence with Julian Prideaux and Robert Latham. On Nicholas Ridley, the M40 and regional committees, M.W. correspondence and conversations with Lord Gibson. On Kinder Scout, M.W. correspondence with Lord Chorley.

Julia Blackburn, *Charles Waterton 1782–1865: Traveller and Conservationist*, 1989.

Len Clark, 'A Strange Sort of Animal' in *The National Trust Magazine*, 1992.

CHAPTER 11

On Dame Jennifer Jenkins, M.W. interview. On the Trust and Archangel, M.W. correspondence and conversations with Sir Angus Stirling and Tiffany Hunt, and their written accounts. On Sutton House, S.W. recorded interview with Robin Mills. On the Young National Trust Theatre, M.W. correspondence and conversations with Sally Woodhead and Tricia Lankester. On 2 Willow Road, information supplied by Ed Diestelkamp and S.W. recorded interview with Martin Drury. On West Penwith, S.W. recorded interview with Peter Mansfield.

Susan Denyer, 'A Sense of Place: On reading the Lake District landscape', in *The National Trust Magazine*, Spring 1992.

Merlin Waterson, 'East Meets West' in *The National Trust Magazine*, Autumn 1992, and 'Conserving Estonia in the New Europe', in *History Today*, November 1992.

Simon Murray, 'Private Lives', in *The National Trust Magazine*, June 1993.

Humphrey Carpenter, *Benjamin Britten: A Biography*, 1992.

CHAPTER 12

Ian McQuiston (ed.), *Call a Spade a Spade*, 1993.

Bevis Hillier, *Fougasse*, 1977.

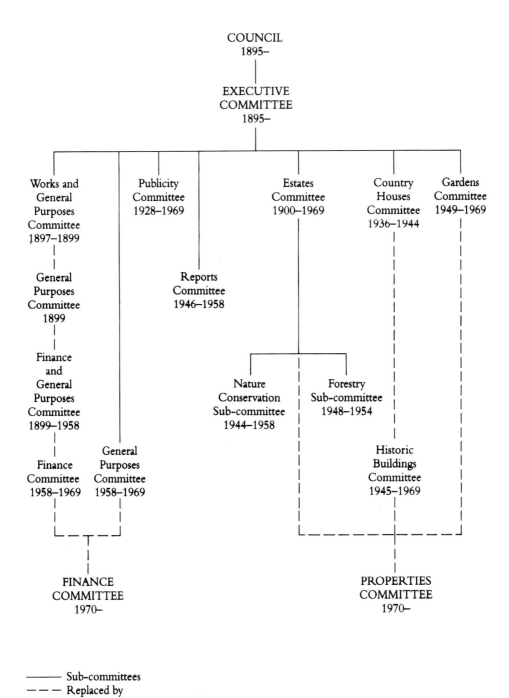

COUNCIL
1895–

EXECUTIVE
COMMITTEE
1895–

Works and General Purposes Committee 1897–1899

Publicity Committee 1928–1969

Estates Committee 1900–1969

Country Houses Committee 1936–1944

Gardens Committee 1949–1969

General Purposes Committee 1899

Reports Committee 1946–1958

Finance and General Purposes Committee 1899–1958

Nature Conservation Sub-committee 1944–1958

Forestry Sub-committee 1948–1954

Finance Committee 1958–1969

General Purposes Committee 1958–1969

Historic Buildings Committee 1945–1969

FINANCE COMMITTEE 1970–

PROPERTIES COMMITTEE 1970–

——— Sub-committees
– – – Replaced by

Present day committees in CAPITALS

ACKNOWLEDGEMENTS

TEXT

The author and publishers acknowledge with thanks permission to reproduce material from the following sources: Faber and Faber Ltd for *Another Self* by James Lees-Milne, Louis MacNeice's *Collected Poems*, 1966 and *Must England's Beauty Perish?* by G. M. Trevelyan; Longman Group Ltd for *The Continuing Purpose* by Robin Fedden; Nigel Nicolson for Vita Sackville-West's Foreword to *The Old Shrub Roses* and the letter by Harold Nicolson; Portmeirion Ltd for *England and the Octopus* by Clough Williams-Ellis.

ILLUSTRATIONS

Sir John Acland 123; Christie's Images 35; The Earl of Crawford and Balcarres 157; Devonshire Collection, Chatsworth, Chatsworth Settlement Trustees 143; Lord Dynevor 224; English Nature and Professor T. ap Rees/John Hammond 82; Fell & Rock Climbing Club 68; Mark Fiennes 211, 264; Francis Frith Collection 40, 50; Mrs Richard Gayner 146; David Gentleman 267; Ray Hallett 226; Artist's family/Herbert Art Gallery, Coventry 251; Gervase Jackson-Stops 192; Lewisham Local History Centre 26, 27; Maas Gallery, London 223; Manchester City Art Galleries 22; Mrs Ruth Maunsell 34; Mrs Ruth Maunsell and Guildford Muniment Room 18; The Hon. Randal McDonnell 169; Roy Miles Gallery, London 39; National Trust 6, 16, 38, 49, 64, 72, 85, 88, 100, 111, 117, 137, 164, 165, 189, 219, 253, 262, 273; NT/Jane Bown 200, 259; NT/Robert Chapman 180; NT/Christopher Gallagher 138, 139; NT/John Hammond 51; NT/Chris Hill 271; NT/Angelo Hornak 247; NT/O. G. Jarman 105; NT/Fred Spencer 188; NT/Mike Williams 206, 207, 234; National Trust Photographic Library 121, 183; NTPL/Peter Baistow 46 (left); NTPL/Oliver Benn 74; NTPL/Mike Caldwell 186; NTPL/Neil Campbell-Sharp 130; NTPL/A.C. Cooper, 66; NTPL/Joe Cornish 62, 190, 255, 274; NTPL/Geoffrey Frosh 250; NTPL/John Hammond 263; NTPL/Angelo Hornak 222; NTPL/Andrew Lawson 134; NTPL/David Levenson, 246; NTPL/Nadia Mackenzie 179; NTPL/Nick Meers frontispiece, 87, 106, 126; NTPL/Alan North 158; NTPL/Ian Shaw 119; NTPL/Rob Talbot 95; NTPL/Andreas von Einsiedel 110, 114, 195, 198, 202; NTPL/Paul Wakefield 90; NTPL/Ian West 178; NTPL/Mike Williams 175; National Portrait Gallery, London 15; Northamptonshire Record Office 148; Private Collection/John Hammond 55, 98; Punch Picture Library 239, 261; Quarry Bank Mill Trust/David Williams 174; Mattei Radev 151; Rosalind Rawnsley 17, 30; Ruskin Museum, Coniston/Bridgeman Art Library, London 31; Mike Smith/Northumbrian Water 256; Society of Dillettanti/John Hammond 147; Trustees of Tate Gallery, London 266; Graham Stuart Thomas 150; Trustees of the Trevelyan family papers 77; University College London 79, 81; Trustees of Victoria & Albert Museum 210; Warne Archive 272; Frederick Warne & Co, 1908, 1903, 1987 46 (right), 47 (top), 47 (bottom); The Wordsworth Trust 71.

INDEX

Page numbers in *italic* refer to illustrations